The Road from Babylon

OTHER BOOKS ON JEWISH THEMES BY CHAIM RAPHAEL

Memoirs of a Special Case
A Feast of History
The Walls of Jerusalem
A Coat of Many Colours
The Springs of Jewish Life

Chaim Raphael

THE ROAD FROM
BABYLON
The Story of Sephardi and Oriental Jews

A Cornelia & Michael Bessie Book

HARPER & ROW, PUBLISHERS, New York
Cambridge, Philadelphia, San Francisco, London
Mexico City, São Paulo, Singapore, Sydney

FIRST U.S. EDITION

Library of Congress Cataloging-in-Publication Data

Raphael, Chaim.
    The road from Babylon.

    "A Cornelia & Michael Bessie book."
    Bibliography: p.
    Includes index.
    1. Jews—Spain—History.   2. Sephardim—History.
3. Sephardim—Israel—History.   4. Jews, Oriental—
Israel—History.   5. Spain—Ethnic relations.   I. Title.
DS135.S7R36   1985   909'.04924   85-42587
ISBN 0-06-039048-4

86 87 88 89 90 10 9 8 7 6 5 4 3 2 1

For Irene and Davide Sala

Contents

Illustrations

the Jews, *c.* 1300 (© *The British Library*).
The seal of Todros Ha-Levi (© *The British Library*).
Illustrations from the Golden Haggadah, *c.* 1320 (© *The British Library*).
Two illustrations from a Haggadah *c.* 1300 showing bread-making and cooking (© *The British Library*).
A detail from a miniature in the Alba Bible showing Rabbi Moses Arragel presenting his Spanish translation of the Bible to his liege-lord Don Luis de Guzman in 1433 (*Mas, Barcelona*).
A carpet page from the Kennicott Bible (© *Bodleian Library, Oxford*).
A page from the Lisbon Maimonides, 1471–2 (© *The British Library*).
15th-century carving in Barcelona Cathedral showing five Jews with distinguishing circles on their hoods (*Mas, Barcelona*).
Sentence being pronounced at an Inquisition in the great square of Madrid (*Mary Evans Picture Library*).
Portrait of the *arrabi mor* of Portugal (*Mas, Barcelona*).
A painting of Ferdinand and Isabella ordering the expulsion of the Jews in 1492 (*Salmer, Madrid*).
A page from an Italian manuscript, *c.* 1400, of the medieval cabbalistic book, the *Zohar* (*Beth Hatefutsoth, Tel Aviv*).
A 14th-century miniature showing a Jewish banker lending money to a friar after his expulsion from Spain (*photo: Osvaldo Böhm,* © *Seminario Patriarcale*).
The printer's mark of Gershom Soncino (*Weidenfeld Archive*).
The house in Leghorn where Sir Moses Montefiore was born (*Mandel Archive*).
The Sanhedrin of seventy-one members summoned by Napoleon in 1807 to work out modern secular forms for Jewish tradition (© *the collection of Mr Alfred Rubens*).
Adolphe Crémieux (*photo: N. D. Roger-Viollet*).
The Grand Rabbin of France, Rabbi René Samuel Sirat (*Keystone Press*).
An 18th-century engraving of the procession of palms in the great Sephardi synagogue of Amsterdam (*Mary Evans Picture Library*).
A portrait of Rabbi Manassah ben Israel by Koning (*Mansell Collection*).
The petition to Oliver Cromwell, 1655, asking for the right of Jews to conduct services in their own homes (*Public Record Office, London*).
David Sassoon (© *the collection of Mr Alfred Rubens*).
Sir Edward Albert Sassoon (© *the collection of Mr Alfred Rubens*).
A painting of the first words of the Ten Commandments in Hebrew and Spanish in the Bevis Marks Synagogue, London (*Keystone Press*).
Portrait of Raphael Hayyim Carigal (*Mandel Archive*).
The synagogue in Curaçao (© *Douglas Dickins*).
The synagogue of Newport, Rhode Island (*Society Friends Touro Synagogue National Historic Shrine*).

Salonika (*Beth Hatefutsoth, Tel Aviv*).
The Jews of Salonika being deported by the Nazis in March 1943 (*Beth Hatefutsoth, Tel Aviv*).

Between pages 208 and 209

The entrance to the synagogue in Rhodes, Greece (*Jewish Chronicle*).
The memorial to the Jews of Rhodes killed by the Nazis in 1944–5 (*Jewish Chronicle*).
A Jewish woman of Gibraltar in a fiesta dress, 1833 (© *the collection of Mr Alfred Rubens*).
An illustration from a book about Shabbetai Zevi published in Smyrna in 1666 (*Mandel Archive*).
Drawing of Moses Hamon, physician to Suleiman the Magnificent (*Beth Hatefutsoth, Tel Aviv*).
A drawing of a Jewish merchant in Turkey, 1568 (© *the collection of Mr Alfred Rubens*).
An engraving of Tiberias (*Mandel Archive*).
Dona Gracia Nasi portrayed in a contemporary medallion (*Mandel Archive*).
A Jewish orphanage in Tchorlou, Turkey, 1921 (*Alliance Israélite Universelle*).
A lithograph of a Jewish marriage in Turkey, 1862 (© *the collection of Mr Alfred Rubens*).
An elaborately carved tombstone in a Jewish cemetery at Altunizade, Istanbul (*photo: J. Powell*).
An exhibition of the work of Jewish schoolgirls in Smyrna, 1926 (*Alliance Israélite Universelle*).
An Algerian Jewish family, c. 1900 (*photo: Jean-Loup Charmet*).
A synagogue in Algiers, from a watercolour c. 1830–40 (*photo: Jean-Loup Charmet*).
A sewing class at an *Alliance* school in Constantine, Algeria, 1895 (*Alliance Israélite Universelle*).
A Jewish bazaar in Tetuan, Morocco, 1868 (*photo: Jean-Loup Charmet*).
A children's school in Tiznit in the 1930s (*The Israel Museum, Jerusalem*).
A Moroccan Jewess in traditional festive dress (*The Israel Museum, Jerusalem*).
The Jewish quarter in Damnat, a village in the Atlas Mountains (*The Israel Museum, Jerusalem*).
A caravan of Jews from the Atlas mountains going on a pilgrimage (*The Israel Museum, Jerusalem*).
The house of Maimonides in Fez (*photo collection of Raphael Benaceref, Paris/The Israel Museum, Jerusalem*).

The Jews of Djerba, Tunisia (*Popperfoto*).

Pilgrims to the *Lag B'Omer* festival, Djerba (*Popperfoto*).

The interior of the old Ghriba Synagogue, Djerba (© *Miss M. R. Bull*).

Solomon Schechter working on the documents found in the Cairo *geniza*, 1898 (© *Syndics of Cambridge University Library*).

An autograph *responsum* by Maimonides found in the Cairo *geniza* (© *The British Museum*).

A page from the Tenth Book of the Mishnah commentary by Maimonides (© *The British Library*).

A richly decorated Yemenite *ketuba*, 1794 (*photo: Hillel Burger*).

Sana, capital of Yemen, *c.* 1900 (*Beth Hatefutsoth, Tel Aviv*).

A Yemenite family in Sana, *c.* 1930 (*The Israel Museum, Jerusalem*).

The shrine of Ezra the Scribe near Basra, Iraq (© *Imperial War Museum*).

18th-century brass and glass oil containers from Baghdad (*photo: Dr K. Meyerowitz*).

A Boy Scout troop at the Rahel Shahmoon Boys School, Baghdad, 1926 (© *the collection of Naim Dangoor*).

The opening of a new wing of the Meir Elias Hospital in Baghdad, 1924 (© *the collection of Naim Dangoor*).

Operation Ali Baba, 1951: a group of Kurdistan Jews in transit to Israel (*Israel Government Press Office*).

Oriental Jews celebrating their first Passover in Israel (*Israel Government Press Office*).

The Aden police supervising transport of Jews *en route* to Israel, 1949 (*Israel Government Press Office*).

Operation Magic Carpet: Yemenite Jews arriving in Israel at Lydda Airport, 1949 (*Israel Government Press Office*).

A Yemenite family on arrival in Israel (*Israel Government Press Office*).

A North African family on its way to a new home in a township in Israel (*BIPAC*).

Oriental Jews receiving intensive schooling after their arrival in Israel (© *W. Braun*).

A synagogue for Bukhara Jews in Jerusalem (*BIPAC*).

A young woman dancing a traditional Moroccan dance at the *Maimuna* celebration in Jerusalem (*Israel Government Press Office*).

Maps
(drawn by Patrick Leeson)

Acknowledgments

I have drawn heavily, as will be seen, on the work of a number of pioneer scholars in this field, whose researches are noted gratefully on many pages of this book. I have benefited too from a flow of guidance offered warm-heartedly by many friends old and new on less formal aspects of the religious, social, political and literary themes explored here. If I list some names – without the glitter of their offices and honours – of those who helped with their expertise, it expresses only a small part of my thanks. From a stimulating stay in Israel in 1984, I think gratefully of good talks with Yitzhak Abishur, Zalman Abramov, Arlette Adler, Ofra Alyagon, Gershon Avner, Issachar Ben-Ami, Abraham Chaim, Joan and Michael Comay, Elie Dayan, Elizabeth Eppler, Ephraim Hazan, Miriam Katz, Nehemiah Lev-Zion, Herzliah Lokay, Jacob Mansour, Shulamit Nardi, Dov Noy, Gordon Robin, Maurice Roumani, Victor Sanua, Amnon Shiloah, Itzik Taub, Ilan Troen, Alex Weingrod, Geoffrey Wigoder and Nissim Yosha. Outside Israel, I have to thank, in addition to the authors quoted, some helpful friends including Martin Aschkenasy, Rose Choron, Michael Kerem, Lionel Kochan, Irene and Davide Sala, Denzil Sebag-Montefiore and Leon Yudkin. I must also say a special word of thanks to Linda Osband, my editor, and Patricia Mandel, the picture editor. None of those listed are responsible, of course, for the way I have presented the subject.

On a more formal level, I should like to thank the publishers of *Jewish Prince in Moslem Spain* (The University of Alabama Press) and *The Penguin Book of Hebrew Verse* (both listed in the bibliography) for permission to print their translations of poems by Samuel ibn Nagrela and Judah Halevi respectively. I am grateful to have been able to quote briefly from translations of Ladino songs in writings by Marc Angel and Raphael Patai, as acknowledged in the notes; and Mr Naim Dangoor was very helpful with pictures in Iraq from his collection.

C.R.

Introduction: Israel's Sephardim

To explain what this book is about, let us start with a few definitions. A 'Sephardi' (plural 'Sephardim') indicates, literally, a Jew whose ancestors once lived in Spain or neighbouring Portugal, *sepharad* being the Hebrew for 'Spain'. Today, however, the name has also come to be applied, especially in Israel, to Jews whose ancestors lived in the Balkans, Asia Minor, North Africa and indeed all around the Mediterranean, and in the Near and Middle East. At first this is confusing, since the links with Spain seem vague. In fact, however, the name 'Sephardi' for all these Jews identifies a central fact about Jewish history in the past, and is of major significance in the life of Israel today.

As for the past, Jewish history until a few centuries ago was overwhelmingly centred in this 'Sephardi' world, in which the *edot ha-mizrach* (eastern communities) were particularly important. Spanish Jewry began to emerge in the tenth century as a remarkable extension of this world, gaining a position of economic, intellectual and social leadership which it sustained for six hundred years, and which resulted in the recognition of the name 'Sephardi' as a token of pre-eminence. The name began to be used in this overall sense when the Jews of Spain and Portugal, expelled from their homelands in the 1490s, found refuge in Mediterranean and eastern countries and soon dominated their life. In the centuries which followed, the world in which the eastern Sephardim lived suffered a great decline, especially in contrast with that of the Jews of northern Europe – the 'Ashkenazim' – who were now poised to take over the leadership of the Jewish world.

The name 'Ashkenazi' arose because from early times Jews lived in the Rhineland, and *ashkenaz* is the Hebrew for 'Germany'. In the Middle Ages, many of the Jews of north-west Europe migrated to eastern Europe, carrying with them the name 'Ashkenazi' and a

German-type language called Yiddish. They increased greatly in number in the seventeenth to nineteenth centuries, and began in this period to migrate in large numbers to western Europe and across the Atlantic, though a very large Ashkenazi population remained in Russia and Poland and other East European countries until slaughtered by the Nazis.

Muslim and Christian backgrounds

The central fact in the early difference between Sephardim and Ashkenazim is that over a very long period the Jews now called Sephardim inhabited a Muslim world, while the Ashkenazim lived among Christians. The Jews of Spain – the original Sephardim – were part of this Muslim world at the beginning, before Christian Spain limited Muslim rule to a very small area in the south. The 'golden age' of Spain's Jewry had first taken form in the Muslim period, and this was an essential element in the unity of what we now call the 'eastern' or Sephardi world.

There was a fair amount of overlapping between Sephardim and Ashkenazim in early times, but by and large they lived separately, and were affected socially and even in their manner of thinking by their different backgrounds. Even though beliefs and prayers were basically the same, differences were maintained over the centuries in rituals and folk practices. But the overriding factor which emerges from the past and still affects the relative position of Sephardim and Ashkenazim stems from the changing role in world history of the different 'host' countries. Until the end of the sixteenth century, the Jews of the eastern communities had lived under the rule of a succession of mighty empires – Byzantine, Persian, Muslim, Mongol, Turkish and so on. After this date, the world they lived in declined, and there was a dramatic rise to power by the northern and western world in which the Ashkenazim lived. It was as a result of this Ashkenazi rise to influence that modern Zionism established and built up the State of Israel. There has now, however, been a remarkable change in this balance: in numbers at least, the East in Israel once more outweighs the West. When one thinks of what this means historically, it is obvious that it is much more than a question of numbers.

Certainly one starts with the demographic fact that since about 1967, Jews who are 'eastern' by birth or descent outnumber the other

Jews of Israel. But this is not a static difference. The Jews of Israel do not exist in watertight compartments. Ethnic loyalties can be strong, but relationships are fluid. No one can say how the outcome will be affected by old influences from the East, but they clearly deserve study.

Balance, East and West

The Sephardi background is not often described in depth because of the recent dominance of the Ashkenazim. The State of Israel came into being as an offshoot of the skills, culture and ideologies of the West. Many eastern Jews were rapidly absorbing some of these western influences in the nineteenth century; but there was never a clear-cut distinction, with predictable effects. One knows, for example, that many of the Ashkenazim brought with them a strong strain of secularism from having lived in eastern Europe during the Enlightenment, while the Sephardim were much more solidly traditional in religious behaviour. At the same time, however, the secularism of eastern Europe encouraged a counter-rigidity – verging on fanaticism – among some of the orthodox, while on the Sephardi side traditional observance carries with it a relaxed, almost humanist, attitude, so that practices are enjoyed in a full-hearted way but without fanaticism. These contrasting elements all have to find a place in the evolution of the new Ashkenazi–Sephardi relationship.

In the foreground, the outstanding issue has been social. When large-scale immigration from eastern lands into Israel began after 1948 it revealed a palpable social gap, which was accentuated by the incredibly difficult circumstances in which the immigration took place. The first phase of Sephardi settlement inevitably included a kind of rapid 'westernization' under Ashkenazi direction. It was not always to the Sephardi taste, and the built-in social and economic conflicts were clearly immense. To a very considerable degree this initial gap has been narrowed, and has been succeeded by more constructive relationships in which the 'easterners' have found their own political and cultural outlets. It took some time for these forces to assert themselves. The easterners needed a breathing-space, in effect, to take into account the full force of their uprootedness from the past.

Jews who had lived for centuries in lands stretching from Morocco to the East had been driven to Israel after 1948 in successive waves of migration, partly through Zionist stirrings, but more powerfully through governmental acts of expropriation and persecution. The scale of migration from these ancient lands of settlement was immense. A striking case was Iraq, where a flourishing community of some 135,000 disappeared almost entirely when emigration got under way. The same happened to the Jews of Yemen, Egypt, Syria and Lebanon, together with a drastic shrinking of the Jewish population of 265,000 in Morocco to no more than 17,000. Leaving aside Iran, where the change was not immediately catastrophic in numbers, a Jewish population of some 856,000 in Arab countries in 1948 is estimated to have fallen to 25,870 by 1976 (for details see Table 1).

Not all these Jews emigrated to Israel, but the great number that did, and their high fertility rate in the early years of settlement, produced a startling change – the emergence of a Sephardi majority – which is, in effect, the *raison d'être* of this book. The incentives to express the change in political terms are not hard to identify. The leadership of the country still lay in Ashkenazi hands, as the Sephardim complained with increasing fierceness. Though the Ashkenazim had become the minority, they still held a large majority of the positions of import-ance, their average incomes were very much higher, their children were much better educated, their housing of a much higher level. Only in one respect was there absolute equality: every citizen has one vote; and as time went on, the Sephardim of Israel began to express a mounting sense of frustration by voting against the well-entrenched Establishment.

Few of the Sephardim – and especially the younger ones born in Israel into a clearly lower position – wanted to be reminded of the colossal work undertaken by the government (largely Ashkenazi Labour) to absorb the immigrants and expand education and welfare programmes, albeit in primitive form, to carry through the new settlement. All they wanted was a way to equality, and this was expressed when many began to support parties opposed to Labour, a factor that helped to bring Mr Begin's Likud coalition to power. There was still no clear-cut voting pattern. Many Sephardim had in the past voted for Labour or religious parties and continued to do so; but small ethnic parties began to grow, and felt free to merge with existing parties, particularly in anti-Establishment coalitions. In the general election of July 1984, with many Sephardim now in better circum-stances, the total ethnic anti-Labour vote was still very strong, though some of it seems to have filtered into support for Sephardi religious parties (see Table 5).[1]

The frustration of Israel's Sephardim was not only expressed politically. It forced upon the Jews of Israel, and to some extent the Jews of the world, the realization that many received ideas relating to Jewish cultural life, and based on the Ashkenazi dominance of the last centuries, are in urgent need of reconsideration. With an open mind one sees two things: first, that the values which shaped Jewish history in the past go back overwhelmingly to the lands from which these Sephardim emerged; and second, that the healthy cultural development of Israel today will have to give full weight to a revivified Sephardi heritage in order to offer the population as a whole, now living in an 'eastern' land, direct contact with much wider traditions than the Ashkenazim knew of.

A new pattern

What has happened to Jewish history can be described in a well-worn cliché: the wheel has come full circle. Ideas that took shape among the Hebrews many centuries ago in the Near East and spread all over the world, have come back to the ancient homeland embodying western experience, and are now open again to influence from the East. The revived eastern influence is not as strong as this statement may indicate, for the great majority of Jews still live outside the Holy Land, and the new Sephardi majority in Israel is itself impregnated with western influences. Yet the romance of a return to the ancestral homeland does seem to acquire an extra dimension by adding in the special element of the ingathering from the East.

One has to note also that even in a world setting the Sephardim have once again become a sizeable element in Jewry. In the early Middle Ages they had constituted the majority of Jews, and seem still to have formed two thirds of their number at the beginning of the sixteenth century. The huge expansion of the Jewish population of eastern Europe in the seventeenth to nineteenth centuries led to an amazing reversal. By 1900 the Sephardim were only 10 per cent of the world population of Jews, but this small proportion was later affected by the Holocaust. The catastrophic loss of lives mostly affected the Ashkenazim, resulting in a proportionate increase among the Sephardim, who today form about 20 per cent of world Jewry.

The decline of eastern Jewry from the sixteenth century on made it all too easy to forget how uniquely important it had been. It was in Babylonia that the Hebrew story began. It was there also that the Jewish people resettled and intensified their distinctive existence after the destructions of Jerusalem by Nebuchadnezzar in 586 BC and by the Romans in the year 70 of the Christian era. For a thousand years after this, Jewish authority and learning flowed from Babylon over the whole Jewish world. When the centre of influence began to pass to Spain in the tenth century, the links with the whole of the Near East were still kept in being; and this was intensified when the Jews were expelled from Spain and Portugal at the end of the fifteenth century. The culture of the original Sephardim rooted itself anew in the Mediterranean and Near Eastern countries, especially in the relatively tolerant ambience of the Ottoman Empire. It was only when the Near East weakened in power, and the Jews living there lost all claim to leadership, that the Ashkenazi world came to the fore in a huge expansion of numbers and influence, culminating, as we have said, in the foundation and support of the State of Israel. But now, in this setting, the Jews of the East have been brought back into a new role. No one suggests that Ashkenazi ideas and leadership must surrender to the Sephardi majority. It is a new balance that has to be attained, with each tradition active and self-reliant in what it has to offer.

This double approach may not seem so unusual when one notes that even in the early centuries, when Jewish life had mainly an eastern axis (from Babylon to Spain), there was always an involvement with the learning and religious ideas of the Ashkenazi world, as we shall see later in this book. Nor must the relatively short period of Ashkenazi dominance lead one to underplay its explosive originality and resilience. As an Ashkenazi myself, I never cease to marvel at how it was that East European Jewry grew so rapidly and set in motion enterprise and talent that flowed westward to such powerful effect in the twentieth century.

But if Ashkenazi dominance and its translation to the life of Israel remains a wonder, it has plainly been insufficient in recent years to satisfy the cultural self-sufficiency of the Sephardi population of Israel. Indeed, it is precisely the self-confidence and aggressiveness projected by the Ashkenazi image of itself in Jewish history that has prompted a critical re-examination of this whole subject in Israel today. It is now nearly ten years since official programmes were launched in Israel to recover and revitalize the Sephardi heritage, injecting the existing work in this field with a new sense of urgency. What is involved, basically, is a reconsideration of Jewish history from the beginning, with the story of the people now called Sephardim in the foreground. This, in effect, is the aim of the present book.

The Sephardi story

Even without the political motivation to give it new attention, the Sephardi heritage attracts compulsive interest because it is a field in which so much has been revealed in recent years. When one is dealing with a past as extensive as that of the Jews, it is often a matter of luck whether this or that period is suddenly illuminated through chance discovery; but when the first clues begin to emerge in this way, the effect becomes cumulative, with scholars standing on each other's shoulders to build up a comprehensive picture of a world hitherto obscure.

One sees this process at work in the study of the origins of early Hebrew history. All Jews – and especially the Jews of Iraq – have a deep interest in going back before Father Abraham to see the world out of which the patriarchs emerged, illustrated magically by archaeology in the last hundred years.

The Bible period itself is self-substantiating, but there are certain areas of a later time where the new unfolding of Jewish history seems to fit perfectly into a fresh presentation of the eastern past.

Perhaps surprisingly, the emergence of the Talmud in Babylon in the early Christian centuries offers a rich focal point of interest, based in this case not so much on the unearthing of lost manuscripts as on the painstaking use of the old methods of Jewish scholarship applied over centuries to texts that have always been available. Here, too, a new field of history has been opened up by the study of old rabbinical *responsa* in which the great scholars, particularly of Babylon, dealt meticulously with current religious and social issues as revealed in questions sent to them from all over the Jewish world.

The history of the 'golden age' of Spain also has been illuminated by new methods of scholarship. Much has been added to the corpus of philosophic and poetic texts long available; but new revelations flow, as we shall see, from the deep study of community archives which have put the story of the Jews in the Iberian peninsula on a new footing.

Something similar has brought about a new awareness of the

community life of the Jews of North Africa during the High Middle Ages (tenth to thirteenth centuries). One feature of great interest is what happened when the lively communities of what is now Tunisia followed the Fatimid rulers to Egypt and enjoyed for some centuries a relatively free life under this dynasty. The story of this period has been enriched in remarkable detail through the discovery of the *geniza*, a vast cache of papers that had lain undisturbed for centuries in a synagogue store-room in Old Cairo. A special feature that has emerged for North African Jews as a whole is the documentation of their links with Babylon to the east and Spain to the west; and from the fifteenth century on these links were extended across the Mediterranean to the newly expanding Sephardi communities of Italy.

The *geniza* papers show that subservience to the authority of Babylon in Jewish law continued for some time; but this is only one aspect of their coverage. The details on travel are perhaps the most revealing, since the Jews of the Near East are shown to have been deeply engaged in trade, mainly by land routes, as far as India and China. And even when the discovery of sea routes to the Orient bypassed the land routes, ingrained skills and family connections meant that new trading patterns were developed in other directions, notably with northern Europe and across the Atlantic.

To some degree this sustained the eastern Jewish world during the period of relative decay which followed. Modernization in the European sense came later; and here there was a give-and-take in Jewish life which gives zest to the story. The Jews of the West, it could be said, now repaid some of their original debt to the Jews of the East. There were some famous instances in which leading Jews of the western world – notably Sir Moses Montefiore – secured an easing of persecution. More generally, the Jews of the West helped to promote infinitely better education for their eastern co-religionists. The outstanding example was the foundation of modern schools in every one of these countries by the Jewish–French *Alliance* organization. Even if this was, from one angle, an element in the colonial policies of France itself, it was, to Jews, a crucial factor in their emancipation. In a less comprehensive way, British Jews did something similar in some of these countries; but in general, French influence was more effective in the whole of the Near East, especially until the outbreak of the 1914–18 war.

Old loyalties sustained

There are special features in the story of the easterners that demand individual treatment. Their trading history has already been noted, and it is remarkable how this surfaces in successive periods: first, during the expansion of Islam, then after the expulsion from Spain, and finally in opening up the transatlantic world in early colonial times. In a very different field, one wants to consider also the internal life of Sephardi Jews as reflected in their customs and folk-songs, a subject receiving very great attention in Israel today.

This brings one back to what is after all the starting-point of this enquiry. Looking at the position today, one has to note that the transcendent focus of interest throughout all the centuries of Sephardi history was the continuous relation with the Holy Land, sometimes purely spiritual in form, at other times directing events to powerful and lasting effect. In this sense, Israel's new Sephardi settlers did not arrive in an unknown land, but were able to pick up the living threads of their own story. To some extent this is true also of Ashkenazi Jews; but if they were sometimes ardent pilgrims and settlers, they never had the continuous physical proximity that exerted its pull on the Jewish residents of the relatively adjacent lands of the Near and Middle East. Perhaps the most dramatic manifestation of this, until the modern rise of Israel, was the upsurge of Cabbalist mysticism that first became evident in Spain and then began to flourish at Safed in Galilee in the sixteenth century, sweeping to a pinnacle of force, first in the Near East and then beyond, with the messianic drama of Shabbetai Zevi. Much that is still powerful in the traditional life of Israel's Sephardim took shape in this context.

There are some other special areas of interest that should lend coherence to the task of opening up the background story of Israel's Sephardim. With Jerusalem at the centre, the Jews who lived for centuries in the lands around it express a sense of endurance that was fed constantly by the link to Babylon, the original homeland of Father Abraham. It is satisfying to come full circle in this way; and it highlights a feature of Sephardi existence that demands a separate word.

In the many countries that formed this world – from Spain and Morocco in the west to Iraq and Iran in the east, and including others from the Balkans to Yemen and India – a powerful element in each case was the attachment of Jews to the places in which they had been born and bred. Objectively, as we shall see, life was not always easy and harmonious, but affection for the homeland and the home town was almost always abundantly evident. In the twelfth century, the poet Moses ibn Ezra bitterly laments having to leave his home town in Moorish Spain for a Christian city in the north:

> O if indeed the Lord would restore me
> To beautiful Granada, my paths
> Would be 'the paths of pleasantness';
> How sweet my life was in that land . . .

In our own day, an elderly Moroccan Jew now living in Canada talks, in a book, about living in *galuth* (exile), by which he means not exile from Israel but exile from Morocco.[2]

These local loyalties have enduring meaning even if, in Israel today, the common purpose might seem to transcend them. There is no more powerful illustration of this than in the theme which has surfaced so often here: the ancient attachment of the Jews to Babylon.

Jews of Iraqi origin seem to have carried into our own times the ethos and dignity that was so potent for centuries in the Land of the Two Rivers. Looking back, they are well aware of periods in which their independence and their very existence suffered grievously; but they still express a loyalty to Babylon which is compounded of two elements: they are active in a practical way to bridge the gap in Israel for Iraqi Jews and their children affected by their tragic uprooting in the 1950s, and they are tireless on the cultural side in promoting the recovery of the Sephardi past in poetry, learning, music and dance. One sometimes feels that their attachment has a quasi-mystic quality, of the kind that is echoed, strangely enough, in the words of an English nursery rhyme:

> How many miles to Babylon?
> Threescore miles and ten.
> Can I get there by candle-light?
> Yes, and back again!

Sephardim from other countries now living in Israel vie with the Iraqis in giving form to their individual loyalties; but even allowing for this, the abiding miracle of Israel is the development that has brought Jews from so many disparate backgrounds into a creative unity. This is all the more remarkable for the Jews gathered in from the East, where local conditions were often primitive and miserable. Above the din of politics one hears a unifying voice, which is the basis of hope for the future.

PART ONE
Jewish Origins in the East

1 *The World of the Patriarchs*

The story of all Jews begins with the Patriarch Abraham whose kins-
folk continued to live in Mesopotamia – 'the Land of the Two Rivers',
Tigris and Euphrates – after he himself had migrated to Canaan. The
detailed picture presented in the early chapters of the Bible is
absorbing in itself and fully consonant with all that has been
discovered by archaeology in recent years.

The Bible story tells us that Abraham's family came from 'Ur of the
Chaldees', which is usually assumed to be the city situated at the delta
formed by the two rivers, and known today as the centre of the fabulous
culture of ancient Sumeria. The name 'Chaldee' helps us to understand
the relation of his family to other clans wandering then or later around
the 'fertile crescent' which leads up the river valleys of Mesopotamia
into the Mediterranean coastal land which is now Israel.

A central name in the Bible story is 'Aram', roughly corresponding
to the Syria of today. The Chaldees were an ethnic group related to the
Arameans, and became the ruling class in Babylonia in the seventeenth
to sixteenth centuries BC. To get an idea of these fluctuating empires,
one can note a few dates broadly related to major elements in the story.

The ancient background

Sumeria's eminence goes back to the fourth millennium BC. It rose and
fell at different times in the third millennium, giving way at one time to
the mighty kingdom of Akkad, which left a different kind of mark on
the history of this area. The military victories of Akkad carried their
language everywhere, and survived as the assumed base (Akkadian)
for subsequent Semitic languages. Stories of Akkad show how far-
reaching was their influence over all the peoples, including the
Hebrews, who came from this world.

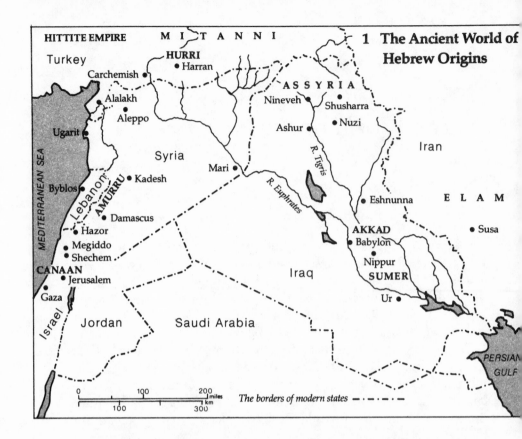

Tradition relates that Akkad was built (*c.* 2300 BC) by a mighty ruler named Sargon, who had been cast out and later rescued as an infant, just as is told of Moses a thousand years later. Sargon created an empire stretching as far as Anatolia to the north and beyond Assyria to the east. In partnership with Ur, he united, with powerful effect for the religions of the Near East, the Sumerian moon-goddess of love and the Semitic goddess of war, Ishtar. When his dynasty fell mysteriously around 2150 BC, Ur re-emerged for a final century of glory, with results that shaped the cultural traditions of Mesopotamia for centuries to come.

Two names that dominate the Bible pages of early times are Babylon and Ashur (Assyria). Babylon comes onto the scene around 1800 BC; its great lawgiver-king Hammurabi lived around 1750 BC. Assyria was powerful at the same time, but made its major mark on history later, with its king Shalmaneser I (*c.* 1263–1235 BC).

The Bible echoes with these and many other names now brought to life in archaeological studies. Much later, Assyria and then Babylon ravaged the kingdoms which the descendants of Abraham established in their own land of settlement; but long before this, Abraham's clan had absorbed a massive amount of history, law, legend, folklore, myth and poetry from the Mesopotamian background, the evidence for which is clearly visible in the early chapters of the Bible.

It is fascinating to see how scholars have given body to clues in the Bible – sometimes just isolated names or word-forms – to bring out the fluid interrelationships of those early times. A case in point is the link of Abraham with the Chaldees. A nephew of Abraham is called 'Kesed' in the Bible. His tribe would be called 'Kasdi', which merges into 'Kaldi', usually transliterated as 'Chaldee'. The Chaldean language was Aramaic, which became the vernacular of the Jews around 300 BC, an interesting return to the original language of Abraham's family.

To mention one more of the innumerable links now demonstrated between Abraham's clan and the Mesopotamian background, we can look at Mari on the upper Euphrates, an archaeological site opened in excavations which began in 1933 and were resumed on a big scale after the Second World War.

The archives of Mari echo much of what we know from the Bible about Abraham's clan. Mari was a city-state throughout the third millennium, in a key position between the empires of Mesopotamia and the rulers to the west and north. When Babylon was rising to power, Mari became a subordinate ally and was later conquered; but it left behind, in the huge *tel* now excavated, the remains of vast palaces, houses and temples, and a collection of archives that paint a detailed picture of politics and social life in this world of nomads and settlers.

The special reference to Abraham's clan is the information in the Bible that Laban, the Syrian kinsman of the patriarchs, lived in this northern part of Mesopotamia. Most strikingly, the scholars have found in the archives of Mari an account of kinship and inheritance laws that exactly parallel incidents in the Bible affecting the patriarchs and their Syrian kinsmen, and that were hitherto without known background.[3]

A new direction

To be linked to the background is only, of course, part of the story. What matters supremely, in considering the origins of the Hebrews, is the new shape that they gave to the memories of the Mesopotamian scene when they had settled in their own land and produced the teachings of the Bible. Through some mysterious kind of inspiration, they looked at the world they had grown out of and transformed it with a moral purpose. The Bible establishes this in its story of Abraham being urged to migrate to a new land. He hears God's voice in words that are very graphic in the Hebrew text: *lekh-lekha* – 'get going'; 'Leave your country, your kinsmen and your father's house, and go to a country that I will show you.' With hindsight, we know that this was to be more than a command to move to a new country to improve his well-being; it was to lead, ultimately, to a wholly new way of thinking about man's existence on earth.

The fullest expression of this would come in the universalism of the Prophets and the Psalms; but it is equally evident in those early parts of the Bible which have strong echoes of the Mesopotamian background. One can pursue this with two brief illustrations.

One, posing many questions, is the account given by archaeology of a great deluge that spread over the ancient world. According to the epic stories of Sumer, transmitted much later by the Mesopotamian writing-schools, there was a gap in Sumerian history of about two centuries towards the end of the fourth millennium, after which they re-emerged with stories of a great flood and a subsequent golden age of even greater city and temple building. When this flood story was deciphered from archives at Nineveh and published in the late nineteenth century as part of the Gilgamesh epic – the Babylonian story of the creation – it was sensational in its Bible parallels. The sensation seemed to gain an extra dimension when excavation at Ur in the 1920s under the direction of Leonard Woolley revealed thick layers of mud that some liked to think had been left by the flood. All these deluge parallels are interesting; but if the Hebrews took this Sumerian memory with them from Mesopotamia, the important thing is what they did with it. It could be said, in one sense, that they took a lot of colour out of the marvellous Gilgamesh epic, which is a novel reflecting a completely polytheistic world, in which human beings mix with gods. By contrast the Bible story is strictly monotheistic; its real drama lies in the way it establishes a moral purpose. The Mesopotamian stories have no clear motivation for the flood, while the Bible links it directly to the evils of a corrupt world which God cannot accept.

A similar distinction has to be made in considering the extraordinary parallels between the law codes of ancient Mesopotamia and the very detailed socio-legal provisions of the Bible, expressed in what is known as the Covenant Code (Exodus 21–23). Questions arising from this go to the heart of Jewish history, which has centred on the moral duty of studying and implementing these ancient social and religious rules, known collectively as the Torah. Where did the original stimulus come from, resulting in the establishing of these comprehensive laws as an immutable basis of social life?

The role of law

For a long time some scholars suggested that the Bible had based its ideas on the famous law code of the Babylonian king Hammurabi (*c.* 1728–1686 BC); in more recent years the question has broadened. The code of Hammurabi is now seen as an adaptation of much earlier law codes copied in the writing-schools of Babylonia. These go back ultimately to the law codes of Ur in the third millennium BC. Scholarly arguments on this are not the main issue, however. What is at stake is whether the emergence of Bible law, from whatever origin, represented a crucial break from the past.

Certainly there are remarkable parallels between the Hammurabi code and the Bible, particularly when case-law is being presented. But overriding all parallels there is, in the Bible, a wholly new element which links behaviour and law to the commands of God; and this in turn is rooted in the concept of a Covenant between God and Israel through which this pattern of moral conduct is established. Behind all the law expressed in the Bible is the belief – wholly original to Israel – that moral action is *imitatio dei*. Israel is to be a holy nation, reaching out to God's holiness.

The Bible texts expressing this are linked indissolubly to the Holy Land itself. They are given as the motivational force behind the exodus from Egypt and the achievement of a homeland fulfilling God's promise to Abraham. Yet one has to note, perhaps with awe, that it was in Babylon, during the first exile from the Holy Land, that supreme emphasis was put on this spiritual aspect of Torah teaching.

At the centre of worship in the Holy Land was the system of animal sacrifice and other rituals which had to be carried out exclusively at the Temple of Jerusalem. The prophets and other moral teachers had denounced those who performed these duties mechanically while ignoring the personal and moral aspects of the Jewish faith.

When the Jews were driven off to their first exile, in Babylon, in 586 BC, they wept bitterly for Jerusalem but at the same time began to intensify their old loyalties in ways other than through sacrifices. The Temple system was restored later by those who returned from exile; but in the meantime life in Babylon had provided new and lasting forms for the spiritual teachings that were to be the hallmark of Jewish life.

2 *Nationhood and Exile*

The exile in Babylon is usually thought of in terms of the conquest of the tiny kingdom of Judah by the Babylonian king Nebuchadnezzar in 586 BC; but it should also be related to the earlier conquest of the Northern Kingdom of Israel by the Assyrians in 722 BC.

In the Bible story, Assyria and Babylon were the two major empires that were always threatening the land of Israel and the adjacent Mediterranean lands, Syria and Egypt. The stories are told with grim sadness, but also, in the visions of the prophets, with a conviction that the ultimate fate of these empires would dramatize Israel's true destiny. To the prophets even the mightiest empires were evanescent in the working of God's will. These great empires might swallow Israel, but they themselves rose and fell in fateful struggles together; and in the end, the Hebrew people – incredibly – would survive them all.

It was doubtless hard to accept this when one was part of a tiny nation now in exile. Assyria had been the first to wreak this fate on Israel. It had been a mighty empire from its base on the Tigris as far back as the third millennium BC, and after various periods of decline had risen again towards the end of the second millennium – not far from the time of the Exodus – to a position of colossal power, supreme in architecture, art, diplomacy and trade, and conducting military campaigns which are thought to be echoed in some of the heroic exploits ascribed to characters in Greek literature. During these centuries they were in the closest relations, through treaties and dynastic marriages, with the successive rulers of Babylon, whose culture they deeply respected. Tradition, going back, as we now know, to roots a thousand years earlier, was always a prime activating force, as it was to become equally with the Israelites.

Conquest by Assyria

In this dizzy world of power Israel was sometimes able to contribute to the defensive alliances of the Mediterranean countries; but in the eighth century BC this became futile. A great Assyrian ruler, Tiglath-Pileser III (745–727 BC), had begun to establish his position by taking over Babylon (adopting the Babylonian name 'Pulu') and other adjacent rival kingdoms. Moving westward to secure timber and mineral resources, he found the kingdoms of Israel and Judah and their allies only small hurdles in his road to triumph. 'And Pul[u], king of Assyria came against the land', the Bible says (2 Kings 15:19). The Assyrian archives mention 'Azariau of Yaudi' (Azariah of Judah) in the alliance against him in 738. Tributes were paid by a number of the western 'states', including Hamath, Tyre, Byblos and Israel; but when they later moved into resistance the Assyrians, now led by Shalmaneser V, decided on a total destruction of the ten-tribe Northern Kingdom of Israel. They took her capital Samaria in 722, and carried out a mass deportation of the inhabitants of the kingdom.

The destiny of these 'lost ten tribes' has never been established, but there are clues to this now that are relevant to the theme of this book. The deportation places mentioned in the Bible (2 Kings 17:6) seem to suggest areas adjacent to Mesopotamia, but too vaguely to identify them. Instead, legend was allowed to take over; and in legend the lost ten tribes have surfaced in every corner of the world, including appearances as Japanese, British or American Indians.

The most popular legend about these lost tribes related that they were living in a land beyond the mysterious river Sambattyon, which on weekdays flowed too fiercely to let them cross, while on the sabbath, when the river was at rest, a crossing was forbidden by sabbath law. This legend was drawn on in picturesque form by medieval travellers, as we shall see later, in the story of the sixteenth-century pseudo-Messiah Reubeni, who appeared at the court of the king of Portugal, claiming that he had come from their distant lands and was a brother of one of their kings.

There is a more intriguing thought for a book concerned, as we are here, with the origins of eastern Jewries. Is it not possible that the lost ten tribes remained distinctive in Mesopotamia and merged later with the Jews of Judah who were exiled to Babylon in 586 BC? One has to take account, here, of the dramatic speech by the Assyrian diplomat Rab-Shakeh (2 Kings 18) in which he tried to persuade the ordinary people of Judah to oppose their king's alliance with Egypt, and instead to recognize the many good things provided by Assyria to their kinsmen in Israel. How can anyone trust Egypt, he asks: a 'bruised reed on which, if a man lean, it will go into his hand, and pierce it'. Instead, trust the king of Assyria, who promises that if you make an agreement with him, your life will be happy: '[I] will take you away to a land like your own land, a land of corn and wine, a land of bread and vineyards, a land of olive oil and honey, so that you may live and not die.'

Rab-Shakeh's audience may well have been suspicious of these promises, but Assyrian records now available seem to show that the deportees did enjoy a decent life in their new home. According to the Israeli Assyriologist Abraham Malamat, the documents indicate that deportees were not treated as slaves, and ultimately swelled the numbers of those returning from the Babylonian exile. This sheds a wholly new light on the lost ten tribes. Far from disappearing, 'they were settled in Mesopotamia as land tenants of the king, while the craftsmen among them were employed in state enterprises'. They had the right to hold land, and above all 'to observe the customs of their forefathers'. The return to Zion under Ezra, therefore, 'included remnants of the Lost Ten Tribes'.[4]

The rise of Babylon

All this is an apt reminder that Jewish migrations have never been clear-cut in operation or predictable in their outcome. On the surface, the Assyrian conquest might have been expected to signal the end of the Jewish people, particularly because in the land of Israel itself the conquerors installed deportees from the east who were due to grow, ultimately, into the anti-Jewish Samaritan people. In the event, however, the tiny Jewish territory of Judah that remained had a renaissance of faith under two remarkable kings, Hezekiah and Josiah. It was Assyria itself that finally was pushed into extinction; and though the Babylonian successor destroyed Jerusalem and carried its people off to captivity in Babylon, this new settlement was to become, for Jews, a restorative and creative force for survival in new ways.

Assyria did not surrender its powers easily. It enjoyed a succession of triumphs during the ensuing 140 years recorded in literary and historical records of enormous interest; yet they chronicled rebellions in all directions. The final alliance that Assyria faced was of rebellious

Medes and Babylonians. In 612 BC these allies captured and utterly destroyed the Assyrian capital Nineveh. Three years later (609), Babylonian forces pushed the Assyrians out of their last outpost in Mesopotamia at Harran, the home town, centuries earlier, of Father Abraham.

This was the base from which the Babylonian kings now picked up the attacks on Israel and the other Mediterranean countries who had long suffered from the Assyrians. When the final assault on Jerusalem came in 586 BC, the city fell to Nebuchadnezzar after a long siege and was put to the flames. The king, Zedekiah, was blinded and taken to Babylon in chains. He died there; but his successor Jehoiachin was, after a while, taken from prison and given a royal allowance. A similar kind of recognition was maintained later, so that a tradition of direct descent from King David sustained the Exilarch (ruler of Exile) in Babylon for centuries to come.

A new era in Jewish life had started, though after a terrible blow. The scale of the shock is indicated by the way Jewish legend built up the figure of the conqueror Nebuchadnezzar, with the prophets depicting him as a direct agent of providence, endowed with almost superhuman powers.

At the same time the teachers of the Jews in exile had to project ideas that would cope with the theological problems that the loss of their independence presented. Somehow or other they had to accept that the God who should have protected them was responsible for what had happened; but, by the same token, they had to believe that one day God would see them worthy of restoration. The deportation had brought suffering, which was punishment; but was it not also part of God's plan that their new home offered a good life and new opportunities to intensify their ancient faith? In sentiment they would weep when, by the waters of Babylon, they remembered Zion; but to some extent they had brought the dignity – and even the royal family – of Zion with them to Babylon.

The Babylonian Empire had, at this stage, only a few years to run before it fell to the Medes; but the healthy roots of the Jewish settlement which had been planted there grew fruitfully under the successive rulers of Mesopotamia, so that 'Babylon' remained a concept of independence and leadership for Jews for the next 1,800 years. In some respects, as we shall see, this special role was maintained for Sephardi and Oriental Jews in more recent centuries too, which makes the memory of Babylon a unique feature of Jewish history.

The way of life which increasingly attached the exiles to their new home in Babylon was helped by the conditions in which the departure from Judah had been carried out.

Unlike the Assyrians, the Babylonians did not depopulate a conquered land and then send in aliens to change its character. They took the leaders with them to exile, leaving the ordinary folk to be, in the Bible's words, 'vinedressers and husband-men'. This difference in treatment meant, as one historian puts it, that 'the Jews who settled in Babylonia represented the cream of their country's political, ecclesiastical and intellectual leadership, which was why they were selected for deportation'. From the few available figures, it seems that the total, including families, might not have exceeded some 15,000: 'but these exiles, though few in number, were the ones who would shape Israel's future, both giving their faith its new direction, and providing the impulse for the ultimate restoration of the Jewish community in Palestine'.[5]

The exiles, it seems, were not dispersed throughout the country but lived in settlements of their own in southern Mesopotamia, not far from Babylon itself. They farmed the land, becoming famous later for their agricultural skills. Above all, they were free to assemble to develop their communal religious life; and it was here that they made their special contribution to Judaism.

New teachings

Cut off from the rituals linked to the Temple in Jerusalem, they would clearly put more pressure on rituals that could still be followed to express their traditional faith, two in particular: the sabbath and circumcision. And even if the Temple was not at hand for sacrifices that were a routine route to ritual purity, they could give attention to ritual cleanliness in other ways, while studying the rules which priests had brought with them to exile.

Here, it seems, are the roots of the priestly code as it finally appeared in the Bible. The Temple had become a supremely sacred memory, with the prophet Ezekiel its key interpreter.

Ezekiel, who was of priestly stock, saw the whole of the Jewish future centred on a restored Temple, with the corollary that the priests, administering the Temple, would be the future rulers of independent Jewish life. 'Son of man,' he hears God telling him, 'mark well, and behold with thine eyes, and hear with thine ears all that I say unto thee concerning all the ordinances of the house of the Lord, and all the laws thereof; and mark well the entering in of the house, with every going forth of the sanctuary' (Ezekiel 44:5).

With equal devotion but greater universality, the prophet who wrote in Babylon under the name of Isaiah saw a deeper meaning in the restoration to Jerusalem.* He wrote at the time of the fall of Babylon in 539 BC to the Medes led by Cyrus, and saw in these cataclysmic events a turning-point in human history, brought about directly through providence. As the instrument on earth of God's purpose, the Jews had a direct role in these events, even if, to an ordinary observer, they were merely pawns.

To Isaiah the triumphant Cyrus was God's chosen agent: his *messiah* ('anointed one'). The first phase of man's restoration would be the return of the Jews to their central role in Jerusalem, but beyond that the whole of mankind was now to feel itself to be under God's wing. In the oracles through which God speaks (Isaiah 45), all mankind is asked to see that the rule of God is universal:

I am the Lord and there is none else . . . from the rising of the sun and to its setting, there is none beside me . . . let the skies pour down righteousness: let the earth open and bring forth salvation . . . I the Lord created it.

---

* Chapters 1–39 of the book of Isaiah in our Bible are by a prophet who lived in Jerusalem c. 740–700 BC, dealing with events of that time, nearly two hundred years before the destruction by Nebuchadnezzar. Chapters 40–66 reflect the experiences of the Jews in exile in Babylonia, clearly by a different author, referred to in discussion as 'the second Isaiah'.

3 Return and Dispersal

The clues that have come down to us about Jewish life during the exile in Babylon are followed by an almost blank period of nearly five hundred years; yet it was in this period that the ancestors of the Jewish people developed their identity, adherents of a faith rooted in the Bible and celebrated in a way of life that was to be common to Jews all over the world.

In trying to work out how this immense change came about, we can take two men, both from Babylon, as guide-posts. The first was Ezra the Scribe, who played a leading part in the return of many Jews to the land of Israel in the fourth century BC; the other, at the end of the 'blank' period, was Hillel, a rabbi who became the leading Torah teacher in Israel towards the end of the first century BC, and was succeeded by family descendants through whom the whole tradition of rabbinic Judaism took shape. Hillel became legendary in Jewish life not only for his authority in determining the laws binding on Jews in accordance with Bible interpretation, but also for his ethical teachings and the gentleness of his character.

In reality the interim period between Ezra and Hillel was far from blank. We are simply short of contemporary historical writings to give us a coherent account of what was going on. In this situation, some political detail provided later by the writings of Josephus and the books of the Maccabees has to be supplemented by what we can deduce from *some* books which have survived from this time, and by what has come down through tradition about the basic acts and attitudes of our two symbolic guide-posts. Ezra's key act after arriving in the ruins of Jerusalem was to read and expound 'the Book of the Law' to Jews who assembled to hear it. By Hillel's time the Torah, which had come freshly to Ezra's audience, had become central to Jewish life. His eminence lay in being able to express the received body of interpretation which generations of teachers had been developing.

Authority from the Holy Land

When the first Temple had been destroyed in 586 BC, authority in Jewish life had lain with the priests who carried out the holy rituals. Ezra was himself of priestly stock; and his authority from the Persian ruler to lead the return allowed him – indeed encouraged him – to restore all the glories of the Temple rituals. It is all the more significant, then, that even at this early date the reading of the Torah, with its moral emphasis, was so important.

In political terms this emphasis became less dominating after the Temple had been rebuilt. Members of the priestly clan exploited their authority to win power and wealth, in an atmosphere of corruption and social unrest. But if this, as the writings of Josephus show, was the public pattern, there must also have been an untold story which flowed directly from Ezra's exposition of the Torah, and which reached back to the beginning of Torah study in Babylon itself. This, in effect, is how it was that a Babylonian, Hillel, could become the rabbinic leader of the Jews in Israel. Bible study had continued in Babylon after 'the return', ready, as we shall see, to reach the high standards of Israel itself.

But in the meantime, in the lead-up to the age of Hillel, authority had to flow from devoted Bible teachers in the Holy Land. Later generations had records of how the traditions on this had been handed down from one generation to another, all keeping alive vibrant oral teachings side by side with the written Bible text. The strength of feeling on this can be seen in the vehemence of the revolt which broke out early in the second century BC against the paganism of the Syrian–Greek ruler Antiochus, and even more clearly still when pious Torah-loving Jews rejected the practices of their own Maccabeean rulers, themselves corrupt behind the mask of their priestly authority. The new monarchs, who brought military glory and expanded the tiny country for a time, were often at loggerheads with the Torah teachers, some of whom were now organized into strictly observant groups called 'Pharisees' ('separatists'). The title 'Rabbi' ('Master') was basically a form of address, but acquired its own dignity. It was as the supreme expositor of the teachings of the rabbis that Hillel became famous.

This, then, was the underlying pattern of the 'blank' centuries from

Ezra to Hillel. It was the period in which the Torah assumed the central role which it has occupied ever since in Jewish life. A perfect illustration of this lies in the contrast between the positions after the two destructions of the Temple. In the first Exile, the Jews in Babylon had to build up elements of the faith which lay among them and dream of a return. By the time of the second destruction, 'normative' Judaism, in its rabbinic form, was strongly established and led by teachers, soon to spread everywhere, who would keep the faith alive.

The very varied contents of rabbinic Judaism were ultimately expressed in the Talmud (law, argument and history) and the Midrash (homily, anecdote, and folklore). Though always Torah-oriented, the vast range of these varied writings showed that Jews had also been absorbing much from their environment during the long unrecorded period. Much came through from Babylon and the Greek–Hellenist world that would form a strong element in the ideas and culture of subsequent Jewish life.

Influences from Babylon

Taking environment influence to the maximum, scholars have argued fiercely on whether the final text of the Bible itself was edited in Babylon (which could have influenced the style of the historical books) or in Israel after the Return, which would have allowed those who held priestly office to give the Bible text a slant which emphasized the antiquity and centrality of priestly authority.[6] But whether or not the Bible was edited in Babylon, there can be no doubt that many of the ideas that were soon to be a familiar part of Jewish legend took shape there, as a natural overflow from the Mesopotamian background.

Much of this surfaced later in Bible commentary known as midrash. Not surprisingly there is much midrash commentary on passages in Genesis that have an archaic setting. The Jews in exile would have become aware of the old Babylonian myths – on the creation, the flood, the early generations of man, for example – and sought to harmonize these with their own traditional reports of these events.

More powerfully, one can see how some very brief and mysterious passages in Genesis acquired body from ideas current in the Baby-lonian background. Two examples are the stories on Enoch and the emergence among Jews of the idea of angels, all drawn from the time of exile.

Of Enoch, all we know from the Bible is a brief suggestion that, as one of the Bible's primeval characters, he never died, 'for God took him' (Genesis 5:24). In later apocalyptic and rabbinic literature, Enoch becomes a powerful and clearly defined character: the creator and bearer of human culture, and the transmitter to mankind of heavenly experience drawn from his regular communication with angels. All this, especially the angelology, reflects Babylonian concepts which must have entered the Jewish oral tradition even though they had only cryptic expression in the Bible.

The link with Babylon here is the influence of the religion of Zoroaster, with its emphasis on one supreme God. Zoroastrianism was not a pure monotheism, but saw a struggle between the Supreme Being and the forces of evil appearing as rival celestial beings. Without taking this too seriously, the Jews borrowed the idea of celestial beings, in various forms.

The outstanding example which comes to mind in this way is Satan (a Hebrew word for 'adversary') who appears in Job as an ingenious plotter arguing with God. The idea of a highly placed opponent of God grew into elaborate drama in sectarian literature.

Very different was the idea of angels, who became very popular. In earlier books of the Bible angels, as messengers of God, are very rare, though we begin to hear of celestial beings, *seraphim*, flying around God and praising Him. From Exile times, however, angels begin to be seen with explicit roles, in particular as guardians of specific people. In Daniel, leading angels (archangels) appear for the first time with personal names – Michael and Gabriel – and distinct personalities. In later sectarian books, such as the Dead Sea Scrolls, the archangels are thought to have special roles in world history.

Greek parallels

The influence from the surrounding Greek–Hellenist background was less in the field of myth or legend (where that of Babylon had been strong) than in current social or philosophic ideas. It was more direct, of course, among the Jews of Egypt who were Greek-speaking and highly assimilated; but Hellenism also made its mark among the Jews of Palestine, despite their strong nationalistic feelings. The truth is that Jews rarely cut themselves off completely from their neighbouring cultures; and this was very relevant to the formative period of rabbinic

Judaism, in which much can now be seen as related to the Greek background. To hear echoes of this in Temple times, we have to consider what surfaced later in the non-biblical 'apocrypha' or 'pseudepigrapha', and in sectarian writings loosely known as the Dead Sea Scrolls.*

The Jews had, it is true, inherited a very distinctive outlook religiously and socially; yet they had been aware of the Greeks as part of their world long before the arrival of the Macedonians under Alexander the Great. Greek traders had been familiar in the coastal towns of Palestine as early as the seventh century BC. There were Greek mercenaries in the Egyptian and Babylonian armies, including the army of Nebuchadnezzar. From the time of its greatness in the fifth century BC, Greece had poured a profusion of explorers, adventurers and scholars into the Near East, and the Jews had responded.

Palestine, writes Elias Bickerman, 'belonged to the belt of an eclectic Greco–Egyptian–Asian culture, which extended from the Nile Delta to Cilicia. Greek painted pottery, Phoenician amulets and Egyptian idols are equally typical of Palestine in the fourth century.'[7] And if contact with this world brought ideas in for the Jews, it also served to spread Jewish influence outward, laying the basis for a widespread Jewish diaspora from early times. This vast expansion of a Jewish presence in the whole of the Near East became, of course, a major element in the spread of Christianity, though the new religion, accepted by many who were only partially Jewish in outlook, was ready to harmonize its faith with ideas from Greek myth in a way that was anathema to older-established Jews.

The common element for the Jews themselves lay in the field of ethics and social philosophy. If one looks briefly at two Jewish books that emerged during the Hellenistic period, one can see how important they were in the consolidation of the rabbinic tradition.

The first is a late biblical work, Ecclesiastes, whose opening words, 'Vanity of vanities, all is vanity', set the tone. Here we have among the Jews an essay in epigrammatic scepticism, very Greek in style, but not necessarily a direct borrowing; for the Jews, like the Greeks, drew on ideas common in the oriental world. Ecclesiastes certainly echoes the mood of Stoic philosophy; but Stoicism had an oriental source. Zeno,

---

* 'Apocrypha' (hidden writings) are for the most part historical and ethical works preserved by the Church, though not included in the Hebrew Bible. 'Pseudepigrapha' are visionary writings in many styles attributed to the ancients and dealing with the mysteries of creation.

founder of this movement in the fourth century BC, reflected the interaction between western and eastern ideas which followed the conquests of Alexander, when many important thinkers came to Athens from oriental cities.

The other book, *The Wisdom of Ben Sira*, also has something of a Greek philosophic tone, but is very different from Ecclesiastes, being profoundly Hebraic in its concept of the moral life. This is expressed in a confidence that free will is fundamental to man – he has to choose between what is right and wrong – even though everything in man's choice is already known to God. This philosophical dilemma would one day receive full expression in the academies whose debates were finally expressed in the pages of the Talmud of Jerusalem and Babylonia. A great second-century rabbi, Akiba, expressed it in a memorable epigram: 'All is foreseen by God, but freedom of choice is given' (*Aboth* 3:16), and it is echoed in another saying of the Talmud: 'All is in the hands of Heaven, except the fear of Heaven' (Bab. Tal. *Ber.* 33b).

These are merely two of a number of books that illustrate the common Jewish–Greek background of the pre-destruction period: and even in themselves they offset the utterly fallacious notion that the rabbis were only concerned with dry legal argument. Study, as exemplified later in the Talmud, was at one level a holy activity, but at another a comradeship absorbed in human issues, encompassing history, anecdote, philosophy, legend – and humour. This alone explains its undying influence on the Jews in whatever circumstances they lived.

Role of the diaspora

This positive aspect of Torah study was evident even under Roman domination, once a *modus vivendi* was found after the wars. Life was never 'normal', with Jerusalem in ruins and out of bounds to them in any case; but in Galilee the Jews began to structure a form of self-government, built around the continuing need they felt to consolidate their inheritance of Torah teaching. They worked from a study centre at Usha (near Haifa), where Jewish religious authority was vested in a Sanhedrin (rabbinic court), headed by a leading rabbi, Simeon ben Gamaliel, a descendant of Hillel who commanded the respect of the Roman authorities as well as of the Jews.

His son Judah, whose life spanned the second half of the second century AD and the beginning of the third, became a key figure in these developments, and was particularly important in the movement to set up norms of law and practice for dispersed Jews all over the world.

The task of exercising authority over Jews everywhere was financed by taxes at home and the collection of funds from diaspora countries, a process which has continued without interruption from that time to this. Administratively Judah's colleagues gave him the right to nominate rabbis and teachers throughout Jewry. The calendar was fixed by his authority for use even beyond the Holy Land; and with Roman approval, the rabbinic courts were given full civil, and even sometimes criminal, jurisdiction.

Judah was known by the title Rabbi Judah Ha-Nasi (Judah the Patriarch). It was as a natural corollary of his status as patriarch that he produced a very systematic code of Jewish law which became known as the Mishnah ('The Study Book'), which then became the formal text for the more discursive discussions recorded in the Talmud, a name which broadly indicates 'learning'.

At its peak the patriarchate could draw on a very large number of adherents in the diaspora. The total number of Jews at the time was less than it had been before the Roman–Jewish wars, but was still very large. A census ordered by the Emperor Claudius in 48 AD is said to have found almost seven million Jews within the Roman Empire, suggesting a total Jewish population at the time of more than eight million, of whom probably not more than two and a half million lived in Palestine.

Of eight million Jews in the world, it is thought that Egypt, Syria and Asia Minor might each have had more than one million, with a similar number in Babylonia, and many more in the Iranian plateau, Yemen and Ethiopia. These figures are, of course, very relevant to the theme of this book, for these many Jews, scattered through the Near and Middle East, were to a great extent the ancestors of the *edot ha-mizrach* now re-gathered, overwhelmingly, in the land of Israel.

Migration had, of course, also spread much further afield. There is hardly a country of Europe – except for England – that does not record the presence of at least a few Jews in Roman times. But the East (the *mizrach*) was still the Jewish heartland; and in this heartland Babylon was now poised to assume an even greater importance as the alternative to Israel, once dispersal was in full flow.

Half-jokingly the Jews of Babylon would claim that they were superior to those of Israel. They would never dispute the basic holiness of Jerusalem, with which nothing could compare; but in material terms they were far more prosperous, and the head of their self-government – the *resh galutha* (Head of Exile) – was a direct descendant of King David. Even their scholars had taken over Israel's former pre-eminence. 'All countries', said one rabbi, 'are second-rate compared with the Land of Israel, and the Land of Israel is second-rate compared with Babylonia.'[8]

If this was not to be taken too seriously, Babylonia certainly had special importance in projecting for the first time a paradigm of diaspora existence in a form that was highly significant for the future.

The uniqueness of the Jewish diaspora lies in its being anchored firmly at two ends – the ancient homeland and the land of settlement. The double connection was organic, in this case, for it was the land of new settlement, Babylonia, that made it possible for the ancient base to be sustained. The remnant left in Judaea might well have disappeared in the face of constant attacks from surrounding nomads if the Persian Empire, which reigned with paramount authority all the way to the Mediterranean, had not permitted – indeed encouraged – the Jews in the Holy Land to find a new form of loyalty to their tradition, an amalgam of what emerged from their own folk history and what was now being brought to them from Babylon.

Elias Bickerman has pointed to another virtue of diaspora life, typified by Babylon. Jews in the Holy Land were guarded against 'spiritual inbreeding' because of the enlargement of their experience in drawing on Jewish living 'outside'. This relationship was re-enacted later in many diaspora situations. Dispersed Jews everywhere always felt a living connection with the Holy Land, but this was never rigid. There was, as there still is, a symbiotic relationship between the diaspora and the homeland, in which what is valuable in the diaspora finds its way back to its source.[9]

4 *Resurgence in Babylon*

It can be taken for granted that the Jews of Babylon accorded Israel full respect during the centuries in which Torah teaching had its centre in the Holy Land; and this was deepened in the period after the wars with Rome when Jewish authority reached a peak in Israel under Rabbi Judah Ha-Nasi. But even at this time the relationship was beginning to change in character because of major political and social forces now dominating the Near Eastern scene.

An advantage was flowing to Babylon because of its relative calm compared with the upheavals of Israel. The large Jewish population of Babylon − it had grown to around a million by the time of the destruction of Jerusalem in AD 70 − were living under the rule of the Parthians, a semi-feudal people who accorded the Jews a kind of feudal independence under their *resh galutha*. In the battles of the Parthians with Rome, the Jews, who were settled densely on both sides of the border and were historically anti-Roman, were regarded as useful allies.

This special position continued when the Persian Sassanid dynasty took over from the Parthians early in the third century AD. The incessant campaigns between Rome and the Persians were part of the cause of the decline of Roman power in this century. When the Emperor Constantine formally recognized Christianity in AD 313, there was an even stronger motivation for Jewish attachment to Persia, where they were free from the vilification that the Church was now beginning to turn in full force on the Jews.

This is not to say that the Jews of Palestine were in total decline. Towards the end of the second century they had begun to benefit from the goodwill of some of the Roman rulers, who worked closely with Rabbi Judah Ha-Nasi and had good relations with the Sanhedrin.

The influence of Torah study

For a few centuries the community still showed considerable strength, expressed in the completion of the Jerusalem Talmud and the collection of books of midrash which were of lasting spiritual value. Economic prosperity is illustrated by the building in the fifth century of some lavish synagogues, excavated in recent times. We also know now that side by side with the creativity that produced the Talmud, Palestine had a profusion of poets at this time, writing the most lyrical Hebrew.[10] The spirit of rebellion was also kept alive through sporadic revolts, in which the Jews sought help – usually in vain – from the Persians.

But the Holy Land was still weakening in its leadership of the Jewish people, compared with the burgeoning strength of Babylon. Reversing the earlier trend, the flow of scholars was now from Palestine to Babylon. The turning-point had come in AD 219 with the arrival there of a distinguished rabbi, Abba Arika, known affectionately, but with respect, as 'Rab'. Working with a Babylonian rabbi called Samuel, Rab founded study centres through which the fame of Babylonian scholarship became universally acknowledged.

These academies soon began to produce their own version of the Talmud, parallel to the authoritative work being produced in the Holy Land, but in many ways more detailed and complete. The Babylonian Talmud which emerged from this after centuries of study was not only crucially important for the *edot ha-mizrach* but was the prime authority for Jews everywhere.

Leaving aside the importance of the Babylonian Talmud in the field of *halakhah* (Jewish religious law), it has an additional interest for us today as a detailed reflection of the kind of life that the Jews developed in Babylon in these early centuries. Those who came together at set seasons – rabbis and laymen – to discuss the *halakhah*, and thus lay the basis for the Talmud, had a very wide field of experience to draw on, if only in terms of numbers. The population of Babylon had been described by Josephus in his book *Jewish Antiquities* as 'countless myriads of which none can know the number'. Philo, the Jewish philosopher of Alexandria, had written in the same vein of 'the very large number of Jews in every city' in lands beyond the Euphrates. A modern scholar, Walter Fischel, who is a leading authority on ancient Persia, says that the great number of Jews in this area was increased through voluntary movements of Jews from the Roman provinces, as well as through forced migration of Jews from territories adjacent to Babylonia, citing a fourth-century Armenian historian who writes of a forced transfer of perhaps seven thousand Jews to the interior of Persia.[11]

It was because of the large population that study sessions could be such a dominant feature of the social scene. The two major *yeshivot* (academies) founded or expanded by Rab and Samuel were at Sura and Nehardea – the Oxford and Cambridge of Jewish Babylonia. Both academies attracted masses of ordinary people who turned to study, side by side with ordinary work, as an enlargement of life. In each year work in the fields came to a standstill in Adar (February/March) and in Elul (August/September); and it was then that the students flocked to the academies. In Rab's time, Sura alone had 1,200 regular students. Nehardea was succeeded after a time by a similar academy in Pumbedita, and additional academies were founded elsewhere in Babylonia. But the two major academies remained the pivot of Jewish life, respected throughout the world.

Picture of social life

It is impossible to understand the nature of Jewish survival in a host of different and often hostile environments without recognizing the nature of study that had been launched in Palestine and was now vastly extended in these Babylonian academies.

Three desires were being gratified, in a form that was original and sustaining. First, there was the desire to express reverence for the Torah. The analysis of every word and action – and every character motivation within each story – was a holy duty. Second, there was the determination to conduct the whole of ordinary life in consonance with what the written and oral Torah had laid down; and this meant analysing daily preoccupations in every field – work, rituals, human relationships, everything – to put life under what might be called a canopy of the Torah. Bringing these two processes together released the third gratification – the absolute delight in the experience of study itself. At one level it was a supremely rational experience; at another it was mystical.

Though the object of Talmud discussion was to determine 'the Law', one cannot but be interested in the case histories within the argument, especially in the light they throw on the Jews of Babylon as a basically agricultural people. The rise of Islam and the expansion of the Arab Empire changed all this, as we shall see. But until then the Jews of Babylon had been settled for centuries on the land, which therefore made agriculture a central issue in many Talmud discussions. Scholars who have analysed the Talmud with this in mind have given us a lively picture far beyond the realm of pettifogging discussion once associated with Talmud study.

In one book which does this to delightful effect, the author offers a list of contents on Talmud agriculture that will be startling to those accustomed to think of rabbinical Jews as simply immured in their studies.[12] In effect, it leaps across the centuries to modern Israel, with chapters entitled 'Methods of Land Cultivation', 'Livestock Rearing', or 'Fishing, Fowling and Hunting'. The case histories cited are sometimes as funny as they are illuminating.

We hear, for example, of one dispute between Rab (head of Sura) and Samuel (head of Nehardea) on how to deal with a barrel of wine found floating in the Euphrates. If one could be sure it was prepared by Jews, it could be used; if it had a non-Jewish origin, it might be associated with pagan ceremonies and therefore ritually barred. Rab, clearly anxious to give Jewish wine-drinkers the benefit of the doubt, argues that if it was found near a town with a Jewish majority, all was well. His rival Samuel argues that the barrel might have floated downstream from Idh-da-Khiri (modern Hit), where the majority were non-Jews. Samuel was clearly a spoil-sport. But in terms of social history, the main point of this and many other stories is the detailed confirmation of what the historians had reported only vaguely, that Jews were now very numerous and closely settled in central Babylonia. Rab, having returned from Palestine, argues in quite a few cases that ordinances laid down in Palestine to deal with close settlement there (e.g. laws on keeping sheep and goats out of cultivated farmlands) should now apply equally to Babylonia, where Jewish land-occupation had become so extensive.

We hear, in fact, both of small farmers (the rule) and of Jews with huge estates. The Exilarch, not surprisingly, was the greatest land-owner. Others with large estates had bought up land from tax defaulters. The farms of Samuel's family were so extensive that when they sold their grain it depressed the market price for a long period. At the same time we hear of distinguished rabbis among small-scale farmers, such as Rabbi Huna, who always carried a spade on his shoulders, saying that hard work was a virtue. He was, however, always ready to take a rest. If people came to him with a *halakhic* dispute while he was working his field, they had to supply a substitute to carry on digging while he listened to the argument. The wide-ranging content of the disputes raises the most technical questions, worthy of being included in a farming handbook, which, to some extent, the Talmud was.

Agriculture was, of course, only one aspect of Talmud study. We shall see later, from the *responsa* sent by the rabbis of Babylonia to enquiries from all over the world, that Talmudic expertise was enthusiastically applied to every aspect of business, communal, religious and personal life, surfacing in material of great interest to social historians.

These are merely some aspects of Jewish study and economic existence in Babylon while the foundations were being laid for its unique role in taking over from the Holy Land in many respects. It was providential that this was carried through so effectively that Judaism could survive and flourish in the totally changed situation that confronted Jews after the rise of Islam.

PART TWO
Changes under Islam

5 Jews and the Rise of Islam

Around AD 570 a boy whom his parents named Mohammed was born to a high-ranking Arab family, custodians of a pagan shrine at Mecca. At the age of forty he had visions related to a belief in one God, which echoed to some extent the beliefs and historical tales of Jewish tribes living in that area of North Arabia. For the next twenty years he gathered followers but, meeting opposition, fled with them to Medina in 622, a journey known as the *hegira* (flight).

Mohammed had admired the Jews and Christians for having a 'scripture', and gathered his own visions and rules into a book, the *Koran*, which would have a similar holiness. With conversion to the new faith as their aim, his followers now set about an extraordinary series of military conquests. Because Jews and Christians had a 'book' of their own, they were excused forced conversion and allowed to live as *dhimmis* (protected persons), though, as we shall see later, subject to humiliations.

Mohammed died in 632, but by now the conquests were fully launched. By 636 his followers had captured all Syria. Two years later they took Jerusalem from the Byzantine Emperor Heraclius, opening an Arab gateway to the west. These dramatic events, crucial to world history, were to have an overwhelming impact on the Jews, giving them experience that added great depth to their own story. The first major encounter with the new world force was in the most 'Jewish' part of the diaspora: Babylonia.

The Jews and Arabia

As the armies of the new faith swept, in little more than a decade, through Syria, Palestine and Egypt and eastward from Babylonia to the gates of India, Jewish communities everywhere looked hopefully to the new invaders and often assisted their progress. This had been true in their capture of Jerusalem, and was even more significantly so in their triumphs in Babylonia.

Islam offered Jews a different world in which to sustain their existence, often with great difficulties but also with new opportunities in the economic and intellectual fields. In due course, the powerful Jewry of Babylonia made the most of this, especially when the new capital Baghdad (founded in 762) achieved its full glory. But when Mohammed had been formulating the new faith 160 years earlier, the Jews he had dealt with in his native Arabia had represented a very different stream of Jewish life.

In the sharpest contrast to the Jews of Babylonia, who had led a settled, sophisticated life for centuries and produced a host of scholars reflecting the authentic traditions of Jewish life, the Jews of North Arabia whom Mohammed knew lived as small tribes or clans linked in uncertain origin to peoples like the Nabataeans in Palestine, remote in experience and outlook from the Jews who thronged the academies of Babylon. But they were fiercely loyal to Judaism in their belief in One God; and the story they knew of their past put an emphasis on great leaders – Abraham and Moses – whom Mohammed clearly found attractive. They had a book – the Bible – which expressed their faith and which they treated with veneration. Mohammed saw himself as a prophet in this Jewish tradition; but though some of the Jews of his world of North Arabia were sympathetic to him on his famous flight to Medina, and many Jews must have converted to the new faith, there was in general strong Jewish opposition. (This may have been, Goitein believes, because they thought that Mohammed had imbibed sectarian Jewish views, and sectarianism is always divisive.)[13]

The Arabian ambience was so important to the Jews then and later that it is necessary to look at the pre-Islamic position more closely for a moment, particularly to note the major differences in origin and outlook between the Jews living in and around the cluster of towns in North Arabia where Islam arose, and those in the south-west, known then as Himyar, and later as Yemen.

The historical material on the pre-Islamic Jewish settlement in Arabia is a subject with its own fascination. There is no direct Jewish source, and even the account given by Arab historians was written down much later and was heavily dependent on legend. Yet this story is illustrated by modern research in two remarkable ways. First, a great many names mentioned in genealogical lists in the Bible, and linked especially to the patriarchs, have been identified with Arabia in recent times through newly found inscriptions or by mentions in Assyrian and Greek sources. Second, the excavation in 1936 of the ancient cemetery at Beit She'arim (near Haifa) revealed a series of graves of the peoples of Himyar going back to the third and fourth centuries, with Greek inscriptions establishing the Jewish presence in Arabia and the link with Palestine over this huge distance.

The Bible names and incidents that are now identified so positively with Arabia prompted some scholars to argue at one time that the Jewish people must have originated in this vast peninsula as Bedouin wanderers, working their way to the fertile crescent and settling in Palestine. This view is firmly dismissed by S. D. Goitein in his lively study, *Jews and Arabs*, as without any historical foundation, and derived largely 'by a false analogy from the conquest of the Middle East by the Muslim Arabs'. More positively he argues that it is misleading to see the wanderings described in the Bible as paralleling the ceaseless desert wanderings of camel-breeding Bedouin. The ancient Hebrews were absorbed in agriculture and cattle-raising. It was as a settled people that they had to engage in forays with the erupting desert peoples of Arabia, of which there are so many echoes in the Bible story.

And it is here that we see the character of the original Jewish presence in North Arabia as described by the Arab historians. Looking back to very ancient times, their legends talk of Jewish settlement in northern Arabia at the time of Moses's war against the Amalekites, and of King David fighting idol-worshippers at Yathrib (the original name of Medina). The first destruction of the Temple in the sixth century BC may have brought in exiles to join Hebrew traders already settled in the oases of this area. They tell of '80,000 priests' among these exiles; and Hebrew names surface from the first century BC among inscriptions in some of these northern settlements.

From early Muslim times the northern area became known as Hijaz; and the Arab historians list about twenty Jewish 'tribes' living there in Mohammed's day, including two – the Banu-Nadir and Banu-Qurayza – who were called 'al-Kahinan' (priests). Many Jews lived in Khaybar and other oases, including Maqna, a trading port near Elath, and of course Yathrib.

The Arabs and trade

Goitein sees the original influx of Hebrews into North Arabia as an overflow from the Negev, hoping to profit from trade. 'For centuries preceding the rise of Islam, Arabia occupied the favourable position of a neutral country prospering as a commercial mediator between the East and the West, the Roman Empire and the Persian kingdom, who were engaged in incessant warfare for 700 years.' Many Jews returning from Babylonian captivity brought back useful experience as traders, as is known from documentary evidence about the growth of commerce at the time.

It appears, however, that there was a very important change in the position of Jews in North Arabia for some time before the rise of Islam, with a major expansion of commerce moving into Arab hands and the Jews moving back to a heavy preoccupation with agriculture. The Arab expansion, both in Arabia itself and throughout the Near East, drew on skills in communication that proved valuable, later, in spreading the new faith. But while Arab trade rose to this peak, the Jews in North Arabia had now, for some centuries, been organized, through their 'tribes', into compact agricultural units, engaged mainly in the cultivation of dates. It may be, Goitein thinks, that severe persecution of the Jewish religion by the Byzantines 'caused the Jewish date-growers of the Jordan valley to emigrate to Arabia and carry on their former occupations there'.

This surmise is relevant in considering a question often raised by scholars as to whether the Jews of Medina, who had such a strong influence on Mohammed, were immigrants from Palestine, with a full awareness of Judaism as it had developed under rabbinic guidance, or immigrants from other Jewish centres, or aboriginal inhabitants of Arabia converted to Judaism.

In those fluid times there may well have been a mixture of all three elements; but the reflections of Jewish thought and experience in the *Koran* are strong enough to indicate that even if Medina did not rise to the standard of Babylon in Jewish learning, there was enough of the authentic tradition present to indicate that at least some teachers or rabbis had come direct from Palestine. This may indeed indicate why, in the end, the welcome that Mohammed had expected from the Jews of Medina was not forthcoming. In disputes with the Jews, Mohammed, the scholars say, often took a literalist view of Bible teaching, which might indicate that he had been instructed by a sect of Jews called 'Karaites', whose teachings concentrated on the written text of the Bible (*kara*, 'reading'), and spurned the oral traditions of interpretation. The rabbis fiercely opposed the Karaites; but their influence grew in some places in the early centuries of Islam, and this may have played some part in the distinctly less friendly attitude to the Jews that emerged after the death of Mohammed in 632.

The Jews of Yemen

During this formative period of Islam the Jews of south-west Arabia – Yemen – had had a very different experience; and their life under Islam was to be very different too.

Unlike the Jews in the north, many of whom were descended from Jews living in wilderness areas in the Negev and Transjordan and ruled by Nabataean Arabs, the Jews in the south seem to have immigrated quietly in very ancient times as a natural result of the flourishing trade down the Red Sea.

Many legends spelt out biblical hints on Jewish links with this area. The queen from the 'capital' Saba (Sheba) had visited Solomon and borne his child. 'Ophir', to which his ships sailed from Ezion-Geber (near Elath), was located here, the centre of his exotic trade with 'all the kings of Arabia' (1 Kings 10:15). Jews had come here, it was said, in the first Exile. They are certainly likely to have been settled there in number by the first century, thoroughly identified with the Arab background yet living separately and with fierce loyalty to Jewish tradition. Even at their distance from the rabbinic learning of Babylon, they must have had strong contacts, as was proved centuries later when the Yemen became a uniquely stable and independent community with strong links to the rabbinic tradition.

Two links from pre-Islamic times establish this. The first is the discovery in Beit She'arim, as has been mentioned, of graves from the Amoraic period of 'the people of Himyar' (Yemen), with Greek inscriptions of Jewish names identifying them as leaders of the community. Whether they migrated to Palestine or were transferred there after death, it indicates a well-established Jewish community in Himyar going back to the first or second centuries.

The other clue to their character is the strong resistance of Himyar, through the activities of Jews there, to Christian missionaries sent there from Palestine in the fourth century. It is said that rabbis were sent from Tiberias to help the Yemen Jews on this. Going even further, it has been established that the last king of Himyar (fifth century) was converted to Judaism, which was perhaps partly conditioned by the growing skirmishes with his Ethiopian (and Christian) enemies across the Red Sea.

There was a period after this in which the area prospered under Persian rule; and at this time the Jews of Yemen were able to re-establish a lively relation with Babylon. There is then a hiatus in their story; but though nothing is heard of Yemen Jewry for a long time, their independent Jewish tradition must have persisted in these early times, as we know now from a number of clues, some relatively minor and one of major historical significance: a letter to them in the twelfth century from the great scholar Maimonides.

The minor clues establish that the Jews of Yemen were in touch with the academies of Babylon in the eleventh century, sending them financial contributions and receiving their religious support. We know also from the *geniza* that they were also in close touch with the currently prestigious community of Egypt on personal and trade matters.

This links up, in fact, with the famed Maimonides letter. Around 1170 the Jews of Yemen had written to Maimonides, resident in Egypt and already famed as a scholar, to seek guidance on a problem that had become desperately urgent for them. The Shi'ite ruler of Yemen had instituted a religious persecution, giving the Jews there a choice of conversion or death. Many converted; and the distress of the community was compounded by the emergence of a wild Jewish orator claiming that he was the forerunner of the Messiah who would arrive soon to save the Jews from forced conversion.

Maimonides replied with a long letter now known as *Iggeret Teiman* ('The Yemen Letter'), discouraging talk of the arrival of the Messiah. (As we shall see later, Maimonides was a rationalist, temperamentally averse to all mystical ideas.) On the broader issue of conversion, he and his father had already given their views in major letters, advising those being forced into conversion to succumb temporarily but to hold to their faith secretly and migrate elsewhere as soon as possible. This was what Maimonides' own family had done during the Almohad conversion drive in Spain.

Authoritative advice from Babylon

The Yemen Letter, which was distributed far and wide to all

communities in the Near East, is just one example of the 'question and answer' system which, as mentioned earlier, had first arisen among Jews through the enormous prestige of the scholars of Babylon and had later become universal.

We shall return to this subject later, but a word on it is appropriate here since it is so closely related to the centralized authority of Babylon that was to prove invaluable everywhere when Jewish communities were increasingly dispersed following the Islamic conquests. In this dispersal the Jews needed to know direct from the *geonim* (supreme scholars) of Babylon how their local conditions were to be related to the *halakhah*. The Babylonian Talmud was known and revered, but copies were not always available for consultation.

The correspondence with the rabbis began in the middle of the *geonic* age (*c.* eighth century) with requests for individual chapters of the Talmud and for specific answers not just on *halakhic* questions but on the widest range of scriptural and moral issues. Questions to Babylon were assembled at various places to be classified, copied and then forwarded, often via Egypt, which was on an established caravan route to Babylon. The *responsa* were also copied and even more widely distributed and studied for their guidance. Questions could cover any aspect of local Jewish life and its relation to life outside; and modern scholars working on the *responsa* have used the material – much of it preserved in the Cairo *geniza* – to paint a lively picture of historical developments otherwise unrecorded.

Though one thinks of this as mainly affecting the Mediterranean and Near Eastern world, the authority of Babylon went much further. There is an interesting example of this in a study of Rhineland Jewry in the tenth century which appears in a classic work by Max Weinreich on the origins of Yiddish.[14] How did the Jews of Northern Europe manage, he asks, to establish contact with Babylonia, the centre of Jewish authority, when the huge sweep of Arab conquest in the seventh and eighth centuries had put an iron curtain between the Mohammedan and Christian worlds. Before then, trade moved dominantly on sea routes; but now, 'even when there was no full-fledged war, the sea was in the hands of the Arab fleets. They would capture the ships, seize the merchandise, and sell the captives into slavery.'

The answer had to come through the development of new land routes, and the Jews pioneered them, aiming always at the Middle East cross-roads where their merchandise could be accompanied by questions to the rabbis of Babylonia.

There were two land routes starting from Cologne and Mainz, where the roots of German Jewry were being sown. The first was up the Rhine, over the Alps to north-west Italy, across the Adriatic to Dalmatia, to the Balkans, to Constantinople, Asia and Syria, and thence to Babylon. A second route went east towards Prague, and thence to Galicia and Kiev, along the eastern shore of the Caspian, arriving ultimately at the same destination.

In one sense this pioneering drive for new land routes – by which Jews from different lands communicated with each other in Hebrew as well as in mangled other languages – was stimulated through the desire to develop trade; but, as Weinreich says (p. 49), there could be an additional cargo:

The Jewish merchants carried with them not only furs, silk, and spices, but also books and responsa. . . . Even the private letters written by Jewish merchants *en route* were not confined solely to business and family matters; . . . [they] travelled the same routes as others did, but frequently carried a unique cargo.

This 'unique cargo' continued in evidence long after Babylon itself ceased, in the eleventh century, to be at the centre of the Jewish stage in a physical sense. The *responsa* system, which had started through the emergence of the Babylonian Talmud, became a familiar process for many centuries of Jewish life, helping to create a living picture that would otherwise have faded from history.

Every distinguished rabbi took part; and as in the original questions to Babylon, enquirers raised every possible subject, in the course of which they described their lives and experience, both among themselves and with non-Jews, in detail that has been a treasure-house for scholars. Of the many examples that come to mind, two *responsa* studies seem particularly relevant to mention in a book discussing Sephardi and Eastern Jews, since one of them uses the *responsa* of a great Spanish rabbi of the thirteenth century to illustrate the history of Spain, while the other deals with the *responsa* of a famous fifteenth-century rabbi of Algiers to illustrate the history of the Jews of North Africa. Both collections offer vivid pictures, as we shall see, of events of their time.[15]

Ultimately, all these *responsa* are part of the legacy of Babylon, which was clearly a major influence in the Jewish world both before and after the rise of Islam. We shall see it in the background as we move in the next chapter to consider how the Jews were affected after the conquering armies of Islam and the force of its teachings had come to dominate the world from Spain to the East.

6 Jewish Life under Islam

Mohammed's formulation of a new religion – Islam – and the wide conquests that followed had specific effects on the Jews, apart from the huge impact on the political and cultural history of the world at large. The Jews were caught up in a myriad ways, sometimes painfully but also benefiting from the economic development that followed the conquests. Their life was, in a sense, transformed, yet in a way that enabled them to strengthen their traditional outlook. Their faith and communal life remained independent; yet they had broadened their horizons immeasurably on issues which they shared with cultured people in the world around them.

This double benefit was possible because, when Islam was proclaimed early in the seventh century, the Jews had already established, through Torah and Talmud, a strong sense of pride and intellectual security. In adjusting to Islam they continued to live their lives under a double aspect. In one sense they gave Jewish unity the highest priority, as expressed in allegiance to Jewish observance and the authority of Jerusalem. At the same time there was the need to adapt to local conditions, which meant being subservient to the dictates of rulers and rival religions, and on the move, where necessary, to seek out a new town or a new land where life would be easier.

This did not make them into non-stop wanderers. Jews were often long-term settlers, in contrast to the upheavals around them; and if they had to move, Jewish kinship was always there to give them stability. It was because their communal loyalty and faith underpinned the uncertainties around them that they could survive in the far-off lands to which they wandered; and it was in this spirit that they absorbed the impact of Islam. Many undoubtedly must have surrendered to the new faith, as some had given way to Christianity; but for the most part the Jews had the individual strength and the communal institutions to survive independently. It was in this guise that they came to play such an astonishingly fertile role in the cultural renaissance that surfaced in the Arab world about two hundred years after the conquests had begun.

Here we reach the 'broadening of horizons' referred to in the first paragraph. But a word of caution is needed immediately. There are some stock ideas about the 'golden age' of Arabic culture which need careful definition before they can be accepted as valid.

The Arabs did not, as it were, bring culture with them and make it available to all, including the Jews. The first results of their conquests in the seventh century were, inevitably, wild and destructive. The Arab armies were on the march in this style for a century or so, after which they began to be subjected in the various areas they had conquered to successive invasions – and takeovers – by fierce hordes, mostly from further east in Asia.

It was only after this that the great surge of culture for which the medieval Arabs are famous began to emerge; and this, of course, was not an explosion of *Arab* culture but a rediscovery and further development in the Arabic language of the cultures of earlier civilizations hitherto unknown to them.

Arabs and the new culture

It was, to that extent, a historical accident; and this is central to an understanding of how it was that the Jews, among others, were able to participate so strongly and broaden their own horizons.

Philip Hitti, a prominent Arabist of Princeton University, spelt this out usefully in his lively – and loving – book, *The Arabs.* In sharp contrast, he says, to the peoples of the Near East, including the Jews, who had been heirs to the great civilizations of Mesopotamia, the Arabs came into the foreground with no cultural – and not much religious – baggage; and it was other nations, including the Jews, who were the foremost carriers of the new learning:

What we now call 'Arab civilization' was Arabian neither in its origins and fundamental structure nor in its principal ethnic aspects. The purely Arabian contribution was in the linguistic and to a certain extent in the religious fields. Throughout the whole period of the caliphate, the Syrians, the Persians, the Egyptians and others, as Moslem converts or as Christians and Jews, were the foremost bearers of the torch of enlightenment and learning.[16]

The careful phrasing about the contribution in the religious field is very relevant when one is considering the impact on the Jews of the rise of Islam. If the faith of Mohammed himself had a clear religious purpose, the armies who surged forward in its name, Hitti tells us, were not so preoccupied. Most of the armies of conquest were recruited from the Bedouin, and 'religion sits very lightly in the heart of the Bedouin'. Whatever their battle-cry, the prime object of the soldiers was booty, and because of this, the conversion to Islam of the conquered peoples was small in scale to begin with. 'Not until the 2nd and 3rd centuries of the Moslem era (8th/9th centuries AD) did the bulk of the people in Syria, Mesopotamia and Persia profess the religion of Mohammed.' And when they did, it was primarily 'to escape tribute and seek identification with the ruling class'.

This does not mean that there was strong resistance to the invaders. On the contrary, the Arabs were greeted by virtually all peoples of the Near East and Mediterranean – including the Jews – as liberators. The fighting was between armies; the ordinary people saw the invasions as the end of centuries of domination by foreign rulers – Romans, Byzantines, Persians – and extended a ready welcome to soldiers who seemed like kin (speaking a kindred language) and without, as yet, the trappings of empire. But this was only one of the factors that produced the truly astonishing triumphs of the Arabian armies who, within a few decades, had spread from the Atlantic to the Indian Ocean.

The most obvious factor was that the Arabs were able to use their highly original raiding qualities, based on the daring use of camels and horses, against the mercenaries of the dying empires. Fighting – the noblest profession in the sight of Allah – brought more than the traditional booty; it also expressed their sense of personal superiority – embedded in their religion – over all in their way. Non-Muslim enemies had to be slaughtered unless they adopted the faith; and even the one exception was to be dealt with by humiliation. Under the *Koran*, non-Muslims with their own religious book (mainly Jews and Christians) were to be allowed to survive in a 'protected' status if they paid a special tax to Muslim communities. The *Koran* dictum was: 'Make war . . . upon such of those to whom the Book [i.e. the Bible] has been given until they pay tribute offered on the back of their hands, in a state of humiliation.'

Socially this meant accepting a degraded status, spelt out in a host of humiliating restrictions. Financially, it meant the imposition of a poll-tax (*jizya*) on every protected person (*dhimmi*) as the price of being free to follow the teachings of one's own Book and in this sense to have some basic rights under Muslim rule.

Effects of the conquests

There was no fixed pattern according to which Jews, in the lands invaded, adjusted to the new rulers; but some common features are clear enough. In the early stage – the first and second centuries of the Muslim era – we must assume upheavals in all directions, though with little that is specific to guide us.

An occasional direct reference in a letter to the effect of Islam on the Jews does surface, one example being found in relation to the conquest of Egypt, a prime target for the Arabs. The Arab general who took Alexandria in 639, only seven years after the death of Mohammed, included a mention of the Jews in a letter recounting his triumph to Omar, the second caliph, in Medina. 'I have captured a city,' he wrote, 'from the description of which I shall refrain. Suffice it to say that I have seized therein 4,000 villas with 4,000 baths, 400 places of entertainment for the royalty, and 40,000 poll-tax-paying Jews.' In contrast, there are no contemporary accounts of what must have been to Jews a far more significant occasion when Omar himself, encamped two years earlier in the Hauran (Syria), had sent in a young officer to occupy Jerusalem and had subsequently readmitted the Jews.

Details of these events are hard to come by. Later historians wrote of the efforts of the Christians to maintain their hold on the city, and of Jewish – or former Jewish – advisers who helped Omar to respond to the holiness of various sites; but at least it seems to be generally agreed by scholars that Jews *were* admitted. A document in Judaeo–Arabic found in the Cairo *geniza* states that the Jews asked Omar for permission for two hundred families to settle in the town. Because of Christian opposition, Omar is said to have fixed the number at seventy families. But this is all very vague; and in the same way, nothing firm is known about what must have been an important event in their institutional life – the transfer of the talmudic academy to Jerusalem from its seat in Tiberias.

Even in Babylonia, where we know that Jewish life looked back on a long tradition of stability, the impact of Islam in the first Muslim centuries has come down only in oral traditions or legends. It is clear that the special representative role of the Exilarch *vis-à-vis* the new authorities was respected, though a legend that Omar honoured the current Exilarch by giving him as wife the daughter of the Persian king seems unfounded. More significantly, the Jewish talmudic academies, under leaders known as *geonim*, maintained their distinction, so that for at least four centuries the rest of the Jewish world could still turn to them for guidance.

On a broader economic front, this first phase of Arab conquest must have been impoverishing for the Jews of Babylonia. They had been largely deprived of their long-standing agricultural base, and found it hard, at first, to gain some kind of compensating position in city occupations and trade. It may well be that this impoverished state accounts for the blank in Jewish history during the first two centuries of Islam.

The Arabs were settling in during this period. It was in Babylon that they first began to encounter the richness of life – physical luxury, intellectual distinction – that flowed from the splendours of the past. If it was a new experience, they certainly responded to it in full, sustained in wealth by the flow of booty and the profits of rapidly expanding trade. In due course the Jews, too, were caught up in this transforming process, which has been called 'the bourgeois revolution'. They responded eagerly to new opportunities over the vast area that had been opened up and integrated through the extraordinary triumphs of Arab conquest.

Opportunity and discrimination

Even in the dark period, the Jews must have retained their resilience, as was shown when their horizon began to expand both in economic terms and by their participation in the cultural renaissance beginning to establish itself through the medium of the Arabic language. In due course, this culture found expression in many places – Baghdad, Spain, Kairouan, Cairo, Sicily; and the Jews, in settlements stretching in an unbroken chain from north-east Persia through Mesopotamia, Palestine and Egypt to the shores of Spain, Italy and France, were heavily involved. With a wholly new status under Islam, the Jews faced a life of mixed blessing and humiliation which was to endure for more than thirteen centuries. Under tolerant rulers, they benefited from social autonomy, religious freedom and economic opportunity, while under fanatics the regulations against them were implemented to the full.

In Babylonia itself this is seen in the contrast in character between Omar I (634–44), mentioned above, and the second Omar who ruled seventy-three years later (717–20). Omar I is known to have been friendly to the 'protected' non-Muslims. Omar II, by contrast, was a religious fanatic who pursued every possible way to bring about the humiliation that the *Koran* ordered for these *dhimmis*. Specifically, he forbade the erection of synagogues and churches, ordered *dhimmis* to wear hats and cloaks which would distinguish them from believers, forbade their using a saddle or employing a Muslim in their service, all in addition to the strict payment of the *jizya*.

These regulations, and many others, were given authority as 'the Covenant of Omar', loosely ascribed to the first Omar but in fact built up from regulations issued by fanatical rulers like the second Omar, and extended whenever a local ruler was so minded. The Covenant assumed a final form in the fourteenth century, and a list of what was included illustrates how severe life could be under Islam from time to time. In addition to the rules of Omar II mentioned above, *dhimmis* were not only forbidden to have a Muslim slave or servant, they were always to stand in the presence of a Muslim and to step aside to avoid any contact in the street. The distinctive clothing rules meant that the Jews had to wear yellow dress, girdles and hats. They were not to bear Muslim names; they were restricted in the use of bath-houses; they were forbidden to carry arms; they were not to ride on horses or mules but only on donkeys, and then without saddle; their houses – and tombs – were never to be higher than those of Muslims. Above all, though this was not carried out to the letter, they were not to be employed in any governmental post or any position – including that of doctor – which would give them authority over Muslims.[17]

If this were the whole story it would be grievous indeed; but there is another side. There were rights under the Covenant of Omar covering the security of life and property, freedom of religion and internal autonomy. To get the issue in proportion one must note, also, that instructions for obeying the Covenant were repeatedly issued, which shows that the conditions were not consistently respected. Rulers made no bones about employing Jews and Christians in essential work as doctors, administrators, specialists in minting coins, and even as viziers, explaining that even in top posts the *dhimmis* only executed orders and never exercised authority themselves. What this transparent excuse really meant was that a *dhimmi* in a top position was always liable to be disposed of ruthlessly.

In this mixed setting the most precious element for Jews throughout the Islamic dominions was the freedom to practise their religion, though this, too, was abrogated at certain periods. An outstanding case was when the fanatical Almohads ('unitarians') swept to power in North Africa and Spain in the twelfth century, putting to the Jews the blunt choice of conversion to Islam or death, which for many Jews – including the Maimonides family – led to pretended conversion and flight. It is relevant that the Almohad fanatics were not Arabs but Berbers, standing outside the normal culture of Arab-speaking Islam; but this was never a consistent distinction.

Despite the religious freedom that was supposed to be accorded by Islam to *dhimmis* who paid the *jizya* and observed the regulations of the Covenant of Omar, life under Islam could be very uncertain. There was a notorious case in eleventh-century Egypt when the Fatimid Caliph al-Hakkim (996–1021), who had been honoured by the Jews as a Messiah-like prince of justice and wisdom during the first fifteen years of his rule, suddenly launched a most violent persecution in 1012, reinforcing all the anti-*dhimmi* regulations and going much further. In all lands under the caliph as far as Tripoli in northern Syria, synagogues new and old were destroyed; in Cairo itself the caliph ordered that the Jewish quarter was to be burnt to the ground on Passover Eve with all its inhabitants. Muslim historians ascribe all this to the caliph being overtaken suddenly by a psychological breakdown; and it is fair to say that after his death all was restored to Jews and Christians, with forced converts allowed to return openly to their faith.

A basis of self-confidence

When Jews living in the Islamic world moved heavily into international trade from the ninth century on, with many becoming prosperous, it was once again a mixed position; their distinctive advantages, arising from the ease of communication and trust between Jews, offset considerably the extra tax burdens and other acts of discrimination. Under Muslim law, for example, a non-Muslim paid double the customs duty of a Muslim, and was subject to a higher minimum tax payment. But discrimination of this kind was small in effect compared with the types of economic discrimination practised against Jews in virtually all fields in the Christian world. As S. D. Goitein puts it, 'the absence of oppressive discriminatory economic legislation in Islam can be judged from the great variety of professions and crafts followed by the Jews in Islamic countries as opposed to the few trades available to them in medieval Europe'.[18]

One can be even more positive on this; for even when all the adverse factors are taken into account, the position of the Jews in the Islamic world was wholesome and rewarding in absolute terms until this world itself went into decline, carrying most of its Jews down with it. In the good times and places, the Jews under Islam did not simply suffer less overt discrimination. They were the beneficiaries of economic expansion that this world brought about, and they benefited from it correspondingly, with the Arabs as teachers.

As Goitein points out, it is ironic that the Jews, who are commonly assumed to have an inborn instinct for trade, were basically an agricultural people, brought into trade through instruction from others. Leaving aside what they learnt from the Phoenicians, he shows the process starting in the first Exile, where they

learnt business from the Babylonians, an old nation of traders. During the Hellenistic period, the Greeks served them as masters. In Muslim times they again found themselves confronted by a highly mercantile civilization but responded to the challenge so completely that they became themselves a nation of businessmen.[19]

One does not normally think of the Arabs as preoccupied with trade, yet in the Muslim tradition this is in fact a strong element, and with a religious angle. The income of the merchant is regarded as 'earnings free from religious objection'. The leisurely pace of trade when pursued in eastern style allows time for prayer and study. If the Jews came to find this attitude compatible with their own predilections, it was a bond of agreement with the Islamic world around them.

The same is true of the ease with which the Jew was at home in the world of Islam even if it was intended, in the *Koran*, that he should be humiliated. There was kinship in origin, in religious practice and in language; and even physically, the Jew did not look like a stranger from outside.

A recent study of this relationship by Professor Bernard Lewis shows that at least in its first phase it was remarkably deep:

In early times, a good deal of social intercourse existed among Muslims, Christians and Jews who, while professing different religions, formed a single society in which personal friendships, business partnerships, intellectual discipleships, and other forms of shared activity were normal and indeed common.[20]

At many levels, it is clear that there was a kind of affinity between Jew and Muslim. In religious and linked folklore, they shared many traditions. In day-to-day contacts they were at ease together in exploiting the economic opportunities that Arab–Islamic expansion brought in all areas of the economic field; and this had a natural overflow when the Jews, benefiting from the links with cultural development, took an equal and fulfilling part in this too.

One could not call this 'emancipation' in the European nineteenth-century sense, since Christian teachings were based on a theory (however disregarded) of human equality, while Islam counted on an acceptance of permanently lower status in many important respects. Yet from another angle Islam could generate a certain sense of independence and satisfaction.

In the early centuries of Islam, when Jews gradually became part of the wider cultural world, they could draw freely and copiously from Muslim civilization yet preserve their identity untouched. This was not the case when the Jews of Europe, and especially Germany, began to absorb the surrounding culture in the nineteenth and twentieth centuries. Jewish culture was never regarded by a really Germanic Jew as reaching the same high and broad level as German culture.

The history of our time has shown the inherent dangers of this subservient attitude, and one sees its contrast with the attitude of Jews under Islam at the time of its magnificent cultural triumphs. The Jews participated to the full in philosophy, poetry and science, but this was as much to the glory of Jewish thinking and feeling as it was a tribute to the culture around them.

Jews living in the world of Islam took it for granted that their inherited Jewish tradition was central to man's progress, and assumed that everything they learnt from the sophisticated culture around them would support this. Without this self-confidence, they would never have been able to lay the groundwork, during the Moorish period in Spain, for the cultural drive that the Sephardim carried with them throughout the Mediterranean and eastern world, with its powerful side-currents further afield.

The dynastic story

These brief comments on the impact of Islam on the Jews who came within its orbit are too general to be applied to every time and place; they serve only as guide-posts for a vast variety of situations. There was, however, one common feature among the powers that governed the Near Eastern world in the first five or six Islamic centuries. Though vastly different in origin, they almost all fell under the spell of Islam as a religion and Arabic as a language, which to some extent provided a common social background.

The Jews met these Islamic empires in a variety of places, of which three were particularly important. The first, obviously, was in the original Middle Eastern setting, when Damascus and Baghdad were a cradle of Islamic life. The second more surprisingly was in Spain, where an offshoot of the caliphate established itself and developed a unique form of culture. The third, more ambiguously, was in North Africa, stretching through Egypt to Palestine. This vast area of Islamic influence might have been still greater, and with further effects on the Jews, if the Arab armies had not been turned back in various major forays further into Europe.

In their first phase of conquest immediately after the death of Mohammed in 632, the Arab armies, waging campaigns which have been called 'among the most brilliantly executed in the history of warfare', swept into the provinces of the Byzantine and Persian empires and seemed irresistible. With a climactic victory in Syria in 636 they had a base for attack against Armenia, northern Mesopotamia, Georgia and Asia Minor. In Persia they took the capital Ctesiphon in 637 and pushed on – though now against stiffer resistance – towards the borders of India. In the west, Egypt fell in 640, and the way was open to the land of the Berbers in Tripoli.

Arab rule of these huge territories never matched the efficiency of its military triumphs. Wealth and luxury had a debilitating effect on the conquerors, intensified by ruthless rivalries over claims to the rightful succession. The first example of strong internal rule came when a shrewd governor of Syria seized power in 661 and established what became known as the Umayyad caliphate, with its capital in Damascus. Militarily, Arab armies failed in persistent efforts to take Constantinople, but in the second phase of their expansion were immensely successful in other campaigns. Eastward they moved beyond the Oxus River, the traditional limit of Persian influence, into

Outer Mongolia, capturing the famed cities of Bukhara, Tashkent and Samarkand, and from there arrived at what is now Pakistan, from then on Islamized for ever. Westward, having reached the limits in North Africa, the Umayyad governor sent a small Berber force under a soldier called Tariq across the narrow strait into Spain in 710. A year later Tariq moved in with a larger force, and the conquest of Spain had begun.

Its progress was very swift, with considerable help from local people, including the Jews, who had found the rule of the local Visigothic Christians extremely burdensome. Sweeping to the north, Arab/Berber armies crossed the Pyrenees in 717 and seemed poised for further triumphs; but though they engaged in sorties quite far into France, they were ultimately pushed back at Tours in 732 by Charles Martel in one of the decisive battles of history.

In Damascus itself the weakening of central government both through the growth of luxury and the enmity of kinsmen led in 747 to a revolt against the Umayyads by their cousins the Abbasids. It was under the Abbasid dynasty, which lasted from 750 to 1258, that Islam, from the new capital Baghdad (founded in 762), achieved its greatest glory. It is true that the area administered from Baghdad shrank in due course. A separate caliphate – the Fatimid – established itself in Tunis in 909 and soon controlled all North Africa and Egypt. The Fatimid era, and the splendour of its capital Cairo, was in many ways very congenial to the Jews, with a character all its own until the dynasty was overthrown by Saladin in 1171. Moorish Spain had asserted its independence from the Abbasid caliphate in Baghdad even earlier. A young member of the Umayyad family had escaped when the Abbasids took over, fled to Spain and seized power there. In 773, his successors established their own Umayyad caliphate, with a resplendent new mosque at their capital Cordoba. This was the host setting that proved so stimulating to the Jews of Moorish Spain.

Glory and fall of Baghdad

These limitations on the extent of the Abbasid caliphate's domains were of small consequence compared with other weaknesses that gradually developed. Before these became paramount, Baghdad was the glory of the world in luxury, commerce, palaces and learning. For the Jews who lived within its orbit it sustained their undimmed pride in

Babylon, reflected not only in the authority of its scholars, the *geonim*, but also in the quasi-monarchical institution of the Exilarch, with his claim of descent from King David.

Even when the Exilarch's role became narrower in range compared with that of the *geonim*, its special quality survived, as is shown in letters from the tenth century describing the lavish ceremonies in which the Exilarch was elected. To be objective, one has to note that this ceremonial glory did not last. By the twelfth century, Baghdad had declined enormously, and with it, inevitably, the status of the Exilarchate. But Baghdad's glory did not disappear overnight. To judge from reports by two famous travellers of the twelfth century, the Jewish position in Baghdad could still be painted in rosy colours.

The first traveller, Benjamin of Tudela (a small town in northern Spain), found the regime 'most favourable to the Jews' with the caliph 'familiar with the Torah and able to read and write Hebrew'. The second traveller, Petahiah of Regensburg, wrote that the 'king' (caliph) loved the Exilarch and 'in his heart' had adopted the Jewish faith. Babylon itself, Petahiah found, was a paradise for the Jews.

> There is not an ignoramus throughout the lands of Babylon and Assyria . . . who does not know all the 24 books of the Bible in their punctuation and grammar . . . Babylonia is an entirely different world, their affairs consisting of Torah study and the fear of Heaven. Even the Ishmaelites [Arabs] are trustworthy. In Babylon there are 30 synagogues.[21]

One speaks mostly of Baghdad, though throughout these centuries there were large Jewish communities all over Babylonia. In Basra alone, in the twelfth century, there were 10,000 Jews, with leaders of distinguished descent who were treated almost as Exilarchs. It was this widespread base in Babylonia that enabled the Jews to ride out the political chaos, even after invasion by the Mongol hordes of Genghis Khan.

In perspective, it was not just the Jews who were able to lead a continuing life of the mind, occupied with issues of lasting moment, while the political world was falling apart. The successive invasions which finally brought the caliphate to ruin never prevented the world of scholarship, science, philosophy and poetry from functioning by its own incorruptible standards of truth. From the middle of the eighth century, scholars (including many Jews) had been absorbed in translating into Arabic the precious heirlooms of Greek and Persian scholarship; and within a century after that this world of scholarship, functioning internationally, had its own system of communication, with retranslations into other languages becoming very important. The languages of translation included Syriac, Hebrew and Latin as well as Arabic.

The rescue of Greek medicine had come first; this overlapped with the boundless lore of Aristotle in philosophy and the arts. Basic works on mathematics from India had been fed into astronomy and geography; the researches of alchemists had pushed chemistry forward. Persian and Indian art had been absorbed to dazzling effect in great buildings throughout the world of Islam. All this could transcend, for a time, the grim story of invasions until finally, in 1258, Baghdad itself was destroyed.

The Jews of the East had been eager participants, where possible, in the renaissance of learning, science and the arts that had reached particular expression in Baghdad; but in Jewish history this shows itself to particular effect in the context of the broad culture that developed among intellectual leaders of the Jews of Spain. We saw earlier that the Jews had welcomed the new presence in Spain from the time of the first Muslim invasion in 711. They were in a position to reap the full benefit when the base established by the Muslim armies became an independent caliphate in 773, with Cordoba, its capital, poised for its own 'golden age'. In the centuries which followed, the Jews of Spain participated to the full (as we shall see) in the cultural explosion that had been proceeding through the whole of the Arabic-speaking world, and helped to carry this into Christian Spain during the 'Reconquest'.

This was, however, only one side of the cultural life that was to become the Sephardi heritage. The Jews of Spain did not simply share general culture with their neighbours – Muslims and Christians. Socially and intellectually their existence in Spain was an integral part of the Jewish world of faith and scholarship that stretched from its roots in 'Babylon' all the way across North Africa and north across the Mediterranean towards the Jewish presence in northern Europe.

Within the dazzling new experiences that came to the Jews in the Iberian Peninsula, their creative power still had personal roots in the world of the Bible and Talmud. For the Jews, the 'golden ages' of Spain always drew on this while they looked outward, also, to the new world around them.

PART THREE
The Sephardim of Spain

7 Golden Ages in Spain

Before pursuing the chronological story of the Jews of Spain and Portugal – a stretch of nearly eight hundred years from the Muslim invasion of 711 to the expulsions of 1492 and 1497 – we should look at some general factors, since the Sephardi heritage reflected not merely the strength of its Jewish constituent but also, in a special way, the tripartite society in which Spanish history had been shaped.

In broad terms we can follow in this the view of the historian Américo Castro that the Spanish character is a unique amalgam of the interaction over centuries of the three constituents: Muslims, Jews and Christians. Religiously, socially and indeed in every significant way each was very distinctive; but they fell into roles which were essential to each other until the time came when the Christian element put Spanish consciousness on an exclusive course.

The interaction of the three elements went through successive phases. When the Moors began their conquests in 711, they could not have established orderly life without the help of Jews and Christians already living there or immigrating. At a later stage, when the Christians themselves took on a conquering role, they echoed the Moorish pattern: 'Centuries of reconquest had accustomed the Christians of Castile to the arts of war and to employing Moors and Jews for all types of artisanry and for the administration of finances.'[22]

Variety of Jewish life

The Jews fell into specialist roles in many countries, but in Spain there was a unique factor, not just in their being intermediaries between two of the three basic elements, but in forging in their own right a positive and proud individuality. It was relevant, in this connection, that their forms of self-government were more highly developed here than elsewhere, and this was because the ruling authority, whether Muslim or Christian, did not weigh so heavily on Jewish life. It was less intent on 'humiliation' than Muslim rule in other lands, and less absolute than the feudalism of Christian Europe, where 'the lord' totally dominated the horizon of the vassal. On this view, one could argue that the usual picture of Sephardi Jews carrying *Spanish* pride into the world may perhaps be upside down. The proud Sephardim of Spain had not borrowed this quality from their surroundings but were themselves an element in the creation of that peculiarly bony hauteur that came to be recognized everywhere as Spanish.

There was a good historical reason for this. The Jews who emerged to leadership in the Moorish south or in the Christian kingdoms to the north carried with them an unshakeable commitment to their Jewish faith, and had no reason, for a long time, to modify this in order to make themselves more acceptable to a dominant social pattern. In this creative period, religious and social differences were taken for granted, both for the small number of Jews who moved freely in royal or other top circles as doctors, financiers and specialist advisers, and the majority who lived in their own Jewish quarters and were engaged in less glamorous occupations. For a long time, they were in no sense despised and rejected by virtue of being Jews. They had enemies; but more characteristically they were free to make the most of their lives in a rich country which respected their difference and recognized their special roles. The news they had of the lives of Jews in less favoured countries must certainly have inculcated in them a sense of pride and independence.

One sees this reflected very clearly in the character of Hebrew literature – serious and light-hearted – that emerged from this background. For a long time it reflected what seemed an open-ended story of progress; and when this assured position was shattered, first by the 'pogroms' of Seville in 1391 and a century later by the Expulsion, the world had come to an end. In the happier time, the faith they had in the arrival one day of the Messiah was vaguely progressive, as expressed, say, in the poetry of Judah Halevi; now, it could carry also a cataclysmic air. Reason gave way for many to forms of mysticism, wrapped up in cabbalistic ideas. But even if desperate, the Jews still clung to the sense of superiority engendered by the Spanish experience. As émigrés, their inbred self-confidence remained unshakeable. They took Spanish pride with them because, in the unique three-layered circumstances of the peninsula, they had helped to shape it.

Américo Castro goes even further in arguing that Jewish pride was a founding element in the very Spanish conception of 'caste'. With the three constituent elements of early Spanish life interlaced, each had to affirm a pride of descent strong enough to offer a countervailing force to the other two. No one could adopt this attitude with greater assurance than the Jews, who felt, as God's chosen, that they had received the Torah uniquely from Him.

One can carry this type of analysis too far, and many will think that Castro does this in arguing that the key Spanish concept of *limpieza de sangre* (purity of blood) was also adopted from the Jews, who laid great emphasis, he says, on 'keeping the blood pure'. In due course, the Spaniards used this concept to attack Jews who converted to Christianity, so that it would be ironic if they had borrowed it from the Jews themselves. In fact, this is not credible; for though the concept of *yichuss* (pedigree) has an honoured place in Jewish tradition, the idea of 'pure blood' never enters Jewish writing. However, if in this case one has to question Castro's approach, the general proposition that Spain emerged from an amalgam of its three constituents, with the Jews as a solvent between the other two, appears undeniable.

Unusual source material

There is a further general consideration about the early Sephardi experience that is worth making before looking at the chronological story. This story is open to us today in unexpected richness because of the truly remarkable nature of the source material that describes it; and this calls for a word of explanation.

The Judaeo–Spanish experience – paralleled to a great extent in Portugal – is documented for us in four broad forms, all of which have been opened up and elucidated by scholars in very recent years, so that the picture of that time is seen in depth in a new way.

First, and most pleasantly, this period saw a flowering of literature in Hebrew, especially in poetry (sometimes intensely felt, sometimes easy-flowing descriptive verse) built around every kind of experience – personal, religious, political and even military – and brought to life in a language that is full of classical allusion, but is also, by its subject matter, immensely informative on the current scene.

Second, the Jews in Spain under both Muslim and Christian rule lived with strongly developed systems of self-government, based on observance of the *halakhah* interpreted by the Jewish courts to fit every possible circumstance of religious and secular life. This broad position was familiar among Jews everywhere throughout the Middle Ages, but was notable in Spain by the very detailed records it left behind. Scholars of our time are equipped as never before with expert knowledge of the varied background – languages, Islamic and Church law, political and social life – which allows them to project the Jewish archives with full understanding of the setting.

The third source, linked with this, is the application of the material found in *she'eilot u'teshuvot* ('questions and answers'), the system through which Jewish communities everywhere sent *halakhic* questions to distinguished rabbis (mostly in Babylonia) arising from their local circumstances, which they described in detail. As mentioned earlier, both questions and answers were copied and preserved, with collections opened to intense study in our own times. They are particularly valuable for the light they throw on Jewish life in these centuries in the Iberian peninsula and North Africa.

Finally, there are the non-Jewish sources. Most obviously this includes state and religious archives, with many direct and indirect references to the Jews. But more intriguing, in a way, is a source which one might not have looked at for accuracy: the records of the Inquisition.

Offsetting one's instinctive distaste, one has to accept the view of the experts that even though the verdict of each Inquisition 'trial' was mostly predetermined, the pictures that surface in the archives are full of accurate raw material. The aim of every Inquisition was to establish whether the person charged, professing to be Christian, had exhibited, in actions or statements, proof of heresy against Christian doctrine; and the enquiry could proceed from the other approach, to see whether the pattern of life of the accused revealed Jewish sympathies, which automatically implied Christian heresy. Inevitably there has been much argument among scholars on how far one can safely draw on this material to illustrate the lives of Jews and *conversos*; but the consensus is that the material is helpful in building up an objective picture, even though the presentation of the accusation was always tailored to secure confession of guilt.*

* There is a fascinating discussion of this by Bruce A. Lorence, 'The Inquisition . . . Historiographic Issues', in *The Sephardi and Oriental Jewish Heritage* (Jerusalem, 1982), pp. 26ff. The author argues that the accused often pleaded guilty, because 'collaboration' helped him psychologically as an act of rediscovering his early innocence. Absolution by untrue confession, he says, is paralleled among Zuni Indians accused of witchcraft; and one can, of course, also cite Arthur Koestler's *Darkness at Noon*.

Among scholars who have used all these types of source material constructively, one in particular, Yitzhak Baer, stands out for the way he has projected a new evaluation of it all. Basic to all study in this field is his publication of a vast collection of archives, which he used in his major works on the history of the Jews in Spain, and which we shall inevitably quote from later.[23]

The early Muslim period

Turning now to the chronological story, there was a Jewish presence in Spain going back to Roman times or even earlier; and when the German Visigoth tribes conquered Spain as part of their attack on the Roman Empire, their adoption of Christianity led, after a time, to anti-Jewish regulations by the Church councils. It was not surprising, therefore, that the Jews of Spain looked with some hope towards the conquests by Islam in North Africa, and made common cause with the invaders when they crossed the Straits of Gibraltar and pursued their military triumphs through the peninsula.

Arab historians record that the relatively small Muslim armies which swept north to the Pyrenees called on the Jews, wherever they could find them, to garrison the newly conquered towns – specifically Cordoba, Granada, Toledo and Seville – and to take a leading part in developing economic life to meet the new needs of the country. In particular, they were entrusted with the running of the estates abandoned by the Visigoth nobles and were soon prospering, despite the discrimination that was supposed to affect them as *dhimmis*.

Little is known in any detail of Jewish history in Spain for the next two hundred years, though it is clear that they began to live well (as testified by large immigration) and became active in many occupations, including medicine, commerce and finance, as well as agriculture. The Muslim rulers in Spain had asserted their independence from the Abbasid caliphate currently ruling from their new capital Baghdad after the Umayyad dynasty had been overthrown in Damascus. As we saw earlier, a young member of this dynasty had fled to Spain, and with great daring had risen to power there, continuing Umayyad rulership as Abd al-Rahman I, with a magnificently expanded Cordoba as his capital. His most illustrious successor, Abd al-Rahman III (912–61), took the full title of caliph and led the country to an era of glory.

It was during his long reign that evidence surfaces of the build-up in Jewish life in Spain that had long been gathering momentum. The seeds had been sown not only for the remarkable development of Jewish cultural life in Muslim Spain but for an ensuing development in this field among the Jews living in the burgeoning Christian lands of the peninsula, now beginning to assert themselves militarily and culturally. As suggested earlier, it was by participating in a give-and-take between Moorish and Christian rule that the uniquely creative life of Spanish Jewry was forged.

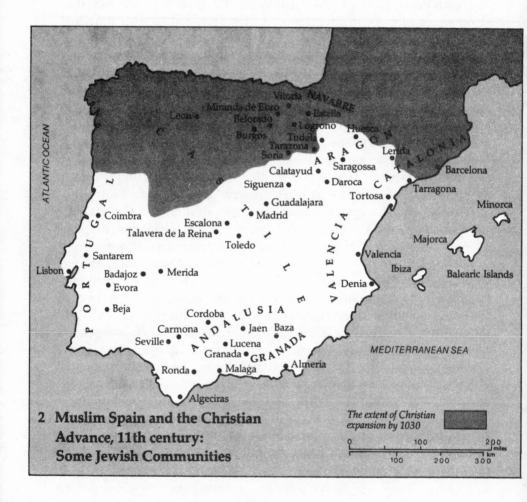

2 Muslim Spain and the Christian Advance, 11th century: Some Jewish Communities

The extent of Christian expansion by 1030

Origins of the Muslim golden age

By the tenth century, when Abd al-Rahman III was caliph in Spain, the Arabic-speaking world was in a position to enjoy to the full the remarkable ingathering and development of culture that had been staged in the Muslim world of the Middle East as a by-product of their vast military triumphs. From their new territories the conquerors had brought into their orbit much of the learned heritage of Greece, Persia and the East. Basic Greek works on philosophy and science had been translated into Syriac and thence into Arabic. Mathematical and astronomical learning from Persia and India was also absorbed; and all was presented in a lively development of art and sophisticated living.

The Umayyad dynasty had started on this road in Damascus, but was overtaken and dwarfed in splendour when their Abbasid cousins rose in bloody revolt in 747 and founded their own dynasty with its new capital Baghdad, due to become legendary for its power and luxury. As early as the ninth century its new generation of learning, literature and science had spread far and wide in influence, and nowhere more fruitfully than in the Moorish world of Spain.

Nothing, perhaps, could match the physical splendour of Baghdad, with its miles of wharves and the bazaars that displayed (as one historian puts it) 'porcelain, silk and musk from China; spices, minerals and dyes from India and the Malay archipelago; rubies, lapis lazuli, fabrics and slaves from the lands of the Turks'. But the *learning* of Baghdad was fully transportable. Translations into Arabic of Aristotle, the neo-Platonic commentators and the medical writings of Galen – to name just a few of the basic writers – were soon to spread, with strong Jewish participation, into the revival of learning in Europe as a whole. The Jews were fortunate that in the setting of those early times their presence in Arabic-speaking lands and their own bent for study gave them a bonus of full participation, both in the Baghdad scene and, when this culture flowered sweetly, in the more varied world of Spain.

The direct links of the Jews of Spain with Baghdad soon made available to them the secular as well as the religious writings of the great Jewish scholar Saadyah ben Joseph (882–942), always known as 'Saadyah *Gaon*'. Another *gaon* of Baghdad, Rabbi Amram, is known to have sent to Spain a copy of his famed prayer-book, which soon became adopted widely. In the view of Yitzhak Baer, these early links with Spain reflected the intensive effort being made by 'Babylon' to encourage diaspora communities to develop ideas that moved with the times. One major principle was the attitude to civil authority. In Roman Palestine, the Jews had displayed nothing but hostility to government; by contrast, the Babylonian Talmud asserted a famous dictum: 'the law of the land is law', and this, though apparently a platitude, was in effect an important statement of a social attitude.

New trends in Spain

Subservience to civil authority found clear expression in Moorish and then in Christian Spain, with both pleasant and unpleasant aspects. The unpleasant side was the principle, which later became quite clear-cut, that the Jews were the 'property' of the ruler (*servi regis*), to be used for his personal ends. The corollary, with wide beneficial results, was that the ruler had to protect the Jews from economic jealousy and religious fanaticism, and give them something like *carte blanche* in their economic operations. This opened the doors to outside society, within which the Jews were able to develop social and political freedoms hitherto unknown.

There were ironies in this. Jews who held prestigious positions close to the rulers, usually as financiers and physicians, stood out in sharp contrast to the Jewish masses; yet they were always intimately involved with them, believing that they had been placed by providence in this position to be of help to the Jewish people in time of need. This was in no sense restricted to what one might call, in modern terms, a 'welfare' role. Their sense of responsibility was intellectual and cultural, as they showed by their devotion to learning, secular as well as religious. As a result, the opening-up of thought spread far beyond the upper-class world of the Jewish courtiers.

There is a striking instance of this in the life of the first Spanish–Jewish leader whom we know about in any detail: Hasdai ibn Shaprut (*c.* 915–70), who rose to a unique position of influence at the court of the caliph Abd al-Rahman III at a time when Muslim rule of Spain was at the height of its power. Its capital Cordoba was famed for its innumerable libraries, bookshops, mosques and palaces, and was linked diplomatically with Christian kingdoms in the north of Spain and other countries and empires far beyond its shores.

It was indeed in this field that Hasdai achieved particular renown. Recruited to the court as a physician, he had later been entrusted with overall responsibility for customs and foreign trade; but his expertise in medicine, which included experience of translating Greek medical treatises into Arabic, remained significant; and in the diplomatic field this was linked to giving medical advice to foreign rulers. It was as a reflection of his wide experience of foreign affairs that he was able to conduct a direct correspondence with the Khazar kingdom of Asia Minor, whose king had converted to Judaism in the eighth century.

Hasdai's life certainly offers a stimulating introduction to the style that was to characterize Jewish life in Spain in the succeeding centuries, and in one respect he left a particular heritage for modern Israel by recruiting two scholars to help in widening Hebrew to enable it to cover its ever-increasing secular use in literature and science. One of the scholars, Menahem ibn Saruk, was a lexicographer; the other, Dunash ibn Labrat, was a poet who developed Hebrew metrical poetry, and thus provided a structure for much of the glorious poetry that was to flourish in Spain.

It is relevant to the theme of this book to note that both these scholars came from Fez, in Morocco, which illustrates the close connections of Spanish Jewry with North Africa, due to be immensely important for the future. In the first phase, the Jews of Spain drew in scholarship from abroad; later, the trend was reversed when scholars from Spain moved out into the world, especially after the Expulsion of 1492.

The growing strength of Spanish Jewry began to show itself when the centralized authority based on Cordoba collapsed some fifty years after the death of Abd al-Rahman III in 1061, and was replaced by local independent rulers. Perhaps paradoxically, the role and life-style of the Jews now became livelier and more creative. They were mostly welcome in the new Muslim centres of Spain and had increased opportunities to work in the various professions in which they had become proficient under the caliphate, as medical and financial advisers, traders, scientists, scholars and poets. This was the time, also, in which their opportunities in the Christian cities of Spain were broadening. There were no absolute barriers between the three constituent elements in Spanish society. In the to and fro of warfare it was convenient, when towns fell to the new conquerors, for the populations to stay put and to draw in refugees with special skills, a situation often very helpful to the Jews.

These sweeping changes in the political scene were never orderly or comfortable. Militarily, there was often chaos, because Muslims of different origins had arrived in the country to meet the rising dangers of Christian attacks from the north. This meant that despotic army leaders – Arabs, Berbers and even Slavs – had taken over in many parts of the country, creating a series of small principalities. Surprisingly, this had lively cultural results. Baer adduces, as a parallel, the political structure of Italy during the Renaissance:

> Both eras were characterized by a high level of culture in scientific and aesthetic fields, by ways of thinking which reviewed critically all historical, political and religious phenomena, and by tyrannical methods of government, devoid of religious or moral conscience.[24]

A flowering of culture

Jews moving from this variegated Muslim world into the relatively austere societies developing in the north – Leon, Castile, Navarre, Aragon, Barcelona and others – took their cultural heritage with them and ultimately developed it further than had been possible in the south. From the end of the eleventh century one has to posit a mixed picture, with as much movement as settlement. In this transitional stage, one sees how, in some cases, a lasting attachment to a small principality could generate a life of power and satisfaction, while in other cases the stimulus came through movement from one milieu to another. A supreme example of the first was Samuel Ha-Nagid (Samuel the Prince) of Granada. Wanderers included many poets and philosophers, as we shall see.

Samuel ibn Nagrela (b. 993) was accorded the prestigious title 'Nagid' – a word used in the Bible to mean 'leader' but with royal connotations – to signal his extraordinary role as statesman, scholar and poet. He had fled his native Cordoba in 1013 following the Berber conquest and had risen rapidly in the service of the ruler of Granada, where he settled, holding the position of vizier under successive rulers until his death in 1056. Unusually, perhaps, for a Hebrew scholar, he was heavily occupied as vizier in leading the army of Granada in almost constant warfare, particularly against Seville. We have a vivid picture of this in his Hebrew poetry which is of very great range, from epic stories of campaigns to songs of love and wine, laments on family tragedies, and thoughts, deep or whimsical, on life and its problems.[25]

Living on a very different scale, the wanderer type is seen in the poet Solomon ibn Gabirol, as it is also, a little later, in the poet Judah Halevi and his friends. Ibn Gabirol, a younger contemporary of Samuel Ha-Nagid, was born not far away in Malaga in 1020, but was brought up far to the north in Moorish Saragossa, a famous old town that was due to fall again into Christian hands a century later.

From the poems of Samuel Ha-Nagid

The War with Yadair ii*

. . . I thank You now with song as when the rebel and king's kin entered the fortress in his folly

And thought to save himself in his stronghold

As he entered therein – even a curse stuck to him like leprosy.

We encamped at its base and his men on the towers were small in eyes like locusts and worms,

But with God's sword my troops were successful while his followers were by the sword cut down.

During the day the heavens were noisy from the tumult of horses while from their movements the earth shook and trembled,

The princes dressed in fine linen touched with red were made crimson by arrows and the assembly of the proud was coloured with blood.

Here I saw a crowd breaking through and hurling stones and then I heard jubilant shouts and trumpets.

And we rose up and climbed to its tip on a ladder made of bows and flying arrows which wearied the tender-hearted

. . . Yadair fled with a trembling and weak heart as one bereft of his senses

. . . He escaped to a mighty potentate while his mind went mad after what he saw happening to his companions.

But sated by our victory we took him from there by a stratagem with a high hand and clear planning.

I drink the cup of salvation, even that of my triumph,

. . . I put my trust and hope in You and my soul knew well your glory and grace.[26]

---

* Written in long rhyming and rhythmical Hebrew lines, many of which are quotations or adaptations from the Bible.

If one is trying to get a rounded picture of Spanish–Jewish writers and the varied worlds they reflected, it is illuminating to consider the contrast between the power and self-confidence of Samuel Ha-Nagid, as expressed in his writings, and the nervous desperation of the poet ibn Gabirol.

As a writer, ibn Gabirol reached out towards the Greek and Arabic philosophies in the air and transmuted them into a Jewish faith that was abstract and mystical as well as devout. Lacking any financial means, he had to seek patrons, and perhaps went south and turned to the Nagid, to whom he wrote some adulatory poems. He was cantankerous as well as clever – a familiar type; but the work that has come down to us has an extraordinary religious intensity, with some of his poems becoming an integral part of the liturgy.

It was a sign of the shared background of medieval religious thought that ibn Gabirol's major philosophical book, *The Source of Life*, which expresses a form of neo-Platonism, disappeared among Jews but became familiar and admired among Christians in the Middle Ages in a Latin translation, with the author's name transformed into 'Avicebron'. He was certainly the most intellectually brilliant of the Spanish poets, but lived a life riddled with perplexity, and was less than thirty when he died, obscurely, in Lucena (Andalusia).

Judah Halevi

The poet Judah Halevi, born just a little later, offers a sharp contrast, for though by this time it was natural to move frequently, as he did, between the Muslim and Christian areas of Spain and North Africa, there was nothing unsettled or turbulent in what he wrote. He expresses constantly a passionate outlook that is always exultantly Jewish. What leaps from the page, also, is a warmth of character that has made him the most accessible and beloved poet in post-biblical Hebrew literature.

Halevi knew Arabic well, having been born (*c.* 1075) in Tudela, an old town in the north still under Muslim control at the time.[27] At an early age he set out southwards to immerse himself in the already legendary atmosphere of the new Hebrew literature in Granada, the breeding-ground of philosophy, scholarship and poetry in a setting of sophistication and wit. He did indeed meet many poets in the south – the somewhat older Moses ibn Ezra and others – all of whom encouraged his prodigious talent. But the good time in Andalusia was ending; the fanatical Almoravid Berbers from North Africa had conquered the area, and the Jews were in flight from the alternatives they offered: conversion or death. Toledo, the most important city of Spain, was now back in Christian hands, and ibn Ezra's family had moved there in 1085. Halevi wandered for a while to many towns in the south, with his fame as a poet growing; but then he too settled for a time in Toledo, where he practised medicine.

Judah Halevi

On the journey to Palestine
. . . The sails quiver and quake,
The beams creak and shudder.
The hand of the wind toys with the waves,
Like reapers at the threshing:
Now it flattens them out, now it stacks them up.
When the waves gather strength, they are like lions;
When they weaken, they are like snakes, who then pursue the lions –
Like vipers that cannot be charmed.

Suddenly, the waves calm down, and are like
Flocks spread out over the fields.
And the night – once the sun has gone down the stairway
Of the heavenly hosts, who are commanded by the moon –
Is like a Negress dressed in gold embroidery,
Or like a violet robe spangled with crystal . . .

From the Ode to Zion
O Zion, will you not ask how your captives are –
The exiles who seek your welfare, who are the remnant of your flocks?
. . . I am like a jackal when I weep for your affliction;
But when I dream of your exiles' return,
I am a lute for your songs.[28]

The high position that Jews enjoyed there may have given him the idea that it was a safe haven, in contrast to the turbulence of Muslim Spain; but he was soon disillusioned by the murder of a Jew prominent at the court and a great personal friend, intensifying his feeling, shown so clearly in his poetry, that the Jew's emotional tie to Jerusalem was the only true security in Jewish life. Recognizing this, he set off on the long journey to Zion, in the spirit of his famous poem:

> How light in my eyes to leave the bounty of Spain:
> How bright in my eyes the dust of the shrine again.

Many of his poems and letters discovered in the *geniza* reflect the excitement of the journey and his warm welcome in Egypt. It was the age of the Crusades, and for a long time legend told that when he finally reached Jerusalem he was trampled to death by a Crusader horseman. The truth seems to be, however, that he died about six months after reaching Egypt and was buried there.

As with ibn Gabirol, Halevi's poetry enshrines a Jewish faith that is also expressed explicitly in a work of philosophy. In Halevi's case, his approach showed belief emerging in direct religious experience rather than by rational argument. He set out these ideas in a book known as *Kuzari* because it is, in form, an imaginary exposition of Judaism before the king of the Khazars, the convert to Judaism who had been in correspondence with Hasdai ibn Shaprut. The role of reason within Jewish faith was to become a central issue in the controversies that arose later over the teachings of Maimonides.

Other poet wanderers

Halevi was inspired rather than tormented by faith, unlike the poet who had befriended him in Granada, Moses ibn Ezra, and who was destined, when he left his native city, to wander disconsolately for the rest of his life. As a poet, Moses ibn Ezra was supreme technically, in work ranging from long penitential poems to clever and often erotic personal verse; but as a human being he was unhappy, especially in having been forced to leave his beloved Granada. 'I am weary of roaming the world, measuring its expanse,' he wrote. 'I walk with the beasts of the forest, and hover like a bird of prey over the peaks of mountains.'

He kept in touch with Halevi and, at one time, wrote – in the usual verse style – that he was considering an invitation from Navarre, in the extreme north, to live in a new town, Estella. Halevi was appalled at the contrast this would offer to the elegance and sophistication of the old life in Granada:

> Eloquent tongue! What wouldst thou among the tongue-tied?
> Why should the dew of Mount Hermon fall upon Gilboa?

Ibn Ezra agreed sadly: 'Fortune has hurled me to a land where the lights of my understanding dimmed/And the stars of my reason were beclouded with the murk of faltering knowledge and stammering speech.' He was never able to adapt himself to the style of life in Christian Spain, and wandered back to Andalusia, to die at an advanced age – over eighty – in Lucena.

The Muslim–Jewish heritage of Spain was lived out more excitingly, it might be said, by a much younger poet of the same patronym: Abraham ibn Ezra. Though not related to Moses ibn Ezra, he was, like him, a close friend of Judah Halevi, and indeed became related to him, as we shall see, by marriage. Apart from the variety of his poetry and commentaries, many journeys gave his life an extra dimension, evoking the underlying unity of the Jewish scholarly world. It was in middle life that he became a persistent traveller. We hear of him in North Africa, Italy, Provence, northern France and even England. In all these lands, he produced, in addition to his poetry, a great assortment of books on the Bible, literature and philosophy, taking the Sephardi experience into the Jewish world at large, a precursor of the process that was to become familiar on a much greater scale after the Expulsion.

Wherever he appeared, Abraham ibn Ezra was welcomed as bringing treasures of knowledge from a major source whose fame had spread. He, in turn, was able to absorb, in his travels, some of the intense talmudic learning for which north-west Europe in particular was celebrated. In due course, scholars from this northern world began to assume teaching posts among the Jews of Spain, which greatly broadened the learning which flowed later into the Sephardi diaspora.

Through the work of men like Abraham ibn Ezra, Spanish Jewry had become, in effect, a hinge, with one arm stretching north to the Ashkenazi countries, and the other eastward, towards Palestine and Babylon. Behind the differences, the Jews were moving into unity. Wandering scholars were one form of this; and the process is illustrated in another aspect of the life of Abraham ibn Ezra, through a fateful journey that his son Isaac made to Baghdad.

In itself, a major journey of this kind was not abnormal. In this case, however, there is a personal side to be evoked, based to some extent on material recently found in the *geniza*. Isaac, we now know, had married the daughter of his father's friend, the poet Judah Halevi.[29] In the course of his journey to Baghdad, he was present for a time with his father-in-law in Egypt, the penultimate stage on Judah Halevi's famed pilgrimage to Zion. From Egypt, however, Isaac went off on his own to Baghdad; and, after he had lived there for a while, he became a Muslim.

To bring these apparently disparate events together, let us use Isaac's journey to Baghdad as a way of looking at the eastern route, a world due to be affected so strongly when many of the Jews of Spain and Portugal moved east after the Expulsion.

8 *The Eastern Hinge*

The personal side of the journey of young Isaac ibn Ezra from Spain to Baghdad seizes one's attention first by its rather startling conclusion: that he became a Muslim. In contrast to the large-scale conversion to Christianity that one knows of, especially in Spain, information on conversion to Islam is scanty, as Bernard Lewis says in *The Jews of Islam*. He adds that there are few recorded instances of when it was undertaken from sincere religious conviction.

The news of his son's conversion was a bitter blow to Abraham, even though Isaac recanted later and claimed that he had always remained a Jew in his heart.

It was, in effect, a by-product of life in glamorous Baghdad. One can assume that Isaac had set out to see what life had to offer away from home, in the spirit in which a young man today takes off for New York. All we know of Isaac's actual journey is that he was present with his father-in-law Judah Halevi in Egypt. If his route there combined land and sea travel, it would undoubtedly have included stopovers – perhaps long ones – in important Jewish communities that lay on the way. In earlier times, Kairouan in Tunisia was one such city, though destroyed and abandoned in Isaac's day. But one city, Fez in Morocco, would have been an obvious first stop; and even if we know nothing of such a visit by Isaac, the early Jewish history of Fez overflows into the theme of this book, with echoes reaching to our own time.

Fez was always a bridge between Babylon and Spain, and thus an expression of the essential unity of the Sephardi and oriental Jewish worlds. The Jews of Fez were a strong community whose rabbis had always been linked to the Babylonian *yeshivahs* of Sura and Pumbedita, sending them financial help and seeking their rulings on talmudic questions. As the Jewish community grew in Spain, it had attracted many scholars from Fez, such as the distinguished grammarians mentioned earlier, recruited in the tenth century by Hasdai ibn Shaprut. But Fez is remembered most, perhaps, for Rabbi Isaac Alfasi ('of Fez'), a renowned talmudist who moved to Spain in his old age and taught, among others, Judah Halevi. His influence went beyond teaching, for he produced in Spain a major distillation of the Talmud called *Sefer Halakhot* ('The Book of Laws'), which was a forerunner of the great *halakhic* code of law – *Mishneh Torah* – written by Maimonides.

Alfasi died in Spain at the age of a hundred in 1103, some thirty years before Maimonides was born there in Cordoba; and it illustrates the unity of this world to note that when the father of Maimonides had to flee from Spain in 1060 as a result of the persecution there by the fanatical Almohad Berbers of North Africa, he took his family to Fez, where the local Almohad rulers were now displaying a more tolerant attitude to the Jews.

Though one cannot include Kairouan in Isaac's travel route across North Africa, one has at least to think of it, since it had been the major Jewish city of North Africa in all respects until sacked in 1057 by an Arab invasion from Egypt. Kairouan certainly remained for him – and remains for us – a key town in Jewish memory, not only for its commercial and talmudic renown, but for its unique role politically in relation to the establishment of the major community in Egypt.

The Fatimid dynasty who ruled Kairouan had seized power in Egypt in 969 (with the assistance of a Jewish or ex-Jewish military adviser) and set up a caliphate independent of the Abbasids of Baghdad and extremely favourable to the Jews. But before this transfer of the dynasty to Egypt, the Jewish community of Kairouan had played a most important part, as Fez had, in building up the Jewish scholarship of Spain. The links were strong, also, at the personal level. Kairouan's most famous scholar, Rabbi Nissim ben Jacob (c. 990–1062), had taught the Spanish poet Solomon ibn Gabirol, and his daughter had married the son of the Jewish 'prince' of Granada, Samuel Ha-Nagid.

In these early centuries, Kairouan had a unique influence over North Africa and beyond. Its leading rabbis were, like Samuel, accorded the title Nagid. Its *yeshivahs* had immense renown. Members of the Exilarch family from Babylon had settled there.

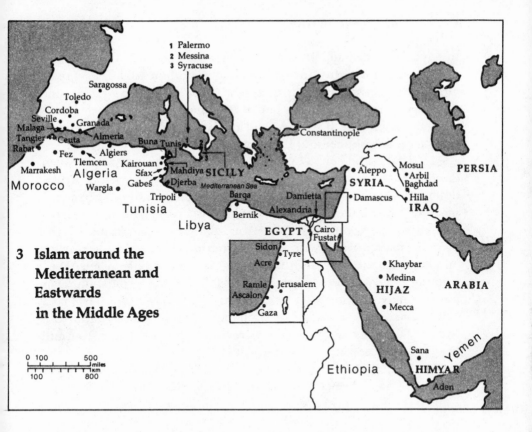

1 Palermo
2 Messina
3 Syracuse

Saragossa
Toledo
Cordoba
Seville
Malaga
Granada
Tangier
Ceuta
Almeria
Buna Tunis
Rabat
Fez
Algiers
Marrakesh
Tlemcen
Algeria
Kairouan
Mahdiya
SICILY
Sfax
Gabes
Djerba
Mediterranean Sea
Wargla
Tripoli
Barqa
Bernik
Morocco
Tunisia
Libya

Constantinople

Aleppo
Mosul
Arbil
Baghdad
SYRIA
Damascus
Hilla
IRAQ

PERSIA

Damietta
Alexandria
EGYPT
Cairo
Fustat

Sidon
Tyre
Acre
Ramle
Jerusalem
Ascalon
Gaza

Khaybar
Medina
HIJAZ
Mecca

ARABIA

3 Islam around the
Mediterranean and
Eastwards
in the Middle Ages

0 100   500
         miles
            km
100   800

Sana
HIMYAR
Aden

Yemen

Ethiopia

The Egyptian community

When the Fatimid dynasty moved its base to Egypt, the Jewish
community there grew in numbers and prestige. In the eleventh
century its leader, too, was accorded the prestigious Nagid title. Our
young traveller Isaac ibn Ezra paid fulsome tribute in verse to the
Nagid of the day, Samuel ben Hananiah, when he arrived in Egypt in
1140. Being under the auspices of his father-in-law Judah Halevi, he
had access to the intellectual and social leadership of Egyptian Jewry.

The visit of Halevi was momentous for them; and we have a vivid
picture of this world from the poetry and letters that centred around it.
For Halevi it was only a stage on his planned journey to Jerusalem; but
he was so stimulated by his welcome and the pleasures of life there that
he stayed for months before taking ship for Palestine. The Nagid had
urged him to stay permanently in Cairo, arguing that Egypt was the
locus of the founding miracle of Jewish history – the Exodus. Halevi
wrote a number of poems to the Nagid, but his heart was in Zion. Only
the storms at sea, recorded in magnificent verse, sent him finally back

to Egypt after he had left.

At some point in this story, young Isaac set off for Baghdad. He was already known in his own right as a poet. In Baghdad he became secretary to the outstanding Jew of the capital, the physician Abu'l-Barakat, who was doctor to the court of the caliph and also a proficient philosopher and Bible scholar.

Abu'l-Barakat dictated his main philosophic book to Isaac, who, in an introduction, wrote a long poem in praise of his patron. It was doubtless out of loyalty that he followed him in becoming a Muslim, a move which was dictated, in Bernard Lewis's view, by court intrigue.

According to one account, Abu'l-Barakat was afraid of the consequences when a wife of the sultan died under his treatment; another account suggests that it was to save his life when taken prisoner in a battle between the armies of the caliph and the sultan. His position may have been uncertain for many reasons. Lewis tells that a Christian rival doctor at court lampooned Abu'l-Barakat, and that a Muslim colleague 'dismissed the pretensions of both the Christian and the Jew' in an appropriately satirical verse;

> ... The one in his modesty rises to the Pleiades,
> The other in his haughtiness sinks to the depths.[30]

In the light of the conversion of Abu'l-Barakat, it is interesting to note that the book of philosophy he had written was criticized later by Maimonides as being too influenced by Muslim theology. Isaac was clearly unhappy about the whole affair. In a late poem, he admitted that he had converted, but said that in his heart he had remained a loyal Jew and had kept the commandments. His father Abraham was still broken-hearted. He survived his son and wrote two laments on his death.

Letters and trading methods

The ibn Ezra wanderings – father and son – were only a tiny reflection of a strange paradox in medieval times: that, superimposed on rigidity and parochialism, there was a world of constant movement and communication. With the Jews the evidence has been preserved in the quantity of their letter-writing, as revealed in the truly astonishing cache of papers discovered in the Cairo *geniza*. When this store of papers was opened up to study towards the end of the nineteenth century, interest was concentrated at first on its formal writings – texts of lost or unknown books, sacred verse (*piyyut*), and other historical documents of great, though uncertain, age. The vast profusion of almost illegible scraps of Arabic writing (in Hebrew characters) that were clearly secular – business and private letters, contracts, invoices, etc. – took longer to decipher and co-ordinate; but this has been increasingly achieved, above all through the brilliant scholarship of Shlomo Dov Goitein, whose books in this field offer a picturesque view of Mediterranean society in the eleventh to the thirteenth centuries.*

This unique source material has significantly amplified another prolific source of information which is found in the correspondence over a period of centuries between scattered Jewish communities and outstanding rabbis, especially those based in the Babylonian academies; for though these *she'eloth u'teshuvoth* are concerned with *halakhic* guidance, the issues they deal with are the practical questions of everyday life, which provides a mirror, therefore, of social conditions. This literature is particularly prolific for the medieval Jewries of North Africa. The books of the leading scholar in this field, Hayyim Ze'ev Hirschberg, offer a vibrant portrait of the world which would have been encountered by any medieval traveller across North Africa *en route* to the East.

North Africa west of Egypt, known as the Maghreb ('West'), was the bridge between the world of Babylon, Palestine and Egypt on one side, and Spain, Sicily and Italy on the other. Kairouan, as noted earlier, was the major destination and crossing-point until its Fatimid rulers moved their power to Egypt in the tenth century; and the lively communication between all these areas emerges very clearly in the *geniza* papers. There is one letter, for example, from a Babylonian rabbi who stops at Kairouan on the way to Spain, and writes about his journey to the *gaon*, Samuel ben Hofni, at home. In the other direction, there is a letter from a merchant of Seville writing from Kairouan to *his* hometown. Journeys could, obviously, take months, with many risks of attack both on land and by pirates at sea; yet given this background it is astonishing how well-organized, and even

* The secular papers had to be stored (and not destroyed) if they carried a mention of God, as they usually did in formal greetings, etc. The store-room was dry enough to preserve them perfectly for centuries. Goitein's major books in this field are *A Mediterranean Society* (3 vols., 1967–78) and *Letters of Mediaeval Jewish Traders* (1973).

relatively swift, travel and communication could be. There were many alternative routes, with trans-desert ones much swifter (if more dangerous) than coast routes. Beacon services along recognized routes conveyed news relevant for the caravans. For Jews, there was a special problem of arranging stopping-places for the sabbath when they themselves made the journeys; but they also used commercial caravans and private couriers, through whom they sent letters to the Babylonian academies.

Despite the speed, there were always delays, discussed in lively terms. A letter from Rabbi Nissim of Kairouan to the merchant prince, Joseph ibn Awkal, in Egypt offers profuse apologies for the delay. Ibn Awkal's name surfaces again in a letter from the *Gaon* Hai in Babylon referring to a most important matter sent to him through a Syrian Jew and to which he needs a reply 'urgentest'.

The larger caravans could be mixed – Arab, Jewish and Christian; but often, it appears, it was most efficient to use 'Ishmaelite' (Arab) caravans, especially those *en route* to or from Mecca on the *hajj* (pilgrimage). It was very important, for example, to deliver a *get* (bill of divorcement) swiftly; and one letter says that the *get* has been sent, wrapped up in garments, in a caravan from Mecca and should arrive soon.

There were many postal services in existence, and the Jews made full use of them, both through well-established agencies and individual couriers, as described in detail in Goitein's *A Mediterranean Society*.[31] In addition, the Jews had a highly developed system of personal representatives in important trading towns everywhere. Other trading nations, notably the Italians, had similar arrangements, laying the foundation for the consular services of later times; but it was uniquely significant among the Jews in relation to a main theme of this book: the inter-relationship of Jewish communities throughout the Mediterranean and eastern world.

Goitein calls the representative system 'the most novel venture in Jewish commercial organization in Islamic times of which we know'. It was natural in the Middle Ages for religious links to be always exploited in trade, and this was particularly true of the Jews. In travel, they would meet in synagogue for prayers and eat together. Their disputes would always be settled within their own religious courts; and the representatives fitted into this system. They had, as their main task, to try to defend the interests of merchants before the multitude of local, often petty, rulers who exercised power of one kind or another along the routes from Spain and North Africa to India. Among their responsibilities, the representatives would rescue merchants, where possible, from the physical dangers of brigandage, and supply banking services for commercial payments or to meet the hazards of swindling, or of death, *en route*.

Trade and mobility

This elaborate financial system reflected the richly productive economies of North Africa in those centuries, though decline was to set in from the thirteenth to fourteenth centuries. In the flourishing periods, as in earlier classical times, the land was extremely fertile, producing wheat, dates, figs, olives and vines. Saffron, cotton, hemp and sugar-cane used the ample water available before the desert took over; the area produced silk and woollen cloth, tapestries and carpets; iron, lead and silver were mined; and wood was freely available from the forests of the Atlas Mountains.

Though the Jews were active in all these fields, they also had occupations special to themselves, one of which was a traditional skill in weaving and dyeing. More strikingly, they had a virtual monopoly in producing jewellery and other products of precious metals. It has been suggested that the reason was that Islam saw gold and silver work, which added to the cash value of the metals, as a kind of usury, a practice which was strictly forbidden to Muslims. For the same reason the minting of coins was originally entrusted to Christians, though Jews later became prominent in this field.

The great range of Jewish trade, centred first in Kairouan and later in Egypt, took Jewish traders as far as India and beyond, as the *geniza* documents show. One aspect of this was the long absences from home of Jewish traders, which was a major factor in letter-writing; another was the sense of loyalty, when families moved, to 'the old land', both of which were to be typical of Jewish history later.

Babylonia inspired particular loyalty, as well as sincere faith. In illustration, there are more than two hundred letters documenting an eleventh-century merchant, Rabbi Nehri ben Nissim, whose family had originally come from Baghdad. He was settled for a long period in Kairouan and then moved (with the Fatimid dynasty) to Cairo, where he was head of the Iraqi community of Cairo and one of the wealthiest Jews in the land, responsible for a huge international trade in precious metals as well as in textiles, furs, indigo and spices, and dealing heavily with Italy and Sicily as well as with eastern countries. In the spirit of the time, he was also a distinguished scholar, receiving and answering questions on *halakhah*. The picture is rounded off perfectly when we learn that, after moving for a while to Byzantine territory, he finally settled in Jerusalem, where he worked piously as a *sofer* (scribe).

As part of their international trade, the Jews (like other traders) employed a number of financial techniques that were to be much expanded later. They had worked out jointly with the Arabs the use of a letter of credit (*suftaja* in Arabic) as a substitute for carrying cash; but as Braudel points out in his great book *The Mediterranean* (pp. 816–17), these financial instruments worked particularly well for the Jews because they had behind them 'a network of mutual confidence and co-operation'. Another bonus for the Jews was their extremely flexible use of *halakhah* to establish an acceptable system of partnership law.

There are many examples of this in Hirschberg's book on North African Jews; and the personal side of this widespread trade comes out in *geniza* letters presented by Goitein in *Letters of Mediaeval Jewish Traders*. Some of these letters concentrate on rebutting claims by the other party. One, for example, is from a Kairouan trader to the rich merchant Joseph ibn Awkal in Cairo (mentioned earlier) contesting a whole series of claims:

I did not send your brazil-wood to Spain for my own profit; indeed I lost on it. . . . You demand that I should send you the 420 pounds of silk: but one-third of this is my brother's investment, and he is entitled to a third of the profit along with you. . . . Then you sent those pearls and I worked hard to collect their price. But how long should this go on! Should I not have taken one-quarter of the profit?[32]

Other letters are more personal, as is one from India. A journey to India from North Africa involved an absence of at least two years, with many potential family problems. In this case, the trader writes to his wife in Old Cairo rejecting her complaints that he has turned his attentions elsewhere: 'I swear by God, I do not believe that the heart of anyone travelling away from his wife has remained like mine, so constantly thinking of you.' She has asked for a divorce. He sends the document, but emphasizes that if she uses it, it will be her choice, not his. He hopes she will wait for his return; above all, she should not act hastily: take advice, and 'act as you think will be the best for you. May God inspire you to the right decision.'[33]

The status of North Africa

The eastern hinge of Jewish life in these early centuries begins to take shape much more positively when the curtain is lifted, in this way, by the research of the new historians; and it is extremely important for the general story, since eastern Jewry was to be a major base for the rescue and rehabilitation of Sephardi Jews when disaster struck them in the 'pogroms' of 1391, and then, a century later, in the major expulsions of 1492 and 1497. Even in these brief notes, it is clear that the glories of the 'golden ages' of Spain and the reinforcement of their achievements later could not have taken place without the existence of powerful, learned and loyal Jewish communities in North Africa and eastward all through these centuries, which must surely be a matter of pride to the modern descendants of these communities.

Yet until recently, the history of these communities was hardly pursued. As Hirschberg says, the African Maghreb, with its strongly individual character, 'was treated as a backwater of Jewish history'.[34] Because the main thread of Jewish life could be followed more easily in certain key areas – Babylon, Spain, Germany and Poland – other areas seemed to offer less attraction to the historians, a position reversed today when material long buried in eastern archives has been opened up to demonstrate the equal vitality of this area.

It is particularly relevant to the theme of this book that new research confirms how closely the Jews of Spain were linked to North Africa, in migration, study and trade. Letters in the *geniza* illustrate this constantly. To take two examples almost at random, there is a short note written in Alexandria *c.* 1100 to a friend in Old Cairo about an errand done in Spain, referring to gold from Morocco, silk from Spain, ambergris from the Atlantic, and musk imported from Tibet or Malaya. In another letter, a Spanish merchant in Fez writes to his father in Almeria (Spain) describing his stratagems in avoiding customs duties, and moving on to personal things, as almost all the letters do. These close links became all-important, of course, when the refugees from Spain in 1492 found a haven in North Africa, either for settlement or as a staging-post for further migration.

This is not to say that the Jews outside North Africa always approved of what they found there. The Maghreb Jews were, for example, very close to their Muslim neighbours in myths and superstitions, which earned them a reproof from the *Gaon* Hai in Babylonia (twelfth century). He had heard, he says in a letter, that Moroccan Jews believed that by the use of magic words, leaves of grass could render a Jew invisible, or bar the way to robbers, or calm the sea. He mentioned stories of a rabbi 'leaping' all the way from Babylon to the Maghreb to give Torah instruction and then returning 'by air' in the same way. 'These and the like are idle things,' is his comment.

There were to be gaps in mutual understanding whenever the refugees from Spain and Portugal settled in these lands. Even Maimonides, who had fled with his parents from Spain to Fez in the later part of the twelfth century, warned his son Abraham later against some of the local Jews of these North African lands. Jews who lived among the Berbers were inclined to be coarse.

Seek company only with our beloved brethren the Sephardim, who are called Andaluzios, for they have sense and perception and a clear brain. . . . You should always be extremely cautious of the people who live between Tunis and Alexandria and who also live in the mountains of Barbary, for they are more stupid in my opinion than other men, although they are very strong in faith.[35]

This wide generalization, one feels, is best understood as one more illustration of the factor mentioned earlier, that uprooted Jews have almost always idealized the country left behind. Maghreb Jewry would never have survived, Hirschberg comments, if the Jews had been as ignorant and coarse as this; nor could they have achieved what they did in the world at large.

9 Background in Christian Spain

If much has been said in earlier chapters about the splendours of Jewish life in Spain, it was always clear that life could also be uncertain and harsh, even before the onset of persecution. We shall see both sides of this in the present chapter sketching the Spanish–Jewish background in the period leading to the full Christian Reconquest.

An early foretaste of troubles to come can be seen in attacks faced even by the illustrious Samuel Ha-Nagid, vizier of Granada in the eleventh century. The vizier of nearby Almeria is known to have published a diatribe against Samuel and to have stirred up much trouble for the Jews in general.

Yet if Jewish life around Granada had difficult times, it at least survived and was the only area that remained in Muslim hands until the Christian Reconquest was completed in 1492. Even so, this persistent corner of Muslim–Jewish existence had its rough side. When the Almohad invaders imposed their rule on Granada in the second half of the twelfth century, Jews were confronted with the alternative of conversion or death. Many fled, after temporary conversion. This harsh position eased later to such an extent that Granada began again to attract the Jews of the north to settle there; but this was a minor turn. The major pattern in Spain from the twelfth century was the increased settlement of Jews everywhere in *Christian* Spain, and the building up there of the Sephardi culture that was ultimately to move out to wider spheres.

Within this pattern, one has to allow, also, for a large-scale migration of Jews from Muslim Spain to North Africa and Egypt to escape the persecution of the Almohad sect, whose military forces had arrived in Andalusia in 1146. Without being able to judge the scale of this flight to North Africa, one is particularly aware of it because (as mentioned earlier) it included the father and family of the great philosopher Maimonides (Moses ben Maimon). Facing Almohad persecution, he left Cordoba with his parents in 1148 when he was thirteen, wandered over Spain and perhaps Provence for the next eight or nine years, and then settled in Fez. His further travels must again be seen as typifying the times. After five years in Fez, continuing his work in the fields of Jewish studies, philosophy and medicine, he and his family left for Palestine, and after some time there settled in Egypt.

The communications between Jewish communities, however wide their dispersion, is illustrated by the fame which began to attach to Maimonides at a very early age, involving him in correspondence with distant countries and stimulating his determination to distil Jewish law and philosophy in forms that would be accessible to Jews everywhere. The brilliant works which he produced with this in mind were not always acceptable to more traditional scholars, as we shall see; and these rabbis may have objected, also, to some of the advice he gave to those who desperately sought his guidance on the subject of conversion, due to become a burning subject in Christian Spain. His father Maimon had allowed the family to embrace Islam temporarily to save their lives; and Maimonides himself, as we saw, argued in his famous letter on conversion to the Jews in Yemen that one might have to accept it as a temporary reality, but only if one were determined to escape at the earliest opportunity and rejoin Judaism.

This attitude makes it all the harder to understand how it was that conversion to Christianity became such a flood in Spain. The 'pogroms' of 1391 were an obvious driving force, but one feels that there must have been other compelling reasons. It may be that the free social life open to many upper-class Jews in Christian Spain during the Reconquest was sometimes translated into an intellectual rapport absent with Islam. When there was conversion to Islam, it seems to have been largely a formality, linked to a place at court, as with the Baghdad patron of Isaac ibn Ezra mentioned earlier. But in Christian Spain, assimilation could produce passionately sincere Christians, who often displayed their new fervour, even in the first generation, in fierce attacks on their former co-religionists. There was obviously a strong latent antagonism to Jews expressed in Christianity and absent in Islam, and the psychological effect of this on the Jews themselves could be bizarre. As far as one knows, there is nothing in Muslim life comparable with the horrible activities of ex-Jews who provided the Church with material from Jewish sources capable of being twisted into attacks on the Jews in disputations and other ways.

This sorry fact can serve as a symbol of the paradox of Jewish life during the centuries of the Reconquest. From one angle, it could be said that the Jews, populous and deeply acculturated in Spain, were completely happy, enjoying a settled industrious life in every occupation, active in business, the professions and agriculture, living mainly, by their own desire, in their own quarters, allotting and collecting their own taxes, ruled by their own religious courts, and led by Jewish notables of learning, wealth and political power. But if much of this emerges from the archives, one knows that underneath it lay a persistent Christian antagonism that exploded with bloody horror in the 'pogroms' of 1391 and ultimately, a century later, in the Expulsion. There is paradox, equally, in the love that the Jews bore for Spain despite these tragedies. It is a measure of this that the Jews took with them, when they were expelled, all the good memories, recalling the freedom and pride of religious life there over centuries, the scholars and scientists who had emerged uniquely in this milieu, the literature, language and music that was permanently to stay with them in their new homes.

This pride was full of nostalgia, but it was also creative in the strength of character it gave the exiles when they spread through the Mediterranean and Middle Eastern worlds. It helps to understand this if we consider how brilliantly they had responded, during the centuries of Reconquest, to the unique opportunities that arose from the Muslim–Christian struggles, and how they had continued to build on this foundation even when, for various reasons, history was no longer favouring them in Christian Spain.

Life during the Reconquest

The Christian march south, which brought many benefits to the Jews when it got into its full stride, took some time to get started. Before this, the Jewish position in the north had been very uncertain. Though settled everywhere, their communities were small, with land the main basis of their livelihoods. It was uncertain in other ways, too. They usually had charters guaranteeing rights, but always at the discretion of local rulers. At this stage, there were many Muslim–Jewish centres in the north-east, adjacent to Christian areas, and with Jews often moving from one to the other.

The first Christian attacks on the south were repulsed by the Arabs with the help of the fierce Berbers who came across from North Africa;

but at the beginning of the thirteenth century, the Reconquest was resumed triumphantly, and with dramatic effect on the life of the Jews.

The Jewish community in Muslim Spain had been the largest in Europe, and widely experienced, as we have seen, in the skills of political administration as well as in the arts and sciences of the Arabic-speaking world. All these skills were needed by the Christian conquerors from Castile and Aragon as they moved south. The land had been devastated in war; new cities had to be founded and developed, and the Jews were uniquely useful in all this. They knew the land and the languages; they could bring to the burgeoning cities industrial and commercial expertise that could promote commerce within Spain and across the sea with Italy, North Africa and beyond. As Muslim areas fell to the Christian conquerors, the dividing-up of Muslim estates included Jews as recipients; and in the charters granted to residents after conquests, Jewish rights were set out covering residence and autonomous courts. It is true that the implementation of these rights would always depend on the ability of the ruler to counter anti-Jewish hostility which was ready to surface in all classes, especially when stimulated by populist preachers. Yet if the Jews suffered grievously from Crusading fanaticism during the early Reconquest, it is the judgement of Yitzhak Baer in his classic *A History of the Jews in Christian Spain* that 'Jewish life came out of these wars revitalized'.

A striking aspect of this, confirmed in documents from the archives, was their distinctive role in building autonomous communities on crown lands in Aragon and Navarre that were mainly but not exclusively agricultural, and were 'unconnected with any Christian town, and independent of any manor, castle or church'.[36]

This was, however, unusual. In general the Jewish quarter was within city walls and often close to the citadel, which the Jews helped to garrison. In Toledo they had their own fortress, a spacious area, virtually a city in itself. Even royal officials could not enter the Jewish quarters without permission. After every conquest the Jews were assigned land for building dwellings, workshops and market-stalls, the last a valuable right, as we see in a contract from Barcelona, dated 1165, in which Preciosa, daughter of Nathan bar Isaac, her husband Nathan bar David, and the latter's brother Isaac sell to Isaac bar Judah 'the stall which we have in the market-place, which had belonged to our father . . . who sat and did business therein all his life'. We hear at the same time that 'the shop of the Christian, Julian the shoemaker' adjoined this stall on one side, while on another was the stall that had belonged to Jacob bar Solomon. It is in detail like this that the archives bring the Jewish scene in Spain magically to life.[37]

In everyday terms the Jews felt free, even if, in the formalities of the time, they were 'the property' of local rulers. The charters laid down that the Jewish *aljama* (community council) paid its taxes direct to the royal treasury. In civil disputes with Christians, their own witnesses had an equal status with those of the opponent, and Jewish officials had the same rights in impounding property following a judgement of the court. There was always a greater difference in criminal cases. The system called for *wergild* (compensation) to be paid for injury and murder. For a Christian, it was paid to himself or his family; for a Jew it was paid to his 'master', the king. This had a dual effect. The ruler was always assiduous in collecting *wergild* from a town if a Jew was killed; but any assertion of power like this by the ruler was always liable to lead to attacks on the Jews.

If the Jewish position was, therefore, precarious, as in other parts of Christian Europe, the heritage of the Muslim age established crucial differences in a number of ways. In particular, the rise of a number of Jewish notables to an exceptionally close relation with the rulers as doctors, political advisers, tax-collectors and diplomats applied to those who had brought these skills from the south, and who combined this, as in the Muslim setting, with a total devotion to Jewish scholarship and a readiness to act as the responsible heads of the Jewish communities everywhere.

Leadership and controversy

From an early date one begins to hear of a number of prominent families in Toledo – Ferrizuel, Abulafia and others – whose wealth and fame in Castile persisted throughout the whole Reconquest period and indeed throughout Jewish history. In Aragon and Catalonia, the Sheshet and Benvenisti families occupied the same roles as doctors, scholars and poets, as well as diplomats. Here, from a surviving document, is an indication of how these things were carried out. In 1200, Pedro II of Aragon sent a member of the Benvenisti family on a mission to the king of Morocco, the journey being financed by a loan from a Christian. The deed, signed by King Pedro, his mother, the dowager queen, and several Christian functionaries of the court, also bears the signatures in Hebrew of Benvenisti and two other Jews.[38]

Spanish–Jewish history is studded with the names of the famous who made the most, in their Christian surroundings, of skills from the Muslim world. In a different way, the rabbis who became communal heads in major cities also enjoyed great authority from the rulers, though this could lead to communal conflict. The *nesi'im* (notables) were not above using their influence at court to secure release from the tax obligations imposed on all Jews by their own *aljamas*, claiming this and other special privileges in respect of their inherited rank. The rabbis were usually prepared to endorse this deference to the élite and fought off complaints. In one case, a trouble-maker who protested against this favouritism was hauled before a rabbinical court and sentenced to confess his sin in synagogue and suffer the lash.[39]

The arguments involving rabbis and courtiers could be more serious than this, as in the famous controversy over the writings of Maimonides, which raised fundamental questions about Jewish beliefs, then and ever since. We saw earlier that Maimonides had finally settled in Egypt. It was there that he produced two monumental works: *Mishneh Torah* (a presentation of the *halakhah*) written in Hebrew in 1180, and his great philosophic book *Guide of the Perplexed*, written in Arabic in 1190. The *Guide* was soon translated into Hebrew by Samuel ibn Tibbon, a member of the great translating family of Provence, so that both books were able to reach the maximum Jewish audience. Once they had circulated, they began to stimulate a fierce argument – no holds barred – on the relative place of reason and faith in the life of a Jew.

It was as a passionate Jew that Maimonides sought, in these books, to present Jewish law and belief in the clear rational language that was second nature to those who had profited, as he had, from the renaissance of Greek philosophy and science through Arabic translations. To his admirers, from Spain to the Yemen, he was an illuminator, a saint. But Jewish learning in Spain and neighbouring Provence now included a strain of teaching, largely imported from northern France and Germany, that saw danger in leaning so heavily on reason. To them, Jewish life had to be accepted on the basis of traditional authority, and not with the help of ordered and often alien ideas. They objected, therefore, even to his careful digest of *halakhah*, which seemed to them to substitute his own judgement for that of the original rabbis. In the same spirit, they found it heretical that he was prepared in the *Guide* to offer 'explanations' of difficult issues – such as God's communication with man, or miracles, or physical resurrection – instead of simply affirming everything in the traditional terms that had always been accepted.

Opposition to Maimonides

The deep issue that divided Maimonides from his opponents was the idea that only through rational philosophy could one 'justify' Judaism. A fierce controversy erupted over this, resulting in a series of mutual excommunications, even though many of Maimonides' opponents were still ready to pay tribute to his intellectual power, and even to his religious sincerity.

The controversy went beyond a straightforward argument over the place of reason and faith in religion. At this level there was always an underlying agreement that traditional Jewish law was God-given and therefore demanded obedience. But within Judaism, there were some who saw Jewish existence explained not just in terms of leading a good life, but as an element in bringing about the ultimate transformation of the Universe. In this view, the Jewish fate is not an accident of history. If the Jews are in exile, God Himself is, as it were, in exile; and a Jew has to grapple with this idea in order to play some role in the restoration of the Universe to its primeval perfection. It was not enough to reject the doubts of a rationalist like Maimonides on miracles and resurrection: one had to look further, exploring the realm of mystical speculation – using numbers, letters and abstruse metaphysical concepts – to bring one into contact with God's plan. The ideas that germinated in this form became known as the Cabbala (*lit.* 'received doctrine') and were due to expand with explosive force among the Jews in the Near East after the expulsion from Spain in 1492.

Jewish thought always had room for those who believed that the tragedies of Jewish existence led one to find refuge in mystical rather than rational ideas. There had been a mild expression of anti-rationalism in the work of the poet Judah Halevi. 'Let not Greek wisdom tempt you,' he had written, 'for it bears flowers only and no fruit. . . . Why should I search for by-paths and leave the main road?' But he was not stimulated to pursue this to its logical conclusion as the rabbis were who saw where the 'Greek' attitude had led a great man like Maimonides. Among the numerous participants in the wild controversies that broke out from about the year 1230 two men, one a scholarly 'notable', the other an exceptionally endowed rabbi, can be taken as indicating the state of this debate in the intense setting of Spanish–Jewish history.

The rabbi was Moses ben Nahman, generally known as Nahmanides (1194–1270). He came from an aristocratic family of Catalonia and had a wide scholarly background, embracing not only traditional learning but also elements of more intensive faith – French talmudism, German–Jewish pietism and Cabbala – that were moving Spanish–Jewish thought towards new paths. He was clearly a man of great courage, as he showed when he was coerced by the king, in 1263, into a public disputation in Barcelona with the Christian ex-Jew Pablo Christiani. In general, his main aim, as he showed in the Maimonides controversy, was to keep the peace between extremists on either side, though in his own writings his mystical views are clearly indicated.[40]

The Maimonides controversy had erupted in Provence, where some scholars liked the 'modernism' of Spanish–Jewish writings in Arabic, now available in Hebrew translations. They were enthusiastic when Maimonides' *Guide* appeared among them in this way, to the fury of extremely conservative rabbis who called it heresy and persuaded sympathizers – notably the 'Tosafists' (Talmud experts) of northern France – to issue a ban against all the writings of Maimonides. This was met by a counter-ban by the Maimonides enthusiasts; and both turned for support to Nahmanides in Gerona (Catalonia).

One sees even from this how the scene was set between disputants; and as a by-product it is interesting to note how the land of Israel came into the story, even before the Cabbala developed there in the sixteenth century. Nahmanides had already shown that he wanted Jewish thought to embrace mystical ideas. It was in tune with this that he elected, late in life, to move to the Holy Land, where he lived in poverty, teaching the Cabbala to a few followers in Acre. This had an interesting outcome. After his death, one of his group, Rabbi Isaac of Acre, went to Spain to make contact with Cabbalists active there, an élite set which included Moses de Leon, now known as the author of the *Zohar*, the central book of cabbalist teaching. Rabbi Isaac claimed later that de Leon had given him some of his writings which became a major part of the book.

This élite group who were attracted to the Cabbala and, by the same token, were strong opponents of Maimonides, were personified in Meir Abulafia, member of a rich and famous family of scholars living in Toledo. Among members of the family who continued to express this approach, the most famous was Todros ben Joseph Abulafia (1220–98), who became a profound student of Cabbala. As head of the family, whose wealth was increased through being allotted large areas of land after the Christian conquests of Seville and Jerez de la Frontera, he was treated as the Spanish 'Exilarch'; but in his writing he took a very personal line, guiding the Jews into exploring new and more esoteric patterns of thought. Many around him followed in turning to messianic and cabbalistic ideas; and this was to have important historical consequences when, after the Expulsion of 1492, the cabbalism of Spain, based on the *Zohar*, spread through the Middle East.

Yet one must see this in proportion. In acknowledging the power that this religious movement generated from Spain, it was small in range, to begin with, compared with the widespread worldliness and prosperity of Spanish Jewry as a whole, intensified on a considerable scale when the Christian Reconquest began to approach completion.

Assimilationist trends

Worldliness in the form of assimilation had long since made itself evident among the rich, in sharp contrast to the Jewish loyalty expressed by leaders like the Abulafias. Baer shows in his *History* the weaknesses that could affect a highly sophisticated society almost automatically, with gifted and privileged Jews all too willing to be drawn into the intellectual and sensual corruption of upper-class life of the time.

To illustrate, he discusses at one point the political stagnation that affected the rich leaders at the end of the thirteenth century, encouraging many who still wrote in charming 'golden age' Hebrew to adopt the corrupt pose of non-Jewish high society. Well-educated in 'all three languages, but principally in Hebrew', these young aristocrats would aim at adapting their style to the ways of the Christian knights:

On their travels they would be accompanied by a retinue of young Jews, and also Christians, whom they pampered with gifts of delicacies and finery. . . . Political rivals among the Jews would heap abuse upon one another in verse, even as the Christian cavaliers did.

Not surprisingly, we learn that 'the dissolute behaviour of this fast set' drew vehement censure from the rabbis around them. The courtiers were only a small circle within the Jewish community, but 'they set the social tone for the Jewish aristocracy' in Castile and Aragon. In Baer's view, one has to see this kind of behaviour as a doom-laden product of religious scepticism, with results spreading far and wide:

The descendants of these highly cultured aristocrats were to betray both their faith and their people during the period of great trial which lasted from 1391 to 1415. The scions of these apostates, in turn, would yet be hauled before the tribunals of the Inquisition, charged with professing no positive faith whatever.

It was all a result, said a contemporary moralist, of Averroism, in which 'the commandments become a subject for philosophic specu-lation, and philosophy itself a rationalization of their indulgence in sensual pleasure'.[41]

Averroes (1126–98) was an Islamic philosopher whose com-mentaries on Aristotle had furthered the spread of rationalism. In their role as translators the Jews had helped to transmit the thought of Averroes into scholarly Christian circles and were themselves exposed to philosophic argument of a kind that did not disturb Jews elsewhere. When many Jews became 'New Christians' but kept up their links with old Jewish friends, argument often took on a new intensity. In some cases, the *conversos* had become passionately sincere Christians and fierce enemies of the Jews; in other cases, the process instilled doubts, leaving many Jews in an ill-defined limbo.

Yet overall this was still a 'golden age' for Jews in terms of faith as well as in the comforts of life. In the setting of the thirteenth-century conquests, they were entrusted as before with the resettling of destroyed areas and towns evacuated by the Muslims. Jews appointed to the court of Castile as doctors, financiers, ambassadors, astrono-mers and so on, received houses, vineyards and land to hold in perpetuity and with limited taxes. The same was true in other states. Jewish land-ownership grew in the fourteenth century not simply among the very wealthy but with an increase in the number of small landowners who built houses and workshops.

In some places the Jews were allowed to convert some mosques to synagogues; and though the codes of law promulgated by rulers spelt out some forms of social discrimination, they always had their own courts, based on talmudic law, and wide-ranging autonomy. To ensure fairness, the ruler would appoint a leading rabbi to sit with palace judges when a Jewish matter came up. In Castile, the cabbalist Todros Abulafia had this role. Leading families were equally prominent in the other states. In Aragon, the most famous name in the second half of the thirteenth century was Judah de la Cavalleria, who acted as the king's bailiff, collecting the revenues, carrying out all expenditures and making huge loans to the king for royal purposes – garrisoning the border areas, outfitting a fleet to fight against the Muslims, and so on. As noted earlier, the Jewish populace both enjoyed the renown of their *nesi'im* and complained of their special privileges.

Mounting attacks

It was more serious for the future that the Jewish notables were beginning to be attacked from the Christian side. When the ruler's interests were at stake, he would defend his Jewish officials, as James I of Aragon did in dismissing a charge by the Dominicans that de la Cavalleria and his son-in-law Bonsenyor (royal secretary for Arab correspondence) had desecrated a crucifix. But in general, the Jewish position was no longer secure, and this was more than two hundred years before the Expulsion.

A major factor was that in many cases Jews were no longer indispensable; as time went on, non-Jews could be found with their financial and professional skills, and the pressure on the ruler to dismiss Jews became harder to resist. The Church always had a hand in the mounting pressure, as when the laws were tightened on rates for money-lending. When Jews secured their economic rights under the established system of law, riots against them were easy to instigate even though the decision had been in their favour.

The Inquisition was already hard at work in neighbouring Provence, with influence across the border. Typical of the increasing bigotry was the instigation in Saragossa in 1250 of a 'blood libel', the monstrous allegation that Jews murdered non-Jews to use their blood for ritual purposes.

For the Jews these mounting dangers stimulated a fear of 'informers', ex-Jews who could make plausible if wild accusations, such as that the Talmud contained attacks on Jesus. These accusations were central to the 'Disputations' staged in the thirteenth and fourteenth centuries, in which Jews were hauled before ecclesiastical courts with the verdicts predetermined.

It was a time, then, of growing insecurity, expressed in legal restrictions, economic discrimination, Church accusations and mob attacks. Conversion to Christianity was beginning to grow, though even with those who took the fateful step, there was much hesitation. A good example was the notorious Bishop of Burgos, who had been Rabbi Abner of Burgos before his conversion in 1321. According to his own account, he had had a vision of the Christian truth as early as 1295: 'I saw the poverty of the Jews, my people . . . this people that had lost its former glory. . . .' A 'tall man' had appeared to him in a dream saying that the teacher of righteousness – Jesus – would save them. It took Abner twenty-five years to accept this, but he then made up for the delay in vehement works (in Hebrew) arguing for conversion on theological as well as practical grounds.[42]

Since conversion on a massive scale was unique to Spanish Jewry and immensely important in its effects, one does one's best to understand its complex character whenever a case is documented. There is a parallel to Abner – and even more revealing – in a conversion about fifty years later that took a scholar called Solomon Halevi into the Church as Paul de Santa Maria, and led him, also, to become Bishop of Burgos. In his case, letters between him and Jewish friends present a lively picture of the mood of the time, but with a sting in the tail.

Solomon had been born into a distinguished family long engaged in tax-farming and other government business, and part of a sophisticated circle of talmudists and intellectuals. The letters which have come to light show him talking teasingly but pleasantly about some aspects of Jewish life; and even after he was converted and became an outstanding polemicist, an old friend of his youth called Joshua Halorki – a doctor and scientist – felt free to write to him ironically about what his true motivation had been. It could not have been a lust for wealth or honour, which he had in abundance, nor could it signify a belief that the Jews had to disappear, for they would go on living all over the world whatever happened in Spain. Then what? Surely Solomon could never believe 'in a Messiah of flesh and blood who eats and drinks and dies and lives again'. Baer provides the full text of this long letter and part of Solomon's reply; but it is the postscript which really matters. In 1412, in the wake of the 'pogroms' of 1391, Halorki was himself converted, and promptly wrote a pamphlet, which he sent to the Pope, purporting to prove the anti-Christian nature of the Talmud. It was this which led the Pope to institute a Disputation with the Jews (in effect a hostile confrontation) at Tortosa in the following year.[43]

A picture of ordinary life

Before conversion became a flood after the 1391 'pogroms', records that have come down to us show the masses of Jews living out their lives in what might be called a typically Jewish way, combining a peaceful devotion to tradition and ritual with unending communal strife, arising from claims and counterclaims before their courts on issues of money or status. One has the same impression in building up a picture of ordinary social life from the collections of long and detailed *responsa* that leading rabbis gave to difficult questions. One collection of a mass of these *responsa* from the distinguished Rabbi Solomon ben Adret of Barcelona shows how involved ordinary Jews were in their synagogues, education and charity, the attention given to inequities in tax-collection, the joyous if sometimes troublesome routines associated with engagement, marriage and divorce. We encounter, also, the grim realities of dealing with heretics and 'informers'. Embracing all, we see how the systems of office-holding were frequently changed to maintain democratic forms of self-government, allowing for the fact that this had to leave room for the special privileges claimed by the *nesi'im* and the appointees of rulers.

It is a mixed picture, but one on which the editor of these *responsa* is prepared to give a favourable verdict:

There were to be found, now and again, men who were tempted to break the religious bond which held the race together. The allurements of wealth seduced others. But through the good and the bad times that were experienced in Spain, the most conspicuous feature of Jewish life was not the infidelity of a few here and there, but the strong fidelity of the masses to the religious institutions which have preserved the Jews through their chequered history, as one people.[44]

One should perhaps qualify this judgment by mentioning the view of Yitzhak Baer (*History*, vol. I, p. 232) that even the ordinary Jews of

Spain were infected at times with Spanish passions untypical of Jews elsewhere. This was particularly true, he thinks, of the stern punishments carried out by the Jewish courts on 'informers', which were influenced, he believes, by the inquisitorial procedures of Roman and Canon Law.

But if these dark hues have to be included, the picture as a whole of these eight centuries remains positive: 'History brought one of the most creative Jewish communities of the Diaspora into collaboration with one of the most gifted peoples of Christian Europe.'[45] The results emerged later to give a unique character to Sephardi history.

10 *Persecution and Expulsion*

In formal terms, Jewish life in the Iberian peninsula was cut off at the end of the fifteenth century: expulsion from Spain in 1492, and forced conversion (leading to flight) in Portugal in 1497. But these drastic acts had been preceded by a wave of persecution in Spain a hundred years earlier in 1391. Indeed, the seeds of the final drama had been sown two centuries before the Expulsion when the period of feudal fighting and constant wars against the Muslims was coming to an end.

When the Christian Spaniards had been preoccupied with rivalries and wars, the Jews had been needed for their many professional skills and had made the most of the relatively free life they were accorded. But now the disturbances within the country had given way to more stable conditions, with most of the peninsula unified in a few large states and administered increasingly by Christian bureaucrats, professionals and businessmen. By this time, too, a positive anti-Jewish drive had begun to gather force, largely at the instigation of powerful Church Orders and mendicant friars, and in accord with the general attitude to the Jews in other parts of Christian Europe. It was in these conditions that conversion to Christianity began to grow among many Jews moving in sophisticated circles, as if expressing a premonition that the Jews of Spain would either have to be fully assimilated or disappear from the Spanish scene.

But though these underlying forces were at work for two hundred years before the expulsion of 1492, the surface pattern of Jewish life still reflected the religious independence, economic power and cultural distinction that had flowered uniquely in the peninsula. The special forms of autonomy, geared closely through rabbinical and lay leaders to institutional life in Spain, were jealously maintained until the fateful Ordinance of Expulsion changed everything.

The distinction of Jewish life

If the numbers of Jewish notables at court began to wane in the fourteenth century, the mass of Jews, consisting largely of a petty bourgeoisie of shopkeepers and artisans, was still prosperous. Even though their lives had more uncertainty, they were still a major source of revenue for the various states. Some figures for the end of the thirteenth century have been unearthed by Baer to show how important this had been. The Jewish *aljamas* in Castile at this time paid collectively a sum of two million *maravedís* in 'fixed tax' in one year, apart from *servicios* (surtaxes) and special levies. A tax register of Aragon for 1294 shows the 'fixed tax' from the Jews yielding 22 per cent of all state taxes, apart from special loans and subsidies imposed on them. As in other parts of Europe, Jews acted as a sponge for the farming of general state taxes – e.g. customs, mintage, monopolies – that would otherwise have been uncertain in their yield.[46]

In these matters, and in cultural life generally, we still hear of leading Jews in every state bearing names that would continue to redound through history. We noted earlier the huge financial responsibilities of two brothers of the Alconstantini family (the name indicates that they came originally from Constantine in North Africa), who were engaged in wide-ranging diplomatic work in fourteenth-century Aragon. They are visible in succeeding centuries as financiers and scholars, until they settled after the Expulsion in Turkey and Italy. We saw the leader of a rival family, Judah de la Cavalleria, exercising great power as royal bailiff of Saragossa; and in this case the family, while still distinguished, slipped gradually (though not permanently) into conversion. The Ravaya brothers, bailiffs of Pedro III, had been central to the whole administration of Aragon, and continued their leadership through family connections. On the rabbinical side, we hear first in Barcelona in the fourteenth century of a great scholar of the Sheshet family, whom we discover later playing a leading part in North Africa after fleeing from the 'pogroms' of 1391.

Combining both wealth and scholarship, the Abulafia family is prominent throughout these centuries. Its leading representative in the thirteenth century – the cabbalist Todros ben Joseph Abulafia – had been saluted in contemporary Hebrew literature as 'the prince of the Spanish *galuth*', and had served Alfonso X of Castile as foreign secretary. In the fourteenth century, the current head of the family, Samuel ben Meir Abulafia, sustained King Pedro the Cruel of Castile through endless struggles with the nobility, and is remembered, ironically, in two contrasting ways. In 1357 he built a magnificent synagogue in Toledo, still displayed proudly (with its long Hebrew inscription) to all visitors as the 'Church of El Transito'. Three years after he had built the synagogue, he was suddenly arrested and tortured to death in Seville.

But perhaps the most remarkable family, epitomizing the origins and future of the Sephardi diaspora, were the Abrabanels, whose wealth, wanderings and scholarship epitomized the whole period, encompassing Portugal as well as Spain, and settling after the Expulsion in Italy and elsewhere. A glance at their history is illuminating in this sense.

The family, whose name appears to be a diminutive of Abraham, is first heard of with Judah Abrabanel, royal treasurer in Cordoba and Seville at the beginning of the fourteenth century, and subsequently revenue collector for the whole of Castile. At least one eminent member of the family – he was treasurer of Andalusia – converted to Christianity during the 'pogroms' of 1391, but reverted to Judaism when the family as a whole fled to Portugal. There the current head of the family was royal treasurer and immensely prominent in overseas trade. A son, Don Isaac Abrabanel, who at first used the huge family fortune in the service of the king of Portugal, became known particularly for his exceptional work as a Talmud scholar and classical humanist, but had to flee to Spain in 1480 following an insurrection of the nobility in which he was thought to have been implicated. Somehow he transferred his fortune to Castile and became financial adviser to Ferdinand and Isabella, who were now getting close to the point of ordering the expulsion of all Jews from the country. Abrabanel, in concert with another eminent Jewish royal treasurer, Abraham Seneor, strove to avert the expulsion decree, putting up a huge loan, though all in vain. Seneor took the road of conversion. Abrabanel secured permission to take a sum of money with him to exile and sailed for Naples. There he continued to work as a royal financial adviser but was mainly occupied, as he had been for years, in writing a large-scale commentary on the Bible. This remarkable combination of finance and Jewish study continued when he settled in Venice, where he organized a commercial treaty between Venice and Portugal, and wrote more books on philosophy and messianism. His son Judah, who was known in Italy as Leone Ebreo, practised as a doctor but was fully identified as a philosopher and poet with the

Platonic Academy of Florence. With some echoes of the same distinction, the family name continued in Italy into the seventeenth century and beyond.

One selects a few family names like this to give a hint of the vast reservoir of talent that had been built up within the Jewish communities of Spain and Portugal in the period before persecution became more and more continuous and then culminated in expulsion. At the mass level and headed by these notables, Spanish Jewry had created a form of Jewish experience that was individual enough to withstand the onset of the dramas of persecution and could still carry away a lasting legacy of pride.

Rise of persecution

In opening this chapter, we noted general factors that had begun to reduce Jewish prosperity and security in the thirteenth century, accompanied by increasing conversions to Christianity. The picture was uneven between individual states and cities until Spain was fully united at the end of the fifteenth century; but the most consistent general factor was the persistent and growing attack on the Jews by a series of Church leaders – mostly popular preachers – who were venomous to all of Jewish origin, whether loyal to their faith or converted. This was often mitigated in its effect through protective action by the rulers; but the underlying power of Jew-hatred, taking the form of libels, public disputations, riots and discriminatory ordinances, was finally revealed in June 1391 when a virulent preacher Ferrant Martínez incited the mobs of Seville to rise openly and murderously against the Jews.

The wave of destruction which followed this riot was extraordinary. In one town after another through the whole of Spain, Jewish quarters were looted and set on fire. Jews (men and women) were slaughtered everywhere: in Barcelona alone more than four hundred; and these 'pogroms' were accompanied by a great many conversions, mostly in mass form by force. Facing continued attacks and the persistent waves of conversion, some managed to find refuge in flight, until the situation eased around 1415. An informed estimate by an historian of this period states that a third of the Jewish population of Spain was slain, a third were converted, mostly by force, and only a third managed to survive, either by fleeing to places of safety in Spain or by escaping abroad, mostly to North Africa.[47]

The mounting effects of this catastrophe were enormous, even though the authorities tried after a time to control the murders and looting. The most crucial damage lay in the desolated towns, where the government needed Jewish life to be restored if only for economic reasons. The most notable effort made to bring this about was in Aragon, where the king and queen wrote to the eminent scholar, Hasdai Crescas, to encourage him to raise funds for the resettlement in Barcelona and Valencia, with the clear implication that Jewish life would henceforth be secure. If Jewish life gradually began to be resumed, it was largely due to the outstanding leadership of Crescas and his associate Rabbi Isaac ben Sheshet, who rallied the spirit of the Jews.

Crescas, who is today recognized as one of the greatest Jewish philosophers of the Middle Ages, had enjoyed a representative position at court as a member of the royal household, and now turned to Jews far and wide to secure support. In a famous letter to the Jews of Avignon describing what had happened, he gave an eye-witness account in which the mood was set poignantly in grim and graphic terms:

...the Lord bent His bow like an enemy against the community of Seville. . . . They set fire to its gates and killed many of its people. Many changed their religion; some of the women and children were sold to the Muslims. . . . Many died to sanctify the Holy Name, and many violated the holy covenant.[48]

The immediate aim of the rulers to restore a Jewish presence in Barcelona proved, in fact, beyond achievement. So complete had the destruction been that after 1396, when some Jews who had tried to return there finally left, not a single Jew established residence in the town until modern times. But Crescas was more successful in stimulating the restoration of Jewish life in Saragossa, which became a rallying-point for all Spanish Jewry. The means adopted was to reorganize the *aljama* in as democratic a form as possible, and to pass *takkanoth* (regulations) tailored to the new situation. The agony of the time and the spirit in which restoration was carried through can be felt in the wording of a *takkanah* of 1397, which refers to the adoption of a tax known as *Cisa*. This tax, the *takkanah* said, is for community expenses in the service of the queen, for the restoration and protection of our holy Torah and for saving the lives and property of our community and of all the other communities of Spain. . . . For if by chance – which God forbid – the *Cisa* should suffer loss and diminution, great harm might be done to our community and consequently to all the other communities dependent upon it.[49]

Gradually, and with resolute courage, the Jews who stayed on in Spain rebuilt much of their lives, unaware yet of the infinitely greater blow that was to fall on them at the end of the century. Many had fled, of course, to other countries, a movement which we will consider later in the context of the Expulsion. Within Spain, survival was part of a much more unusual drama that was played out around the many thousands who had converted to Christianity. Passions were being stirred through this that would, in the end, be a major element in the final Expulsion.

Mass conversion

According to Christian doctrine, the converts should have been treated as equal, now, to all Christian Spaniards; in the event, however, the 'New Christians', as they began to be called, found themselves faced with a wholly ambiguous social position and with new forms of discrimination. There was still a wall between them and the Old Christians, arising partly from suspicion as to their religious sincerity, but more directly from the surviving – and indeed magnified – hatred of them as Jews, despite the baptism they had undergone. It was not surprising that the barriers remained, for the *conversos* continued to live in the same dwellings in the Jewish quarters and had mainly the same occupations. To some extent, it is true, they could now enter new professions, for instance as notaries or judges; but by and large their old occupations remained, and these included their role as tax-farmers, which was not likely to make them more popular with their Christian co-religionists.[50]

The term 'Marrano' by which these 'New Christians' came to be known reflects this dislike, since it is thought to be derived from a Spanish word meaning 'swine', used as a term of contempt. In Hebrew, the term used was *anusim*, meaning those whose change of religion was 'forced' upon them.

A Mesopotamian terracotta of a husband and wife, dated 22nd–21st century BC, illustrating the background out of which the patriarch Abraham emerged c. 1800–1700 BC.

A figure representing Hammurabi, the great Babylonian lawgiver, who was roughly a contemporary with the patriarch Abraham. There are significant differences between his laws and those in the law codes in the Bible.

The ziggurat of Ur, the Sumerian capital, rediscovered in our time.

Israelite prisoners from Lachish taken by Assyrian invaders, 8th century BC.

Left A reconstruction in the Berlin Museum of the Ishtar Gate of the Babylonian palace of the 7th-6th centuries BC.

Below Catacombs at Beth Shearim, Israel, showing a man dressed in a Roman legionary's tunic holding a *menorah* over his head, 2nd-4th century AD.

The inner courtyard of the Second Temple, as reconstructed in the model at the Holyland Hotel, Jerusalem.

The ruins at Ostia, near Rome, of a 1st-century synagogue, probably the oldest in Europe.

Mordecai hanging the sons of Haman, from a book in Judaeo–Persian written in 1332 by a Jewish poet and illustrated by a 14th-century painter, copies of which were made in the 17th century.

A 16th-century miniature, at the Topkapi Museum, Istanbul, showing Jews being defeated at Medina.

Bishop Ildefonso in a disputation with the Jews of 7th-century Spain. Christian rule had become onerous and the Jews welcomed the Moorish invaders a century later.

A 4th–6th-century tombstone in Tortosa, Spain, with an inscription in Hebrew, Latin and Greek recording the death of a girl called Meliosa.

A bilingual Hebrew–Arabic inscription in Ferdinand III's royal chapel in Seville Cathedral, with the two passages paying homage to the Christian king separated by a panel bearing the arms of Leon and Castile. The Jews often acted as intermediaries between Christians and Muslims.

Decorative panels in the synagogue of Cordoba.

The highly decorative work inside the synagogue of El Transito, Toledo, built *c.* 1357. It is now the Transito Church.

A plaque commemorating the generosity of Samuel Abulafia in building the magnificent synagogue of El Transito. Some of the words are in Arabic in Hebrew characters; the royal coat of arms is of the king of Castile.

Exterior of a house built in Toledo by Samuel Abulafia (c. 1320-61), treasurer to Pedro the Cruel of Castile, who was later arrested and executed. The house has few windows and is fortified, reflecting the insecurity felt even by those Jews who reached high positions. The house is now the El Greco Museum.

The expulsion of the Jews from Spain in 1492 had a long background. This illustration from a Haggadah written in Castile c. 1300 shows the king of Castile's advisers urging him to expel the Jews.

The seal of Todros Ha-Levi, son of Samuel Ha-Levi (who was treasurer to Pedro I). Jews played an important economic function in medieval Spain as financiers and merchants.

Illustrations from the Golden Haggadah, *c.* 1320, showing from left to right, top: the distribution of *matzah* and *charoset*; Miriam and maidens playing and dancing; bottom: preparing the Paschal lamb and cleansing dishes; searching for the leaven bread.

Illustrations from a Haggadah written in Castile, *c.* 1300, showing bread (or *matzah*) being made at home; it would be baked in a communal oven. A communal cauldron would be used for cooking.

A detail from a miniature in the Alba Bible showing (bottom row) Rabbi Moses Arragel presenting his Spanish translation of the Bible to his liege-lord Don Luis de Guzman in 1433. In the row above, Christians offer charity to the Jews.

A carpet page from the Kennicott Bible, illuminated in Corunna, Spain, in 1476. The use of micography was unique to the Jews at that time.

A page from the Lisbon Maimonides, 1471–2. This manuscript marks the beginning of the Portuguese school and shows the influence of Italian illumination.

15th-century carvings in Barcelona Cathedral showing five Jews with distinguishing circles on their hoods, in compliance with the decree of the Lateran Council in 1215 that Jews must always wear some clothing to distinguish them from Christians.

Sentence being pronounced at an Inquisition in the great square of Madrid.

Above A painting of Ferdinand and Isabella ordering the expulsion of the Jews in 1492.

Left Portrait of the *arrabi mor* (chief rabbi) of Portugal (holding a Hebrew bible), included in a panel attributed to the painter Nuno Goncalves, 1460, showing leading figures at the court of Henry the Navigator.

Below A page from an Italian manuscript, *c.* 1400, of the medieval cabbalistic book, the *Zohar*, illustrating the '*10 Sefirot*' ('emanations') which are basic to existence. Cabbalism was widely studied in Spain.

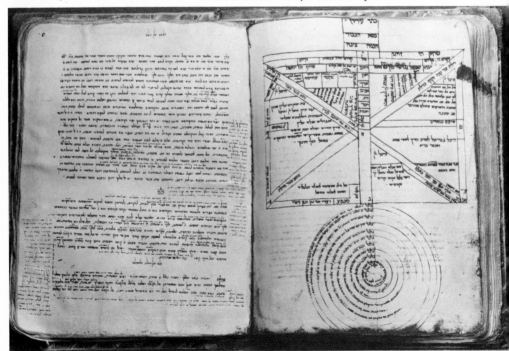

A 14th-century miniature showing a Jewish banker lending money to a friar after his expulsion from Spain.

The printer's mark of Gershom Soncino (d. 1534), the outstanding member of the German rabbinic family which settled in Italy in 1454 and expanded the printing of Jewish books all over the Sephardi world.

The house in Leghorn where Sir Moses Montefiore (1784–1885) was born. Leghorn (Livorno) became a major Jewish trading community after the ruler issued an invitation to Jews in 1548 to live there without persecution.

The Sanhedrin (assembly) of seventy-one members summoned by Napoleon in 1807 to work out modern secular forms for Jewish tradition. In the picture, the Sanhedrin is being addressed by Abraham Furtado, a notable who had emerged from a Marrano Jewish family.

Adolphe Crémieux (1796–1880), French statesman, who fought for Jewish rights and secured French nationality for the Jews of Algiers in 1870. His family had lived in Crémieu (near Lyons) in medieval times and moved in the 16th century to Carpentras (near Avignon).

France now has a Sephardi majority since the inflow of Jews there from North Africa. The Grand Rabbin is now a Sephardi, Rabbi René Samuel Sirat.

An 18th-century engraving by Bernard Picart of the procession of palms at the festival of Succot (Tabernacles) in the great Sephardi synagogue of Amsterdam.

A portrait of Rabbi Manasseh ben Israel by Koning, after the portrait by Rembrandt.

The petition to Oliver Cromwell, 1655, asking for the right of Jews to conduct services in their own homes. It is signed by seven Jews living in London, headed by the Dutch Sephardi rabbi Manasseh ben Israel who was aiming at the free settlement of Jews in England.

David Sassoon (1792–1864), son of the founder of the family Sheikh Sassoon ben Salah (1750–1830), left Baghdad for Bombay in 1832 and opened up huge Sassoon businesses all over the East. His son settled in England in 1870 and became a baronet in 1890. His grandson, Sir Edward Albert Sassoon, drawn here by Spy in 1900, was very active in high society and at court.

A painting of the first words of the Ten Commandments in Hebrew and Spanish, thought to have been painted by Aron de Chavez in 1674 for the Sephardi synagogue, Bevis Marks, in London.

Above Raphael Hayyim Isaac Carigal travelled immense distances in the 18th century preaching in the cities of North America and the very large communities in the Caribbean. This portrait by Samuel King, in 1772, hangs in Yale University Library.

Right The synagogue in Curaçao, which was the largest community in the Americas when visited by Raphael Carigal in 1762–4.

Below The Jewish community of Newport, Rhode Island, was founded in 1639. It was Sephardi during an era of great prosperity. After a decline, the synagogue (shown here) was restored with the help of the Touro family and is maintained as a national monument. Raphael Carigal also preached at this synagogue.

Salonika, captured by the Turks in 1430, attracted Jewish immigrants from many Ashkenazi countries, but became predominantly Sephardi after the expulsions from Spain and Portugal. The community rose to immense strength in trade and learning in the succeeding centuries until it was destroyed by the Nazis.

Jews of Salonika being deported by the Nazis in March 1943, many to the death-camps.

The Jews who remained loyal to their faith undoubtedly viewed the wave of conversion with dismay, though there was not, it seems, much overt hostility. Everyone knew the circumstances; and there was a general assumption, widely shared by many of the *conversos* themselves, that it was all a temporary phase, due to be ended when 'redemption' came. With this in mind, many of the *conversos* held on secretly to Jewish rituals by, for example, not cooking on the sabbath and not eating bread at the Passover. The social bar to their acceptance in Christian society flowed to some extent from a strong feeling that the *conversos* had not severed their links with their former religion; and a host of tests were described in these writings to identify 'secret' Jews. In this atmosphere, riots against New Christians had become frequent by the middle of the fifteenth century, and were greatly increased when Isabella and Ferdinand, heirs to the thrones of Castile and Aragon, were married in 1469, uniting the kingdoms and identifying the new nationhood with passionate Catholic feeling.

It was as an expression of this that the Inquisition, run by the Dominicans, was invited to extend its coverage over the now united nation, and began its work in Seville in January 1481. Tomás de Torquemada, confessor to the queen, was appointed Inquisitor-General in the autumn of 1483. In the first flush of activity, many Jewish *conversos* were identified as guilty of heresy, for which the penalty was to be burnt at the stake, unless sincere repentance was established. If those guilty were not available to be burnt in person, they were burnt in effigy, which involved confiscation of their property and other penalties.

Path to Expulsion

The number of Jews condemned is difficult to establish. According to one chronicler, more than 700 *conversos* were burnt at the stake between 1481 and 1488, and more than 5,000 'reconciled' after enduring various punishments. Though the Inquisition covered all heretics, Jews were the main targets for years. Cecil Roth, examining all the figures in a classic article in *Encyclopaedia Judaica*, quotes another chronicler who states that up to 1525, when Moriscos (ex-Muslims) first began to suffer, the number of those burnt in person came to 28,540, those burnt in effigy 16,520, and those 'penanced' around 304,000, a total of almost 350,000 condemned for Judaism in less than fifty years. Later figures have to include those burnt or condemned in the Spanish colonies overseas, and in Portugal and its colonies, including Brazil.[51]

Many of the *conversos* had doubtless become sincere in their new faith; but with others the Jewish attachment still remained strong. The authorities felt, with some reason, that this was liable to persist as long as there was an open Jewish community in Spain to turn to for support. This was doubtless a major reason for the Order, issued on 31 March 1492, expelling all practising Jews.

Nothing in Jewish history is more surprising than the ultimate effects of this single-minded attempt to root out the form of Jewish life that had developed in Spain. The main avenue of escape seemed across the border to Portugal, for those who fled across the sea in pitiful conditions would face a bleak prospect. Yet within a relatively short time those that survived the sea migrations were able to re-establish themselves in new lands, building up, as we shall see, a Sephardi diaspora of remarkable distinction.

But it was perhaps from Portugal that the most surprising results were to flow. Here, too, the foreground is full of brutality and sorrow; yet out of it emerged a settlement that not only developed a character all its own, but was to play a major role in giving the Sephardi story a world-wide dimension.

Portugal, though less independent than the other peninsula provinces, had developed on similar lines, and had a number of populous Jewish communities in the twelfth century when its national identity was emerging. In the thirteenth century, when full independence was attained under King Afonso III, Jewish life had a familiar pattern, with self-governing councils and courts fully established under a royally appointed *arrabi mor* (Chief Rabbi), and with financial advisers in prominent positions at court. Though the Jews were burdened with exceptionally heavy taxes, and met envy and religious persecution repeatedly, there was nothing corresponding to the fanatic anti-Jewish activities that had led in Spain to the 'pogroms' of 1391 and mass conversion. By the fifteenth century the Jews were sharing in the economic prosperity of the country, with its important foreign trade, but were socially separate from their neighbours in a marked way and proudly loyal to their faith.

Role of Portugal

It was natural, therefore, that when the blow of expulsion fell on
Spanish Jews in Spain, thousands should flee across the border to take
refuge in a country that was culturally akin and seemed at first to
welcome their presence, offering residence rights for a few months in
return for a relatively small fee. According to some accounts, 100,000
fled there; other accounts talk of 150,000.

Within a short time the bright hopes began to vanish. Residence was
to be only temporary; and those who could find no boats with which
to continue their escape were proclaimed slaves by the king, with the
young men shipped off in hundreds to colonize desolate islands off the
coast of Africa.

This was only a prelude to something worse in 1495, when the new
king, Manuel I, secured the hand of the Spanish princess as bride, on
condition that he followed the action of his bride's parents in expelling
all Jews. Being anxious not to lose the economic benefit of the Jews'
presence, he offered conversion as a way out; and when this failed,
produced a terrifying programme of forced conversion. All Jewish
children were seized and baptized in March 1497; and subsequently
some 20,000 adults who had assembled at ports with a promise of
shipping were also forcibly baptized. When many of these New
Christians sought ways to escape later, the right of emigration was
forbidden by an edict of 1499.

There is a relatively happy end to this story, though only after a long
period of bitter experience. The Portuguese New Christians, who had
never dallied with full assimilation, clung firmly to their old religion in
secret, which led inevitably to the establishment of the Inquisition in
Portugal. They were, however, given a breathing spell of twenty years
(later extended to thirty) to allow them to adjust to the new situation,
with the result that crypto-Judaism in Portugal took deep roots,
enabling these New Christians to revert to their faith whenever they
managed to escape to free lands. They were already playing a major
role in the Portuguese economy, and influential connections, especially with Rome, enabled some families to delay or escape the mounting
toll of the Inquisition. Even when it was operating against them with
total ferocity, bribes on a huge scale could occasionally secure some
remissions; but the figures are still horrifying. In Spain up to this time,
as we have noted above, some 350,000 were brought before the
Inquisition, of whom some 28,500 were burnt at the stake and 16,500
burnt in effigy. In Portugal, with a very much smaller population,

more than 1,100 were burnt at the stake and 630 in effigy.[52]

But now, having contemplated the horrors, we can consider the other side of the coin. The establishment of strong Jewish loyalties in Portugal, combined with considerable cultural and economic freedom for those who could survive as titular Christians, seems to have given them a remarkable self-confidence. When they moved through trade connections to freedom in Amsterdam and Salonika and many places across the Atlantic, they were able to re-establish themselves with dignity and independence. In addition to these direct escape routes to a new Jewish life overseas, the relatively free background in Portugal enabled many Jews brought up as Christians to move with unusual confidence to Spain, and from there, after a time, to migrate to new homes across the Mediterranean, especially in Italy.

Portugal was, indeed, unique to the Sephardi experience, as the later story will show. There was no set pattern of adaptation to the new situation; but the long-term process worked its way through in distinctive ways, as we can see, looking ahead to the story of two Cardozo brothers, who emerged from Portugal in the seventeenth century and made strikingly different contributions to Jewish history.

Isaac Cardozo (1604–81) was born in Portugal at a time when many New Christians could, with caution, work and live there with a certain freedom, though in some ways less 'broadly' than in Spain. It was perhaps for this reason that his parents moved in his youth to Salamanca, which was known as a discreet centre for Hebrew studies and where he acquired a solid Jewish background. At the university there he studied medicine, becoming, at the age of twenty-eight, physician to the royal court of Madrid. He held this position for eight years, prolific in scientific and medical writing, and participating to the full in the social glitter and intellectual excitement that presence at the court engendered. But the potential danger, with friends continuously denounced by the Inquisition, finally became too much for him. In his early forties he fled to Venice, where he was joined by his younger brother Abraham, and where they reverted openly to Judaism.

The Portuguese connection

The two brothers, as they developed, expressed between them the two opposite strands in Jewish intellectual life which we saw operating in the controversy over the teachings of Maimonides. Isaac, the older brother, settled down comfortably in Verona, where he was doctor to the community and highly respected as a leader. Late in life he published (in Spanish) an important theological work (*Philosophia Libera*) and a comprehensive study of Jewish life refuting calumnies and extolling Jewish virtues.[53]

The life of his younger brother Abraham offered a very different picture to this settled existence. Abraham is particularly significant to our story in the way he integrated cabbalist ideas which had surfaced in Spain with the cabbalism coming to fruition in the more esoteric lands of the Near East. As a medical student in Italy, he had been assailed by religious doubts, and at thirty-three had started a life of wandering, living in Cairo for five years, where he studied Cabbala, and then moving to Tripoli (Libya) where he had messianic visions and espoused the cause of the widely acclaimed 'Messiah', Shabbetai Zevi, persisting in this even after Shabbetai had converted to Islam. Abraham's outpourings of extremist writings on these subjects led to his excommunication by more conventional rabbis as he wandered to Constantinople, Salonika and indeed all over the Near East. His 'respectable' brother Isaac was in total opposition to everything he wrote; but Gershom Scholem, historian of Jewish mysticism, sees Abraham as a major figure, standing out 'in his originality and eloquence of thought'.

One is constantly tempted, in talking of the Sephardi diaspora, to look ahead in this way, picking up the trail in successive centuries with some notable of the same name whose origin lay in Spain or Portugal. With the Cardozo brothers, for example, it is tempting to think of Benjamin Cardozo, the eminent lawyer who was appointed a member of the United States Supreme Court by President Hoover in 1932. Was he a descendant? All that one biography says is: 'his ancestors settled in New York prior to the American Revolution'. Which of the two brothers would he have liked as an eponymous ancestor? A link of three hundred years is short by Sephardi standards. There are families who are heard claiming direct descent from the great Rabbi Hillel of the first century, and even from King David.

The Portuguese connection, as shown in the origin of the Cardozo brothers, can be seen as dominant in the Sephardi story in two important respects: first, that the roots of Judaism had been very secure there even after the forced conversion; and second, that the Portuguese trading empire furnished unique facilities for the widespread migration of Sephardi Jews. One has to mention this to offset the quite understandable impression that, historically, everything Sephardi centred around Spain. In the Marrano diaspora, especially to northern Europe and across the Atlantic, the Jews who surfaced were most commonly identified as 'Portuguese', and retained this identification among themselves by using Portuguese in many 'official' ways for the conduct and recording of meetings, and for the naming of functions and officials within the community until very recent times. Portugal is important, also, in relation to a breakthrough by post-Expulsion Jews in the writing of Jewish history, in which the force of the dramas through which they were living impelled Jewish writers to consider the meaning of their existence in a wholly new way. It is relevant to describe this change – albeit briefly – and the special place within it of Portugal.

Explorations of history

It is always surprising to note that until the expulsions from Spain and Portugal, no Jewish writer for many centuries had felt impelled to record current Jewish history in objective style. In the Bible, the historical books had been superb, but had ended with the destruction of the First Temple (586 BC), with only a brief postscript dealing with the return of the exiles from Babylon under Ezra and Nehemiah in the fifth century BC. No broad Jewish history was written after that, except for books by Josephus in the first century AD, unknown to Jews in general until a derivative work called 'Josippon' appeared in the tenth century.

A few quasi-historical works on Jewish tradition had surfaced, but history writing in general terms had dried up. It was not that there was a shortage of Jewish dramas to write about, and Arab historians might have furnished a stimulus for imitation. The silence had, perhaps, a twofold source. First, there was no unified Jewish story to be written up as with the Arabs who, to begin with, were chronicling military and dynastic triumphs. Second, the Jews seemed to feel that the essentials of their story had already been told very adequately in the factual account of the Bible and the historical glosses (sometimes factual, sometimes legendary) of rabbinic writings. Apart from the hoped-for arrival, one day, of the Messiah, history was, for them, accomplished. The central events of Jewish existence – the Exodus, the giving of the Torah and the conquest of the Holy Land – were what mattered. In daily life the laws of the written and oral Torah governed everything. Some facts found their way into chronicles which would be drawn on later when history writing came into its own; but there was no attempt to produce a coherent story carrying forward the Bible account of Jewish origins.

This attitude was expressed in the oft-quoted remark of Maimonides pouring scorn on history writing as practised in his time:

It is sheer waste of time, as in the case of books found among the Arabs describing historical events, the government of kings and Arab genealogy, or books of songs and similar works which neither possess wisdom nor yield profit for the body, but are merely a waste of time.

He was ready to accept history writing which authenticated the Jewish *halakhic* tradition, and had himself written in this vein in his *responsa*. But this had a religious purpose. He had good cause, Salo Baron says in a study of this subject, to look down on 'the anecdotal type of history which filled many volumes with lurid tales of intrigue and the love affairs of caliphs and viziers'.[54] Also, by virtue of his rational mind, he had no patience with writing that linked historical developments in the past or future with astrology. The writings of the great Arab historian ibn Khaldun (1332–1406) – the first to explain history in what might be called sociological terms, dealing with motivations and power objectively – had not yet emerged as a more potent stimulus.

But now, with the expulsions from Spain and Portugal, the stability of Jewish existence had suffered an unprecedented shock, and the impulse became strong to record it and assess its significance. The priority in Jewish life was still practical: one had to find a way of surviving, either under a form of conversion or in flight. But this was no longer a temporary, limited disturbance. The Jewish world seemed to have come to an end, or certainly a turning-point; and facing an upheaval on this scale, a serious Jewish writer was impelled to respond. It was for this reason that there was a sudden emergence in the sixteenth century of a number of Jewish historical books of a new kind, starting as before with the biblical and rabbinic story, but incorporating some elements of general history, and continuing to contemporary times, in which the writer drew on personal experience or used information received from participants at first or second hand.

The search for meaning

History writing was thus given a new impetus. A study by Yosef Hayim Yerushalmi shows that of eight authors who produced between them ten major historical works within a span of a hundred years, five were either exiles from Spain and Portugal, and two – one in Crete, the other in Prague – were profoundly influenced by them. Only one of these major studies, that of Azariah de' Rossi in Italy, had a different source.[55]

It is not surprising, in view of what was said above about Portugal, that much of what emerged in this new form bore the mark of this country's intensive Jewish feeling. The most unexpected, in some ways, was a book of genealogies (*Sefer Yuhasin*) by Portugal's most celebrated astronomer, Abraham Zacuto (1452–c. 1515). His ancestors had come to Castile as refugees from France in 1306 and, though basically a scientist, he had acquired, while at the University of Salamanca, a deep expertise in Jewish studies, as all Jewish students did at the time. Expelled with his fellow Jews in 1492 and moving to Portugal, he had become astronomer to successive kings of Portugal, and is famed for the decisive use made of his astronomical tables and his perfected astrolabe on the voyages of discovery by Portuguese sailors and Christopher Columbus. Despite this, he had to flee from Portugal with other Jews who refused conversion in 1497, and spent the rest of his life living in Tunis and other towns of North Africa before moving to Damascus and Jerusalem.

It was surely Zacuto's own bitter experience and forced wanderings that impelled him to try to give his fellow-Jews some sense of assurance through understanding their own history. First, he showed in 'scientific' style the authority of the Jewish tradition; but then he moved on to deal with general history and basic theological argument in a style that would help the Jews, uprooted as he himself was, to hold their own in discussing religious questions with their neighbours. This, he said in his introduction, would promote their sense of self-confidence.

But the times were sad; and this was expressed in the title of another of the history books that is linked to Portugal and written, in fact, in Portuguese: *Consolaçam as tribulaçoens de Israel* ('Consolation for the Tribulations of Israel'). Little is known of the author, Samuel Usque, except that he moved with his family from Spain to Portugal in 1492 and was a man of broad culture, thoroughly at home, as the book shows, in classical and post-biblical literature, Jewish and Christian. The book, which is said to be 'a classic of Portuguese prose', is dedicated to Dona Gracia Nasi, member of the great Portuguese banking family Mendes, whose international influence was to be a remarkable feature of the Sephardi diaspora. Usque's aim in writing the book was to persuade Marranos, wherever they might be, to return to Judaism as soon as they could; but the argument is presented, with Renaissance grace, in the form of a pastoral dialogue between three shepherds. Their latinized names reflect Zechariah, Nahum and Jacob; and their talk brings out not merely the history and tragedies of the Jews until that time, but the thoughts that this story promoted among people of Usque's generation.

It was after reading this book that another historically minded refugee called Joseph Ha-Cohen (1496–1578) decided to tackle the same subject in Hebrew, to reach a wider audience. His book projects, in fact, a very different approach, though the mood is expressed in a similarly sad title, *Emek Ha-Bakha* ('The Vale of Tears'). Joseph's parents had fled in 1492 from Spain to Provence and thence to Italy, where he practised medicine. At the same time he immersed himself in historical studies, leading him first to write a book called *A History of the Kings of France and Turkey*. Jewish experience was fitted obliquely into this context; but this was, of course, dealt with much more deeply in *The Vale of Tears*, which used the general background to take the Jewish story further along the road to straight historical writing. Yet there are still strong traditional elements in the presentation. The author, it is true, tells us that he is striking new ground: 'The chroniclers ceased in Israel until I, Joseph, did arise . . . to write of the troubles that have been visited upon us in gentile lands until the present day.' Yet there is still a hankering for the familiar messianic solution: 'This bitter exile [from Spain] has aroused me to compose this book so that the children of Israel may know what the gentiles have done to us in their lands . . . for behold the days [of the Messiah] approach.'

Varieties of new experience

More significant for the future was another book, *Shebet Yehudah* ('The Sceptre of Judah'), which had its origin in early experience in Portugal, but moved from the traditional approach to what

Yerushalmi calls 'a precociously sociological analysis of Jewish historical suffering generally, and of the Spanish Expulsion in particular'. The author, Solomon ibn Verga, had fled in 1492 from Spain to Portugal where he was forced to convert in 1497, escaping in 1508 to Flanders where he died.[56] His book records persecutions of the Jews from the destruction of the Second Temple to his own times, and finds no answer in messianism or a quasi-philosophic acceptance of suffering. Two distinctive features of the argument which strike new ground, in the view of Lionel Kochan, are his notion of religious relativity and the attempt to comprehend Jewish suffering 'not merely in terms of divine judgment but also in naturalistic terms, inspired by the interaction of political forces and the conduct of the Jews themselves'.[57]

These and other historical books in the new vein all serve to illustrate the extraordinary impact of the expulsions in forcing Jews to re-evaluate the experience that they had once thought secure against all question. Nothing like it had happened in Jewish life since the loss of Jerusalem to the Romans in AD 70; and nothing after the Spanish and Portuguese expulsions was so overwhelming in its impact until the Nazi tragedies of our own time.

This feeling was carried by the exiles wherever they travelled. Ultimately the Sephardi influence was due to spread world-wide, though most directly, of course, in the Mediterranean area. The long-existing links between Spain and the Jewries of North Africa and further east found new expression in cultural influences that have been sustained under the Sephardi name to this day. The overflow of this influence into folklore and music has often been noted, and to close this chapter we can add a footnote from another field – that of Hebrew book illustration – to show how highly the Sephardi tradition was valued. It was in the Sephardi outposts that this precious heritage was often preserved.

In the splendid collection of medieval illustrated manuscripts published by Bezalel Narkiss in Jerusalem in 1969, Spain is, naturally, the dominating source on the peninsula, with a number of magnificent manuscripts of the Passover Haggadah coming from Barcelona in the fourteenth century.[58] But Portugal, too, is rich as a source. The British Museum displays proudly two remarkable illustrated manuscripts produced in Portugal in the fifteenth century: the *Mishneh Torah* of Maimonides (1472) with its superbly decorated opening page; and the famed 'Lisbon Bible' which has eighty-three decorated pages with wide painted borders and its evocative colophon to volume 2: 'Samuel ha-Sofer [the Scribe] wrote the Bible for Joseph b. Judah, surnamed al-Hakim [the Wise], completed on a Friday in the month of Kislev 5243 [Nov.–Dec. 1482].'

It is pleasant to dwell on these and other manuscripts from Portugal for their own sake as works of art, and as a further illustration of the importance of Portugal to the unique Jewish world created in the peninsula. But they are directly relevant, also, to the theme of this book, which is to look at the Sephardi world as a whole. At every point these beautiful books show us intriguing interconnections. The British Museum's great Maimonides manuscript, for example, was obtained from Smyrna in 1724; the Lisbon Bible was bought in 1882, Narkiss tells us, 'from Benjamin Cohen of Bukhara'.

But the links in this field between the Jews of the Iberian Peninsula and the rest of the Sephardi world emerge most dramatically, perhaps, in the rescue of the great Sarajevo *Haggadah*. This wonderfully illustrated book originated in Aragon in the fourteenth century but was only discovered in 1894 in Sarajevo, when a child of the city's Sephardi community brought it to school to be sold after his father had died leaving the family destitute. In origin its thirty-four pages of miniatures dealing with Jewish history from the creation to a scene in a Spanish synagogue, reflect the richness of Spanish–Jewish imagination before the disaster struck. In emerging, after four hundred years of concealment, in the possession of a poor Sephardi of Sarajevo, it is one more indication of the mysterious unity of the wide Sephardi world.

PART FOUR
The Turning-Point

11 *The Sephardi Diaspora*

Up to here it has been natural to tell the story of the Sephardi and eastern Jews as projecting the central themes of Jewish history, even though one has always been aware of developments among Jews in the north, due in time to change the balance completely. Before this happened, however, it was still from within the southern world, in response to the expulsions from Spain and Portugal, that changes flowed, revolutionizing the Jewish scene. In this first phase one sees the unique Jewish experience of Spain and Portugal being transformed in lands around the Mediterranean; but soon this was merged into a broader picture linked to the north, and due ultimately to open up new horizons in a variety of lands across the Atlantic.

We shall look at individual features of these migrations, but a few general factors have to be noted in advance to help one to understand how it was that the expulsions from Spain and Portugal, which began in tragedy and anguish, brought in their train, for those involved, a remarkable story of pride and self-respect. We shall see this spilling over into some, though by no means all, the traditions of those who are known today as Sephardim.

The first general factor to be borne in mind is that the main Sephardi diaspora was not a finite act of the 1490s but a prolonged process which achieved its full force only much later when the original exiles began to be reinforced by those who had become Christian, under various forms of pressure, and now sought to return to the faith of their ancestors. This delayed return had brought hardship but also some advantages in that the *conversos* were able, before escaping, to sustain and even strengthen their economic position, and could develop it still further once they were free.

Yet it would never be an easy path. In personal terms, their position was ambiguous in relation both to the Jews and the Christians. And behind this there was for a long time the danger of the Inquisition,

IRELAND

Dublin
1660

ATLANTIC

OCEAN

To America

To America

PORTUGAL

SPAIN

Fez

MOROCCO

Oran

ALGERIA

DENMARK

Copenhage
1622

Amsterdam 1597

The Hague

ENGLAND
Bristol

London
1656

Rotterdam
LOW
Antwerp
Brussels COUNTRIES

Altona

Emden

Hamburg
1612

GERMANY

Rouen

Paris

FRANCE

La Rochelle

Bordeaux

Lyons

Turin

Milan Venice

Padua

Ferrara

Genoa Lucca

Leghorn
1593

Marseilles

Pisa

Florenc

Ancon

CORSICA

ITAL

Ron

SARDINIA

Algiers

Tunis

Palerm

TUNISIA

AUSTR

4 The Sephardi Diaspora, 16th–17th centuries

- •   *Main Sephardi communities*
- ------▶   *Early emigration (15th– 16th centuries)*
- ——————▶   *Later emigration (17th–18th centuries)*

R U S S I A

POLAND

● Zamosc

● Cracow

Vienna ●

● Budapest

HUNGARY

ROMANIA

BLACK SEA

● Belgrade

YUGOSLAVIA

● Split

BULGARIA

Sofia ●

● Ragusa
1544

● Adrianople

● Constantinople

Naples

● Salonika

GREECE

CORFU

Smyrna ●

Athens ●

Messina ●

SICILY

RHODES

CYPRUS

Beirut ●

● Damascus

Acre ●

● Safed
● Tiberias

CRETE

● Jerusalem

Gaza ●

E
R
R
A
N
E
A
N

S
E
A

● Alexandria

● Cairo

E   G   Y   P   T

0 50 100   400
                                miles
                              km
       100   600

which was on the alert within the peninsula and in many other parts of the world to uncover Jewish links that could be interpreted as Christian heresy, for which the penalty could be to be burnt at the stake. Yet this danger from the Inquisition was itself a factor in opening up the Sephardi world. The Portuguese Marranos in particular seized every chance they could find to travel as financiers or traders to countries where the Inquisition could not operate, or if at all, perhaps less fiercely. This often led the émigrés into a twilight role as 'Portuguese', before coming out openly as Jews. The connections established before the final return to Judaism, and the ensuing build-up, were vital elements in the expansion and strength of the Sephardi world.

Among innumerable instances, this process is seen in powerful form with the Portuguese Marrano family which bore several names (de Luna, Mendes, Nasi, Migues, etc.) during a long series of trans-European migrations before its two most outstanding members, Dona Gracia Nasi (*c.* 1510–69) and her nephew (and son-in-law)` Joseph Nasi (*c.* 1524–79), made Turkey their base of operations some seventy years after the expulsions of the 1490s. Of Spanish origin, their family had been among the forced converts of Portugal, where they increased their already substantial wealth as bankers and dealers in precious stones, with strong connections in Antwerp. In 1537, after her husband's death, Dona Gracia led the family – still ostensibly Christian – to a sojourn in northern Europe (including England), where they moved in high society but also used their connections to try to stop the ravages of the Inquisition in Portugal. After being denounced as secret Jews in the Low Countries and then in Venice, Dona Gracia fled to Ferrara, where she secured Turkish diplomatic protection and emerged openly as Jewish. Her final move was to Constantinople, where she continued to promote Marrano emigration and to prevent persecution of the Jews in their havens of refuge.

Dona Gracia's nephew Joseph, who had served as financial adviser to various royal houses in Europe, expanded her rescue work when he joined her in Constantinople and became adviser to the Sultan. Appointed Duke of Naxos (an archipelago of islands off the Turkish coast), he was tireless in trying to find permanent homes for the refugees; and with the land of Israel now in Turkish hands, one of his projects was to rebuild the once-famed Galilean town of Tiberias and establish a silk industry there.[59]

Rise of Ottoman Turkey

This particular family was, of course, quite exceptional in its power; but its history focuses attention on the central importance of Turkey at this time, and this is the second general factor in the development, during the sixteenth century, of the Sephardi diaspora. By an accident of history very fortunate for the Jews, the expulsions from the Iberian peninsula had coincided exactly with the continued rise to power of the Ottoman Turks, following their momentous capture in 1453 of Constantinople, capital of the Byzantine Empire. The rule of the Byzantine Christians had always been a grievous burden to Jews living in their lands. Long before the fall of Constantinople the Turks had shown that their rule as Muslims would be applied in ways that were kinder to the Jews. In 1326 an Ottoman ruler, capturing the town of Bursa in Asia Minor, had expelled the Greeks and invited the Jews to settle there, with full freedom to build synagogues, own property, engage in business and have their own independent courts. This attitude to Jews led to a pattern of tolerable life that spread through the whole of the Turkish domains during the vast Ottoman expansion of the ensuing century when the Balkan lands – Bulgaria, Romania, Yugoslavia and Greece – came under their rule. There were, of course, many disadvantages in living under Muslim rule, as we saw in earlier chapters. As *dhimmis* the Jews paid a substantial poll-tax, here called *kharaj*. This was designed to indicate their inferior status, and was accompanied by a host of humiliating living conditions. Yet in this place and time, life under Islam still had many compensations for the Jews compared with their position in Christian Europe.

Jews long resident in Byzantine lands had become known as 'Romaniot' (or 'Gregos'), reflecting their ancient connections there going back to Graeco–Roman times. Their ritual traditions were in origin akin to those of Spain, and this affinity was strengthened by immigration from Spain after the 'pogroms' of 1391. Not all the Jews there were Sephardi, however. The good prospects also attracted immigration from France, Germany and Italy. The Ottoman lands, which included Jews of Hungary and Romania, presented therefore a mixed assortment of Jews, dominantly Sephardi but with a strong Ashkenazi element, and also including a substantial community of Karaites, a sect of Jews long resident in this area who were opposed to talmudic interpretation of the Bible.

Until the fall of Constantinople to the Turks in 1453, Adrianople, which they had captured in 1380, had functioned as their capital. This city, which had a long history going back to the times of Hadrian, became an important city for Jews; but the major development had come with the Turkish capture from Venice in 1430 of the port of Salonika. Under Venice the Jews there had been mainly Romaniot, augmented by immigrants from Germany. Under the Turks it grew swiftly into a major Jewish city, immensely successful in trade, and thronged with Jews from every part of Europe, all maintaining their own synagogues and traditions, yet fully ready to absorb and exploit the scholarship and connections that the immigrants from Spain and Portugal brought with them.

The good fortune that made the Ottoman Empire, at this time, a uniquely favourable haven for the Sephardi exiles flowed, to a great extent, from the readiness of the Turks to use the skills of other peoples – Jews, Armenians, Greeks and other non-Turks – as doctors, traders and administrators, so that they themselves were free to pursue their own skills as conquering soldiers, and to live sumptuously on the immense wealth that flowed from this. As the Ottoman Empire expanded to include Palestine and Syria (conquered in 1516) and Egypt (1517), the Jews of this eastern part of the world began to feel for a time that Turkish rule of the Holy Land might be pointing the way towards a messianic age. Long before, the fall of Constantinople had seemed sensational enough to be looked on as, perhaps, a messianic harbinger. With the Holy Land itself now open to the Jews in a new way through the Turkish conquests, they began to settle there in increasing numbers. Safed in Galilee was soon a thriving centre for textile industries overflowing from Salonika, while at the same time an increase in Cabbala studies, with redemption of mankind as a powerful theme, attracted scholars to Safed from Spain and Portugal and the whole of the Near East.

The Ottoman world was wide enough by itself as a major focus of the Sephardi diaspora; but to see its full range one has to note how Turkey was accommodating itself, often through the Sephardim, to revolutionary changes in the pattern of trade and finance outside. One sees an example of this in the way Sephardim now settled in Amsterdam were able to use their old connections with Spain and Portugal to give them an entry to the immensely valuable trade across the Atlantic and, at the same time, to ship goods to the rich markets of Turkey. When this happened, they could work in association with Sephardim living in Turkish lands. It is important, of course, not to exaggerate the part that the Sephardim played in these new patterns of supply and finance, linking northern and southern Europe. Nor should one overlook the significant participation of Ashkenazi Jews settled in key places in Germany and Italy. But speaking in very general terms this was, in its early phase, mainly a Sephardi movement; and if its coverage was small in absolute terms, it was a major element in the Sephardi diaspora and, within its limits, a distinctive factor in world trade history.

Jewish adaptability

There was, as noted earlier, an element of coincidence in the timing of Sephardi success in these fields; but outweighing this was a much more positive factor. The Jews concerned would never have been able to adapt so productively to the new economic forces emerging in Europe and beyond if they had not themselves contributed qualities that their long experience in Spain and Portugal, and, later, in the linked American communities, had developed in them. This adaptability of the Jews is the general factor which dwarfs all the others, as the French historian Fernand Braudel stresses in his magisterial study, *The Mediterranean*.[60]

To get the issue into proportion, one has to note his observation that the Jews were not the only people to whom the Turks were turning at this time. There was an appreciable inflow of Christians willing, unlike the Jews, to embrace Islam, 'where there was work and money to be had'. The Turks 'were opening doors just when Christendom was shutting them'. It was through the immigrants that Turkey 'completed its western education'. Doctors, cartographers, gunnery experts and other specialists were highly prized. In trade, the Turks needed artillery and gunpowder, metals and other raw materials which flowed in from Adriatic countries, Germany and even England (tin, lead and copper). Jews in the North African countries also played a useful role; for though these lands were not rich in themselves, they were 'closest to new developments of western progress', being influenced by immigrants from Spain and Portugal and, later, through connections with the Dutch. The famous 'Barbary pirates' provided a flow of captive manpower; the Andalusians who made their way to Turkey included skilled craftsmen who could manufacture as well as fight with the carbine.

But though the inflow of specialists came from many directions, the Jewish potential was particularly strong, as Sultan Bayazid II recognized in welcoming the Jews immediately after the expulsion order had been issued by King Ferdinand of Spain in 1492. An earlier sultan had developed a pro-Jewish policy in 1453 by issuing a welcoming proclamation immediately after the capture of Constantinople, drawing in Jews to the capital from all Turkish lands. The similar proclamation in 1492 is embellished with an anecdote. 'Can you call such a king wise?' the Sultan is supposed to have said. 'He is impoverishing his country and enriching mine.'

Braudel argues that the Sephardi migrants owed their success in trade to the sense of community that had developed among the Jews in Spain and Portugal, a pattern that has always been characteristic of Jewish history. There are parallels with other successful migrant groups (e.g. the Parsees, or the Armenians), but the Jews, wherever they settled, brought with them, he says, a coherent 'Jewish civilization' which united scattered groups and developed an adaptability that was the key to their progress.

This coherent and almost unified pattern of life gave them a special resilience, even though they were always a minority with powerful adversaries. It was impossible for attacks against them to be wholly successful: 'one prince might persecute them, another protect them; one economy might ruin them, another make their fortunes'. Within this overall pattern they succeeded in preserving their basic personality: 'they remained enclosed within their beliefs, at the centre of a universe from which nothing could dislodge them'. Scattered groups found it natural to communicate with each other. Even when not numerous, these small communities 'were linked by education, beliefs, the regular travels of merchants, rabbis and beggars (who were legion); by the uninterrupted flow of letters of business, friendship or family matters; and by printed books'.

We saw above, in mentioning the Nasi family, an example of these wide connections at a very high level of politics and finance. Braudel gives an evocative illustration at a humbler level by looking at the life of a rabbi called Jacob Sasportas. A North African born in Oran (then held by the Spanish) at the beginning of the seventeenth century, Sasportas became rabbi successively at Tlemcen, Marrakesh and Fez, was imprisoned there, escaped to Amsterdam where he was a professor at the Pinto Academy, accepted a post as *haham* (rabbi) of the Sephardi community in London in 1664 (but left after a year because of the Great Plague!), moved on to become rabbi of Hamburg (where he fiercely opposed the messianic pretensions of Shabbetai Zevi), was called as rabbi to Leghorn (at the peak of its power as a trade link with North Africa and London), and finally returned as chief rabbi to Amsterdam, where he died. Among other things, the wide range of Sasportas's life shows that there was no rigid barrier between the Sephardi and Ashkenazi worlds.

The story of Sasportas leads one to consider also, in mentioning his travels, how one should assess the contacts of Jews, in this period, with the world outside. Although one thinks of the Jews of the Sephardi world as having particularly free access to their neighbours, there was no set pattern to this; the contacts were often freer, as it happens, in Ashkenazi lands. The forced segregation of the Jews by residential or clothing ordinances was never observed uniformly. The establishment of the Venice ghetto (described below) never prevented the Jews from living all over the city, as repeated complaints at this show. Turkish Jews had to wear a distinguishing yellow turban at home, but they boldly disregarded this on their travels by turning up in white turbans, like 'ordinary' Turks.

In general it was accepted that Jews worked their way round – or just disregarded – many of the discriminations against them. Adaptability to the host society was always the key element, then and in succeeding centuries, though never, in Braudel's view, weakening the firm internal standards which sustained their kinship and in this way promoted the strength of the diaspora.

Steps in the Sephardi diaspora

By looking at the general factors at work in the remarkable spread through the world of the Jews who had roots in the Sephardi tradition, we have seen how interrelated all the elements had been. This may run counter to the widespread idea that the Sephardim fall into two quite distinct classes: an élite from Spain and Portugal who maintained their distinctive superiority in north-west Europe and North America and, in sharp contrast, a very mixed assortment of very poor and disadvantaged Jews from North Africa, the Near East and beyond, whose commercial and cultural links with Spain and Portugal have always been very faint. There are plenty of examples to fit this polarized picture, yet taken by itself it misses the dynamism which brought these disparate elements of the Sephardi world together in significant ways, and makes its presence felt as soon as one looks at the individual stories of Sephardi experience after the expulsions of the 1490s.

The influence was not uniform in expression. In some cases, particularly in Turkey and the Balkans, the 'original' Sephardim passed on much of their sophisticated culture to the countries of refuge; in others they were absorbed and lost much of their individual tradition. Yet, as noted in the introduction, a sense of common identity not just as Jews but as Sephardim began to define itself, especially as the contrast with the Ashkenazi world took place.

We have already seen that the most far-reaching effect of the expulsion from Spain in 1492 was the flight across the border to Portugal. It was the major emigration in terms of numbers, involving at least 100,000 – perhaps even 150,000 – Jews. It was also unique in its influence on Jewish life; for though the shelter in Portugal offered only a brief respite before the forced conversion to Christianity of its now expanded Jewish population, the Jewish loyalties of the Portuguese *conversos* were deep-seated and this made the Portuguese contribution all the more solidly based when they returned openly to Jewish life.[61]

But important as the Portuguese story became, it has still to be evaluated in the context of the other flights from Spain, all of which affected the life of the recipient countries.

A dominant image in one's mind of the expulsion from Spain is of hordes of refugees putting out to sea (the French border was closed to them) in leaky boats, subject to all the dangers of piracy and murder, and with no known destination. In some major respects this is a true picture, covering some 50,000 or more who fled from Spain in the first phase, and a greatly increased number when Jews who had been forcibly converted in Portugal began to escape. But the hope of finding welcoming havens was not as black as might have been supposed. Closest at hand were the lands of North Africa, with links long expressed in commercial and rabbinic exchanges, and used as escape routes from earlier persecutions in Spain, as after the 'pogroms' of 1391. The welcome in North African lands varied in warmth; but the migration there provided many with a base for long-term settlement, or as a potential point for embarkation to other havens – Italy, the Balkans, Turkey and Palestine – to which the refugees were travelling also by direct routes. Looking further ahead, the expanding range of

Portuguese commerce soon began to open a channel of escape, also, to northern Europe, and thence to the Americas.

Among North African countries, Morocco, then as now, was a special case. In early times the Jews of Morocco had had a major influence on Spanish Jewry, and had also been very prosperous, with their control of the Sahara gold trade and a dominant position in trade with Christian countries. For more than a century before the Expulsion, however, Muslim power in this part of North Africa had declined, and with it the position of Moroccan Jewry; and though they were, as an adjacent community, a natural haven for many of the refugees, adaptation to life in this very large country was not easy. The sultan, it is true, extended a welcome to the Jews, and some estimate that as many as 20,000 may have arrived, after much hardship. At first, leaders of the *toshavim* (residents) were rather hostile to the new arrivals, some of whom found ways of returning to Spain, while others moved on to further countries. The refugees themselves found it easier to establish their position in the south of the country; and even when they finally achieved some power among the residents in the north, they kept themselves distinct from the old *toshavim*, speaking Castilian, and maintaining their own synagogue in Fez with *takkanoth* based on Spanish customs.

At one level the Jews of Morocco epitomized the humiliation and poverty often associated with the Sephardi masses; at another, the country's isolation from the Ottoman orbit and its access to Spain, Portugal and the Atlantic gave some leading Jews there an important mediating position in the changing pattern of world trade and diplomacy. The trade side was particularly enhanced for the Jews when Portugal occupied Morocco's Atlantic coast in the sixteenth century, developing new trade in world markets. The Portuguese authorities there co-operated readily with refugees from the Iberian peninsula, and Morocco itself appointed Jews as ambassadors to Spain and Portugal. Jews from Morocco had long settled in the Atlantic islands, including the Azores, Madeira and the Canaries; and with Sephardi links extending to Holland it was a Jew, Samuel Joseph Palache, the first Jew to settle freely in Amsterdam, who was appointed Morocco's ambassador there.

Other North African countries

Morocco's neighbour Algeria developed its Sephardi experience differently. Being active in trade with Catalonia and the Balearic Islands, it had accepted a great influx of refugees from Spain in 1391 from the 'pogroms' of that year, but took few in 1492. In the earlier immigration the inevitable conflicts between local Jews and the 'superior' immigrants had been eased through the ministrations of two outstanding rabbis who settled there, Rabbi Isaac ben Sheshet Perfet of Barcelona and Rabbi Simon ben Zemah Duran of Palma, whose *responsa* paint a vivid picture of the time.[62] Though Algiers was a relatively small country, its experience highlights some of the under-lying constants of Sephardi life. In earlier centuries, the Jews of Algiers had been a bridge between the Babylonian academies and the great Jewish centres of North Africa in Kairouan and Fez. Now, through the influence of these two rabbis from Spain, Algiers became again a distinguished religious and intellectual centre.

In another field Algiers, through a strong link with Leghorn in Italy, played an important role in the revolving pattern of trade across the Mediterranean, and thence outward to the West Indies and northern Europe. In the first phase Jewish traders from Algiers were among those who made their way to Italy and helped to build up the flourishing enterprise of many of Italy's city-states. In the 'return' phase Jewish traders in Italy found it useful to have bases in North Africa; and Algiers was particularly important when Jews from the great port they had helped to establish in Leghorn crossed the Mediterranean to settle in Algiers (perhaps with members of their families still there), and moved later across the Atlantic where the valuable trade of the West Indies beckoned.

A couple of well-known family names illustrate the way this revolving process developed. The family of Sir Moses Montefiore were straw hat manufacturers in Leghorn in the eighteenth century before the father of Sir Moses set off for England, where his famous son (having made his fortune) subsequently led the fight for the persecuted Jews of the world, beginning, as it happened, with the Jews of the Near East. In a circle of moves in the other direction, members of the eminent Spanish Sephardi family of Lousada migrated in the seven-teenth century from Leghorn to Algiers, and thence to a high position in Jamaica, as a prelude to a dignified life in England.[63]

The underlying issues were the same in Tunisia to the east, though with special features reflecting the historically rich character of Tunisian Jewry. In classical times this area had fed Rome and Constantinople with wheat and other foods, a trade which the Jews came to dominate, having been settled there in Phoenician Carthage from the days of the Second Temple. (Earlier still, Tunis may have been the 'Tarshish' to which King Solomon sent his fleet.) In the seventh century they had resisted the sweep of Arab armies westward, in alliance with the defiant Berber princess Kahina, sometimes said (though wrongly) to have been Jewish. In flight to the mountains, they had mingled with the Berbers, giving substance, indirectly, to the legends of the Berbers' Jewish origin.

We have already seen that this area enjoyed a golden age flowing from the foundation in 670 of the new town of Kairouan, its population built up by the transfer there of 1,000 Jewish families from Egypt on the orders of the sultan in Damascus. The wealth and learning of Kairouan is echoed in many *geniza* letters; but this had long become only a memory by the time of the expulsion from Spain. Tunis itself was still prosperous, however, and had indeed developed good relations in trade and diplomacy with the Christian rulers of Spain during their rise to power.

Like all the other North African countries, Tunis experienced the initial communal conflicts that surfaced when refugees arriving from Spain had to come to terms with local residents. In this case, however, the drama came later and in sharper, long-lasting form. The direct influx in 1492 had been only moderate, and though it generated a bitter quarrel over their respective systems of *shehita* (animal slaughter), this was soon settled. The real conflict arose when Sephardi Jews now settled in Italy had crossed the Mediterranean from Leghorn to settle in North Africa for business reasons. In Tunis, the *toshavim* had at first alloted a special place in synagogue to the *megurashim* (refugees) from Spain to enable them to practise their rites in their own company, and perhaps also in recognition of their 'superiority'. But when the immigrants swelled in number with arrivals from Italy, the separation between the Tuansa (Tunisians) and the Grana (Jews from Leghorn) developed into a split that could not be healed.

As described graphically by André Chouraqui in his book on the Jews of North Africa:

the Grana looked with derision upon the Tuansa calling them 'Turks with the black cap and the violet turban'. The Tuansa in turn put pressure on the Bey to expel these 'wearers of the perruque', whose religious practices and unbounded conceit were offensive to the dignity of Jews living under the protection of Islam.[64]

The immigrant Grana, expelled outside the city, turned this to their advantage by operating profitably from newly-built markets and expanding their international trade. They also gave more weight to their identity by building a number of separate synagogues. It was not until the middle of the eighteenth century that this bitter quarrel was smoothed over in a treaty between the rival rabbis, allotting to the Tuansa all Jews of Muslim countries, and to the Grana all those of Christian countries. But even with this, the dead of each group had to be buried on opposite sides of a dividing wall.

Libya, as it is now called, presents a more obscure picture of the reaction to the arrival of refugees from Spain. Little is in fact known of Libya's Jewish history between the seventh and fifteenth centuries, though its city Tripoli certainly had a substantial Jewish community. A special feature soon after the Expulsion was the occupation of Tripoli by Spain during a war in 1510, and the swift flight of some 800 Jews to avoid their former persecutors. Under Ottoman rule soon after, the conditions for Jews improved, with many Sephardi Jews arriving to exploit the new trade connections with Leghorn. One assumes some difficulties of adjustment as with Algiers and Tunisia; but it was in Egypt, to round off the impact in south Mediterranean countries, that the community picture was most decisively changed, and in particular by the reversal in Jewish fortunes caused both by the arrival of the Spanish Jews and the rise of the Ottoman Empire.

Major changes in Egypt

For several centuries before this, the position of Jews in the Muslim lands had worsened disastrously. The rise of religious fanaticism had led to intense persecution of infidels, with 'an unending list of edicts', as Goitein puts it, 'to humiliate the *dhimmis* and make lives unbearable'. Jews serving in public positions (e.g. customs posts) had to choose between conversion or dismissal; and many Jews, at this time, did adopt the Muslim faith. Sadly, this was particularly true in Baghdad, long the fortress of the Jewish faith; but it applied everywhere.[65]

It was by the direct impact of the Jews from Spain that this decline in Jewish life began to be reversed, particularly in Egypt. The change had begun a century earlier, Goitein says, when Jews from various Christian lands settled in the countries of Islam, bringing with them the skills, learning and self-confidence that had atrophied in these countries. The impact was more telling when the flight from the Iberian peninsula provided a more intense stimulus. North Africa was the first to benefit from what Goitein calls this 'inner Jewish migration'. But in the sixteenth century there was a general revival of the Jewish communities under Islam, with Egypt an important part of this movement.

At the time of the Expulsion, the Jewish population of Egypt, so rich and well-established in the Fatimid era, had fallen to no more than 650 families, totalling perhaps 5,000 persons in all. There was an immediate increase through the arrival of refugees (including a number of distinguished scholars) from Spain; but it was in the context of constantly expanding Ottoman rule that the Jews of Egypt (which was conquered in 1517) found a new revived life. The Turkish rulers of Egypt welcomed the Jews, who were free to develop their trade and were widely used in the dependent areas in finance and administration. The financial ministry of Egypt was henceforth almost always in charge of a Jew, though this also brought danger, as his term of office was often ended by execution. The Jews of Egypt had their own system of self-government, headed by a Nagid appointed or recognized by the Turkish authorities in Constantinople.

The community of Egypt, like others in North Africa, remained dominantly Arabic-speaking. All these communities were still attached in one form or another to traditions, including music and folklore, that had grown among them in the Muslim world. In the conflicts that inevitably arose with the older residents, the Sephardi immigrants usually established leadership after a time, but without turning the residents, so to speak, into 'full' Sephardim. The main characteristic of these areas of North Africa was a working fusion between old and new. It was in Turkey that a palpable transformation of Jewish life into a new Sephardi frame took place. Its two main features, as we shall see, were the establishment of a common Sephardi tradition in rituals, language and folklore, and the build-up there, as elsewhere in the eastern lands, of a new kind of mystical enthusiasm, with a special attachment to the community of Safed in Galilee.

The new Sephardi developments

Sephardi immigration into Turkey had been reinforced by an inflow from other countries – including southern France and Italy – of Jews already brought up with much of the sophisticated style that marked the Sephardi Jews. Those who were personally Sephardi in origin bolstered their nostalgia and also their pride by maintaining independent synagogues with names linked to their places of origin (for example, Catalonia, Castile, Cordoba, etc.), and printing their own prayer-books to include certain rites to which they were attached; but the Sephardi label now covered all in the area, whether originally Sephardi or not.

This dominance was not achieved without resistance at first from the original residents (the Romaniot), who sometimes saw the Sephardim as dissident; but the Sephardi style in prayers and practices, and the almost universal use in a short time of Ladino, the Sephardi form of Spanish, won through, carrying before it most of the variations in language and traditions that had existed among the scattered communities of Hungary, Bulgaria, Greece, Rhodes and Yugoslavia. Apart from local folk variations, a Sephardi pattern became uniform throughout Turkey and the Balkans, establishing a distinction from the Arabic-speaking Jews of North Africa, Syria and Iraq, and also from those speaking other languages still further afield.

But though these distinctions, and especially that between the use of Ladino and Arabic, are important, they can also be misleading in that they may obscure one of the major elements unifying the post-Expulsion world, which was the new impetus given everywhere to the central place of the Holy Land in the religious motivation of Jewish life. This was an element common among all Jews of the Near East, including the smaller Ashkenazi communities; and it provided a focus for the new importance of Egypt which rapidly became, with Constantinople and Salonika, a rallying point for travel, settlement and Cabbala studies whose drive pointed mainly to the cabbalist centre at Safed in Galilee.

It was the Ottoman capture of Palestine and Syria in 1516 and Egypt in 1517 that drew many of the Sephardi refugees to this whole area. Salonika, with its rapidly growing Jewish population – half the city was Jewish – provided a major flow into Palestine, though Jews were attracted there also from other important cities (Constantinople, Cairo, Damascus, Aleppo, Izmir, etc.) as well as from Italy and even from eastern Europe. Egypt had a special role in this movement, not only as a place to stop off *en route*, but as an exciting centre of Jewish culture in its own right.

The free communication between different areas, with Safed as the magnet, is illustrated in the life history of a number of leaders who helped to create the new mysticism. One was a scholar named Joseph Caro, known mostly today as the author of a very popular guide to Jewish practice called *Shulhan Arukh* ('The Table Set'), but who was deeply involved in the new Safed developments. He had been born in Spain in 1489, had been taken with his family to Portugal in 1492 after the Expulsion, and had then lived in Egypt and Salonika, where he gained some renown as the author of an *halakhic* commentary. Together with his talmudic studies, he also engaged in cabbalist speculation, and was told by his *maggid* (a mysterious tutor who spoke to him in dreams) to move to Safed, which he did in 1535.[66] His pupil there, the cabbalist Moses Cordovero (1522–70), was also of Spanish origin (the name means 'from Cordoba'), and was the first to create in his writings a fully worked-out Cabbala, a major step towards the system created later by Isaac Luria (1534–72), the most famed of all the cabbalists of Safed. Luria, known as 'the Ari', had also, like Caro, spent part of his creative life in the now lively Jewish centre of Egypt. He had been born in Jerusalem, had been taken as a child to Egypt where he lived as a hermit and poet, and had finally gone to settle in Safed in 1569.

The messianic movements that began to flourish in this ambience had started with the appearance in Venice in 1523 of the adventurer David Reubeni, who aroused wide interest in a number of countries by fanciful tales of his royal origins. This ultimately led one disciple, Solomon Molcho, who had studied Cabbala in Salonika and Italy, to believe that he (Molcho) was the awaited Messiah. The messianic peak was reached more than a century later with Shabbetai Zevi, whose claims stirred the whole of the Jewish world.

Shabbetai had been born in Smyrna (Turkey) in 1626 and had been brought up in Salonika and Constantinople with an intense if somewhat unbalanced attachment to the cabbalism of Luria. When his fame spread and he proclaimed himself Messiah in 1665, it was at the instigation of a brilliant Egyptian Jew called Nathan of Gaza, who believed in him passionately. The movement spread rapidly, with only a few doubting that a new age was dawning. Even when Shabbetai Zevi allowed himself to be converted to Islam in the following year to save his life, some of his followers, including Nathan, continued to believe in him.

All these movements centred, as we see, in the freely communicating area of Turkey, Egypt and the Holy Land. Egypt comes into the picture, too, in the life of a remarkable refugee from Portugal mentioned earlier, Isaac Cardozo. After studying medicine in Spain and Italy and falling prey to religious doubt, he had wandered desperately to a number of countries including Egypt, where he had finally restored his Jewish faith through intense study of the Cabbala. These are but a few examples of the many diverse teachings developed in the Near East by the Sephardi diaspora.

Life in Venice

Italy has been mentioned here so far because of the flow of some of its Jews southward into the lively Sephardi world of Turkey, with its open door to Palestine. But the Jews of Italy had their own distinctive role in the Sephardi diaspora after the 1492 Expulsion.

Jews had been settled in Italy since the days of the Second Temple, with a large community in Rome that continued to grow after the end of the Roman–Jewish wars in the first two Christian centuries. In Sicily, subsequently, they had developed a distinctive Jewish culture, with strong links to the Near Eastern Jewish world; and from the eleventh century Venice in particular had become a familiar stopping-place for Jewish traders *en route* between east and west.

The Jews had varied fortunes during the early centuries in different Italian cities until a distinctive role as small-loan merchants (or pawnbrokers) began to be allotted to them through city authorities who needed this function undertaken for the sustenance of poor and rich alike. (Christians somehow overcame the usury prohibition in large loan deals, but left the field relatively free for Jews in consumer help.)[67]

Many foreign merchants, who must have included Jews, had established depots in Venice in the years before its dramatic emergence as queen of the Adriatic. As a rule the merchants (and certainly the Jews) were predominantly from Germany, though some were 'easterners' from Byzantine lands. Jewish communities had proliferated also in other cities on the Dalmatian coast and in Greece; and as the Venetian Empire developed, with the growth of a powerful merchant navy, Venice assumed a protective role over trade within its bounds. We know, for example, that Jewish traders in Constantinople paid a tax to Venice for this benefit. Jews had gradually solidified their trading position in the whole area; to take one example, the silk industry was almost exclusively in their hands. They were, it is true, increasingly squeezed out of many occupations, with only money-lending and some specialist activities like medicine fully open to them; but the record during this period of their religious activities and participation in the cultural life of Renaissance Italy points to a prosperous and free-ranging existence much in tune with the spirit that the exiles were to bring with them from Spain and Portugal.

In earlier times the Jews had not been allowed to live in the heart of the city, but only on the island of Spinalunga, across the channel opposite San Marco, and known as the Giudecca. These restrictions were gradually eased in practice, if only to enable Jews to attend the sales of pledges on the Rialto. Permits to this effect were issued in 1366, though Jews involved were called on to wear a yellow badge, in line with the regulation of the Lateran Council of 1215. (Jews in the Muslim world had been ordered to wear distinctive clothing centuries before this.)

The broadening life that Jews could enjoy in Venice was paralleled in a number of other famous cities which, like Venice, were in a position to offer a sympathetic background to refugees from Spain and Portugal after the expulsions of the 1490s. In many of them Jews were famous, under friendly rulers, as bankers and patrons of the arts, while at the same time concerning themselves very actively with Jewish philosophy and scholarship. In Mantua for example – a community visited by the poet Abraham ibn Ezra during his tour of Europe in the twelfth century – the great Norsa banking family living there had been called in originally by the Gonzaga rulers. Lucca had had a famed Jewish community, led by the Kalonymos family, as early as the tenth century. The Jews of Ferrara, a very old Jewish community, had risen to prosperity under the enlightened and friendly rule of the Este family. It was in cities like this that the flood of exiles in the 1490s, bolstered later by a steady inflow of Marrano Jews, was due to make a very distinctive Sephardi mark in the sixteenth and seventeenth centuries, though the original Ashkenazi base in northern Italy would also continue to remain very significant.

The response to the exiles in these and other Italian cities varied in different circumstances. The most illustrious of the early arrivals had been the banker and scholar Don Isaac Abrabanel, in a class of his own both as financier and scholar. As noted earlier, he was born in Lisbon in 1437, and had been financial adviser to the king and queen of Spain at the time of the Expulsion. When his efforts to avert the catastrophe had proved unavailing, he had fled to Naples where he became banker to the king and continued to write the books on Bible study and philosophy which were his main preoccupations. Moving to different Italian cities, he died in Venice in 1508, one of the great men of Jewish history, at home in every branch of politics and culture. His rounded attitude was characteristic of many of the leading Jews of Italy, whose highly professional studies in the Jewish field seemed to integrate naturally with the philosophy, poetry, music and theatre of the time, to the great satisfaction of historians (like Cecil Roth) who have seen Jewish life in Italy as a paradigm for cultured Jewish life everywhere.

The absorption of the exiles raised serious questions of accommodation in the crowded territories of Venice. Within a few years the Jews began to be attacked and plundered in many areas. Relief was finally secured only by huge 'subsidies' (i.e. bribes) to the authorities, organized by the leading financial (and rabbinic) family of Meshullam, whose origins lay in Provence, and who were ancestors, as it happens, of the great Ashkenazi banking family of Warburg. Against the picture one has of a friendly welcome in Italy, it has to be noted that payments of this kind, on a very large scale, had frequently to be repeated to counter efforts that were often afoot to expel the Jews from Venice.

Within the community itself the disparate elements – German, eastern (Levantine) and Spanish – had to find workable forms of co-existence. In 1516 it was ordered that the Jews, largely from Germany, should reside henceforth in a walled area north of the city known as the *ghetto nuovo* (new foundry), which is how the term 'ghetto' is thought to have originated. Jews from the eastern Mediterranean, whose position was more independent, came to live separately in the *ghetto vecchio* (old foundry) area. When the 'Third Nation' of Spanish and Portuguese Marranos – accepted as Jewish though still ostensibly Christian – began to arrive in the 1520s and 1530s, they gravitated to this area too. The German Jews, with their numerous synagogues, had clung originally to Ashkenazi rites; and though they gradually accepted 'Italian' rites, they were still distinctive as part of the 'German Nation'. They were, of course, never subject, as the Marranos were, to constant spying by Inquisition agents, to see if they could be brought before its court as heretics. The Jews here wore red hats, which led to a witticism that the Marranos were former Catholic priests who were now taking on the air of cardinals.

Other Italian cities

If life could be difficult in Venice, there were always outlets to other Italian city states. The Este family ruling Ferrara had always protected the Jews, defying the interventions of the Pope; and they immediately offered settlement to refugees when they began to arrive in 1492 and established a 'Spanish' synagogue. The Marranos, who lived there with an ambiguous status from the 1520s, were finally allowed to return openly to Judaism in 1553. This chronology illustrates the history of the powerful Nasi family mentioned earlier. Having been pursued by Inquisition agents and expelled from the Low Countries and Venice, they were given Turkish diplomatic protection in Ferrara before returning openly to Judaism and settling in Constantinople.

Ferrara, though the scene of a burning of the Talmud in 1553, was a good example of the merging of cultures that distinguished the Italian–Sephardi world long before the emancipation of northern and western Jews in the nineteenth century. Typical of this were two brothers Abrabanel (of the family already mentioned): Samuel, a financier, and Joseph, a physician, who settled there when, like their father, the great Don Isaac, they had been forced to leave Naples. Though distinguished in their own right, the cultural standards they embodied show up even more clearly in the fame of their brother Judah ('Leone Ebreo'), who lived mostly in Florence, and as physician, poet and philosopher was a distinct figure in the Italian Renaissance. Among others in Ferrara, one notes the presence of Amatus Lusitanus, a Portuguese Marrano who taught at the university and is one of the greatest names in the history of medicine.*

Samuel Usque, whose family had fled Portugal as Marranos, wrote one of the first 'modern' books of Jewish history while living in Ferrara, recording the tragedies and searching for its meaning. The background into which the Marranos fitted is also illustrated by the residence there of the polymath scholar Azariah de' Rossi, whose family claimed to have been settled in Italy since Roman times, and who wrote books of the greatest originality, embracing many of the arts and sciences of the time.

De' Rossi also lived for a time in Mantua, where Jews, whose cultural interests were widespread, showed among other things a great

---

* Amatus 'the Portuguese' (1511–68) settled as a professing Jew in Ragusa and then in Salonika. At one stage he lived in the Papal States, where the Pope was one of his patients. He was particularly famed for his work on blood circulation.

talent for the theatre, with the Portaleone family helping to make Mantua the leading Italian city in this field. Mantua was the largest community after Venice, and followed Venice too as a great producer of Hebrew printed books. De' Rossi, while living there, wrote *Me'or Enayim* ('A Light for the Eyes'), another of the pioneering works that had now begun to emerge, under the impact of the Expulsion, on the relation of Jewish to general history.

It seems fair to assume that it was the variety of life in the Italian city states that made it easier for the refugees to find a more agreeable background than would have been possible elsewhere. Unlike, say, medieval Germany, where political life offered uniform – and usually uniformly adverse – conditions, trouble in one Italian city was likely to be local, offset by good conditions elsewhere. Society – even high society – could be more receptive because the city rulers (e.g. the Medici) had often risen quickly, like Jewish leaders, from success as bankers or cloth-merchants, and not because of ancient feudal rights. Communication was therefore easier; and this was helped because the Jews in the post-Expulsion era were on the move, bringing with them new currents of thought.

A further point is that the Jews of this time, rich and poor, were fulfilled by the Jewish side of their lives. The masses were doubtless poor, struggling as refugees to find their feet; but speaking generally, they all seemed to have great confidence in their faith, turning from their outward life as bankers or pawnbrokers, merchants or pedlars, to their full identification with the synagogue, where even for the sophisticated, their Italian names and carefully turned verses still took second place to the comforts of kinship.[68]

The Sephardi diaspora developed in a special way, therefore, in Italy; and one example of this is the story of the city state of Ancona, which highlights both the freedom with which the Jews tried to operate in Italy and the limits on this, even when exercised by leaders as powerful as the Nasi family.

Ancona, on the Adriatic coast, had become important when the Jews of Naples and Sicily, both under Spanish rule, had been expelled in 1492 under the same ordinance which expelled them from Spain. Some 37,000 had been obliged to leave Sicily, and a great many had found their way to Ancona, encouraged to settle there by the current Pope, Paul III, who made Ancona a papal territory in 1532, and was keen to develop it, with full Jewish participation, as a free port. The number of Jews among its traders had been increased by the arrival later of Marranos, including in 1541 about a hundred Portuguese Marrano families from Naples, encouraged by a guarantee from the current Pope, Julius III, that the Inquisition would not operate against them there. The trade of the city all over the eastern world had prospered; but in 1555, the Pope who had now come to office, Paul IV, suddenly instituted anti-Jewish measures, setting up a ghetto for Jews, imposing trade restrictions on them, and, above all, putting the Inquisition into action there, with fifty-one Jews arrested immediately and twenty-five burnt at the stake. To fight this, Dona Gracia, head of the Nasi family in Constantinople, saw to it that the sultan wrote a stern letter to the Pope claiming that the Jews of Ancona were under his diplomatic protection and had to be left free. When this failed to produce a result, Dona Gracia sent messages to leading Jewish traders throughout the eastern world, asking them to boycott all trade with Ancona until the anti-Jewish regulations were withdrawn by the Pope. Not all the Jews to whom she wrote were willing to support the boycott; but the effort was a measure of the wide-ranging trading freedom that was now evident over most of the eastern world under Turkish influence.

Leghorn, North Africa and Holland

Looking further ahead to the end of the sixteenth century, the port of Leghorn, already mentioned many times here for its contact with the Jews of North Africa, was poised at this point to assume major importance in the Sephardi world, not only for its trade with eastern countries, but as one of the cities which were to open the way to Sephardi emergence in northern Europe and the Americas.

Until the middle of that century, Leghorn had been an unimportant Tuscan port which the Medici ruler, Cosimo I, had been unable to develop, despite an effort made in 1548. In 1593 a successor, Ferdinand I, stepped up the pace of development by issuing a general proclamation addressed to 'Levantines, Spaniards, Portuguese, Germans and Italians' – which was in effect an open invitation to all kinds of Jews – to come and settle in the town where they could return to Judaism, enjoy full religious liberty, be exempt from the yellow badge and receive Tuscan nationality. The effort this time was triumphantly successful. Trade boomed, and in 1675 Leghorn was declared a free port. The Jews were the largest group of inhabitants, totalling 3,000 by 1689, including Spanish Jews from North Africa and Turkey, and Marranos from Portugal. They grew to 5,000 by the end of the seventeenth century, with Portuguese and Spanish their main languages.

To take advantage of their expanding trade, the Leghorn Jews sent members of their families to Smyrna (Turkey), as well as to Tunis and Tripoli in North Africa, as noted earlier. This was the time, of course, when Spain and Portugal, following up their explorations and conquests, were developing an immensely valuable trade across the Atlantic. They financed this partly by their own funds, but also through special arrangements with the rapidly expanding facilities now available in Amsterdam. Leghorn's link with North Africa, which also encompassed the Portuguese Atlantic ports of Morocco, made them part of these evolving trade movements. A particular example, though very surprising when one first hears of it, is the very large trade from Leghorn in coral, which became, in due course, a link, through London, with the exclusive import of diamonds from India (then the only known source in the world), and itself a link with the pre-eminent diamond centres of Holland and Belgium.[69]

In the earliest phase, Amsterdam had emerged with a uniquely valuable link with the Iberian peninsula because the Low Countries had been part of the Holy Roman Empire, headed at this time by the Spanish royal family. Marrano traders from Portugal (like the Nasi family) had used the Low Countries as an escape hatch; and when the northern provinces of the Low Countries – later to become Holland – were asserting their independence from Spanish rule, many Marranos were among the 20,000 merchants who moved north from Antwerp in 1585 to enjoy the greater trade advantages developing there.

To begin with, Jews were not free to resume Judaism openly in Holland. Amsterdam itself was barred to them, and they had to live in Rotterdam. But gradually freedom to live and work in Amsterdam, though with an undefined status, began to emerge; and fuller rights then followed. For a while they were excluded from certain occupations and they could not become burghers; but they did join in expeditions which began at this time to explore – and trade with – some lands of Central and South America, in competition with the hitherto dominant Spanish and Portuguese. It was as an offshoot from a brief Dutch settlement in Brazil, as we shall see, that the first Jews arrived in New York in 1654.

Amsterdam and London

The Sephardim in Holland had risen quickly in standing and economic strength from their informal presence in the sixteenth century. They founded a community only at the beginning of the seventeenth century, but they had soon become active in industry and diamond polishing, participating in the Dutch East India Company and in exploratory trade missions in the Americas.

In the wake of the Sephardim, who were largely Portuguese, Ashkenazi Jews had begun to arrive in 1620, first from Germany and subsequently from Poland and Lithuania; but Sephardi leadership was dominant. They recruited leading scholars, and were stern in maintaining orthodoxy. The most notable dissenter in their midst, Baruch Spinoza (1632–77), was ultimately excommunicated.

Proud of its new independence, the community felt strong enough to send a mission to England in 1655, led by their rabbi Manasseh ben Israel, to attempt to persuade the then government of Oliver Cromwell to reverse the Order expelling Jews issued in 1292, and thus hasten the arrival of the Messiah.* The Expulsion Order was not revoked; but a number of Sephardi businessmen already living quietly in London were given a nod of encouragement by being allowed to meet for prayers and buy a burial ground. (This informal status broadened in time, but did not become complete until well into the nineteenth century.)

England had come into the profitable transatlantic trading picture in the latter part of the sixteenth century, and was soon to make further progress which would ultimately lead it to outstrip the position of Holland, just as Holland had taken the place of Portugal in many areas, including the East Indies. At first it was as 'privateers' (government-sponsored pirates) that England's bold sailors, from the days of Queen Elizabeth, had taken a slice of the enormous wealth carried from the Caribbean in convoys of Spanish galleons.† In time, the gains of the English through legalized piracy were replaced by profits made by capital investment, in which they followed the Dutch.

---

* This would happen when the word of God filled the world. The Jews, expressing this, were now to be found everywhere, including the Americas, but not in England. This had to be corrected.

† The favoured route was to transport gold and silver up the Pacific coast to 'the Spanish main', the land bordering the Caribbean, and thence to Europe. To take one example, it is estimated that silver worth £1½ billion came from Peru this way (*Enc. Brit.*, 14th ed., 1929, vol. 4, col. 862).

Braudel explains in *The Mediterranean* that Spanish commerce had originally been financed by the capitalists of Genoa, and that when this source of money dried up, the exporters of Seville were lent cash by firms in the Netherlands, who took their gain when the Indies fleets returned from the Americas with silver. It was in this process that Sephardim in Amsterdam, and subsequently in London, began to amass capital that would be put to further profit in trading missions in which they were allowed to participate. The merchants of Seville, Braudel says, had become merely commission agents, never risking their own property but taking a percentage of the profit. This passive role, he believes, was 'only a step to total inactivity' and Spanish decline.[70]

When the authorities tried to prevent this infiltration of Seville's trade, the Spanish merchants continued to operate in this way secretly. Indeed, they furthered their own decline by negotiating large deals for their goods directly with the English privateers, though not always successfully, as Braudel shows. In 1596, for example,

sixty ships lying in Cadiz harbour laden from the Indies were surprised by the English fleet which sacked the town. They contained a total of 11 million ducats' worth of merchandise. The English offered not to burn them for a payment of 2 million. The Duke of Medina Sidonia [the Spanish admiral] refused the deal and the ships went up in flames.

But if this deal failed, it was clearly typical of many which succeeded. It is ironic that English history books used to tell schoolchildren (and perhaps still do) that this particular raid was a proud moment when the English sailors 'singed the beard of the King of Spain'.

Skills of the Marranos

The Marrano merchants did more than get involved with Holland's ventures in the Americas. They took also, Braudel says, an earlier lead in ventures from Portugal itself; and they were prominent, too, as was noted earlier, in promoting trade from the north with the Mediterranean:

Preparing and perhaps easing the way for the Dutch, sometimes involuntarily, the rich Portuguese Marranos came onto the scene, the Ximenez of

Lisbon and Antwerp, for example, and their associates the Andrade and the Veiga, who arranged deliveries of northern grain for the Grand Duke of Tuscany after the 1590s, making considerable profit for themselves out of it. They also had a hand in the spice trade of Italy.

A correspondent of the time records in a letter that 'these Portuguese controlled everything'. Among examples given, we hear that in 1590 'they had a ship come from Brazil to Leghorn with 600 chests of sugar'. We get an illustration here, too, of the increased migration of the Sephardi exiles from Holland to Italy. It had become difficult to sell pepper by the Atlantic routes, which led to it being diffused in Europe via Italy, 'and it was therefore to Italy, for a while, that Portuguese emigrants flocked'.[71]

The overflow of Sephardi enterprise from Holland to London found a very profitable channel in the strong trade links already existing between England and Portugal. English consumer goods, especially woollens, had a large market in the Iberian peninsula generally, and they were also absorbed into transatlantic trade on ships that brought back agricultural products (dyestuffs, coffee, sugar, etc.) as well as gold and silver. However, Gedalia Yogev, who has studied detailed trade records of the time, makes it clear that Marrano participation, though important, was always limited in area and scale. Jewish trade, he says, was determined by the things they specialized in – precious metals, diamonds and currencies. They were not involved, it seems, in other areas of trade, such as industrial manufacture, transport, distribution, or even banking.[72]

The prime advantage of the Portuguese Marranos of London was that they were in a position to benefit from Britain's traditional trade with Portugal at a time when Jewish traders in Lisbon itself (ostensibly Christian) were being driven out by the newly rampant Inquisition. For this reason subterfuges and aliases had to be used when Marranos in London dealt with old partners in Lisbon. The British were ready to arrange agents quietly on their behalf, particularly when the Methuen Treaty of 1703 opened up the market for woollens and other goods by lifting all restrictions on their import to Portugal. With this free flow of goods, British capital began to dominate the economy of Portugal and her trade with Brazil. By this time Britain no longer needed to import sugar and tobacco from Portuguese territories, as she now had her own sources in the British West Indies. As a result, she now imported gold from Brazil and, after their discovery there in 1730, diamonds.

The growing success of the Sephardim in London soon attracted Ashkenazi immigration, small to begin with, from areas adjacent to Hamburg; but though there were some major Ashkenazi financial houses, the Sephardim continued to be dominant among Jews in the City. As Britain's colonial empire expanded in the eighteenth century, replacing Holland's dominance in the East, some broad differences of function developed. The Jewish businessmen of London active in Latin-American trade were mostly Sephardim from the Portuguese community, while the Ashkenazim (including those in Holland and Germany) were prominent in the trade with India, stimulated partly by the emergence of the great East India Company.

Trade with India in coral had ramifications, as Yogev shows, involving both Sephardim and Ashkenazim, and is worth spelling out briefly. Jewish traders in Leghorn arranged for the collection of coral from the Mediterranean for shipping to India, where it was very highly esteemed for working into jewellery. The coral was taken to India (with other British goods) in British ships which brought back diamonds in exchange. These were then sold via Anglo–Dutch dealers to Amsterdam, where they were polished and sold throughout Europe. All this interlocking trade, with its involvement of traders from Leghorn and the linked communities of North Africa, was just one more instance of the development of what one might call the main-line Sephardi diaspora, linked in origin to Spain and Portugal, and finding new expression and staying power in major countries of the world.

Offshoots of the western diaspora

The reason for Jewish success in the West was that the Sephardim involved were located in growth countries and were able to make the most of their economic and social freedom. This was clearly true in Holland and England, where a number of families enjoying early settlement were able to expand their wealth during the ensuing centuries. Some used this solidified position to help disadvantaged Jews elsewhere, especially the poor Sephardim of the Near East. This attitude was not uniform, however. It was particularly notable among British Sephardim, led by Sir Moses Montefiore, though not, it would seem, among the rich Sephardim of Holland, despite their earlier dominance in the Sephardi diaspora. In France, by contrast, the tiny group of Jews descended from old Provence families produced a leader in Adolphe Crémieux whose bold policies as a government minister were to be of decisive importance, as we shall see, to the Jews of North Africa.

If Jewish history moved along predictable lines, one might have expected to see a strong Sephardi participation in the exploration of Central and South America in the sixteenth and seventeenth centuries, resulting in the foundation and persistence of Sephardi communities from that time on. But Jewish history is never as predictable as this. In the event, the early settlements of Portuguese and other Sephardi Jews in South America soon faded out, though the Sephardim became visible again in a small way when immigration began to flow on a large scale in the twentieth century.

Argentina is an example of this. The early Spanish–Portuguese period left few records of Jews, though we know of their presence through attacks by the Inquisition. When we hear of Jews there in the nineteenth century, the struggle for 'rights' is being led by the British 'colonizers' on behalf of their protégés the Protestants, with the Jews ignored. The real foundations of the present very large and strongly pro-Israel community in Argentina were laid by the heavy immigration of Jews at the beginning of the twentieth century, under agricultural programmes financed by the Jewish Colonial Association (ICA). Most of these immigrants were Ashkenazim from eastern Europe, though some arrived from North Africa and the Ottoman Empire. The ensuing story, which includes the major immigration effects of the Nazi period, indicates an established, if small, Sephardi community. Recent figures showed that of fifteen orthodox rabbis in Argentina, five were Sephardim.

The early period of Jews in Brazil had much stronger links for a time with the 'mainline' story of the Sephardi diaspora, and produced a twist at the end which has won Brazil a permanent footnote in the Jewish history of the United States.

The Brazilian Sephardim had two sources. The first was from Portugal itself. The admiral who landed in Brazil in 1500 had at least one Jew on board; and this presence soon expanded. A consortium of New Christians had obtained a concession in Portugal in 1502 to colonize the new land, developing sugar plantations on a large scale; and though most of them were ardent Catholics, some were secretly practising Jews, as we know once again from Inquisition records. At the same time 'open' Jews, mostly Sephardim, were arriving in northern Brazil from Amsterdam, as part of Dutch colonizing expeditions. The first had arrived in 1624; and within fifteen years they had expanded very successfully, achieving prosperity in sugar plantations, tax-farming and the slave trade, and importing rabbis for their spiritual needs.

The Portuguese had not looked kindly on this Dutch presence. Sending for military reinforcements they mounted a series of attacks; and finally, in 1654, the Dutch capitulated. Most of the Europeans – about half of whom were thought to have been Jewish – were permitted to go back to Amsterdam; but some, though at grave danger from the pirates, found bases for settlement in Caribbean islands, where they developed the same prosperous occupations. Among these refugees, one boat contained twenty-three Jews who were able to make their way to New York (then New Amsterdam), where they were permitted, after some delays, to land in September 1654, the founding fathers, or at least the precursors, of what was to become the largest concentration of Jews anywhere in the world.

As in Argentina, the early Sephardi settlement in Brazil had vanished; but when immigration there began again, at the beginning of the nineteenth century, the first settlers came from Morocco, establishing the first of a number of Sephardi synagogues in 1824. After this the great inflow was of Ashkenazim, though, as in Argentina, there was always a persistent Sephardi presence.

Elite Sephardi strains

The Sephardi presence in the United States, which had started with the boatload of twenty-three Jews (including some Ashkenazim) in 1654, expanded in New York and along the Atlantic coast generally during the colonial period. In the fortunate background of political freedom, they became prominent culturally as well as in industry and business, constituting about half of the estimated 2,000 Jews living in the American colonies.

Numerically the American Sephardim were swamped by Ashkenazi immigrants in the nineteenth century, but their well-established pride gave them a special place; and when prosperity made the USA a lodestar to Jews elsewhere, there was a particularly interesting immigration of some streams of Sephardi Jews from less favoured countries around the Mediterranean. The first stream came from the Balkans, Asia Minor and Syria during the first two decades of the twentieth century, and numbered some 50,000/60,000 Sephardim. The second stream, also numbering several thousand, arrived from Morocco, Egypt and Iraq after the Second World War. Though well integrated by now, these Sephardim have taken great pride in maintaining some individual traditions, in line with similar attitudes among Sephardi immigrants to Israel from these same countries.

The United States experience in recent Sephardi immigration is echoed, though with significant differences, in the relatively small Sephardi community in neighbouring Canada. Here Jews were first given residence permission in 1759, when the British conquered the country from the French. The first synagogue, founded in 1768, linked itself to the pioneer Sephardi synagogue of London, and took the name (*She'arith Israel*) of the Sephardi synagogue in New York. There was perhaps a mild snob element in this. In view of the proud position of the Sephardim in London and New York, it was no doubt prestigious for the synagogue to be called, as it still is, 'Spanish and Portuguese', even though the founders were, in fact, all Ashkenazim. However, they enlisted some Sephardi rabbis; and a further Sephardi link has now been established in an unexpected way. In the 1950s there was a substantial Sephardi immigration to Canada from some North African and Near Eastern countries, with the common use of the French language, especially in Quebec, as one bond. Here, as in a much larger immigration from North Africa to France, the Sephardim of less favoured lands have moved into a more prosperous orbit without the deep social problems that have accompanied the migrations into Israel from these lands.

These examples of cross-currents in Sephardi life, with different strains meeting and mingling, are very common today, running counter to the old picture of two socially separate communities, a superior one descended directly (or so they say) from old families in Spain and Portugal, and an inferior one that reflects the lower levels of Jewish life in the Near and Middle East, and constituting the majority, in origin, of Israel's Sephardim today. But if this picture has some broad relevance at any given moment, it fails completely to convey the dynamics of Jewish life which, over a period, have always operated against rigid polarization of this kind. In particular, wealth has never been the sole dividing line between groups: many other factors come into the picture as criteria of the élite.

Most obviously among the Sephardim there is pride of ancestry, for which there is a Hebrew/Aramaic word '*yichuss*'. Two examples will illustrate this. One is linked to the steady migration of Sephardi families to the land of Israel for religious reasons over the centuries, which led to the emergence of what one might call a Holy Land élite, not rich but cultured and highly respected. Yitzhak Navon, an early president of Israel, belongs to one such family; and there are many others who are authentically 'Near Eastern' yet in no sense of secondary status.

A somewhat different style of Sephardi distinctions can be seen in the family of Mosheh Castel, the Israeli painter. The family believe that their ancestor carried their name to Jerusalem from Castile immediately after the Expulsion of 1492; but the relevant factor is the way this lineage is reflected in the character of the work that Castel has developed, as if reflecting hundreds of years of residence on the soil of the land of Israel.

History, as we have seen, shows how vibrant the Sephardi diaspora was in the West. In our own time the eastern Sephardim of Israel draw on this, as on their own traditions, with old divisions and categorizations fading in importance.

12 The East: Rise and Decline

In the previous chapter we pursued the story of the Sephardi diaspora in the West, taking a bird's-eye view of main developments that carried the story to our own day. Let us now return to the eastern stream of the Sephardi diaspora, to note how it first surged into unusual distinction in the post-Expulsion period and then, in some cases, relapsed into decline.

Although the two streams flowed into each other in many ways, there was an historic difference. At the time of the expulsions from Spain and Portugal in the 1490s, the mass of the Jewish people were in the East. With hindsight it is clear that the future, in terms of numbers, political freedom and economic power, was to lie with the West; but for a relatively short period the eastern Jews were themselves poised for a period of very distinctive self-expression that was to hold the centre of interest on the world Jewish stage.

In the West, Jews would look increasingly outward for political and intellectual self-assurance. Among the Jews of the East there was a strong movement to look inward. Having to come to terms with the drama of the expulsions, they set out to explore their own resources with a new intensity. In Spain itself this tendency to look inward had surfaced in some élitist circles as a reaction to the spread of conversion, and had been marked, as we saw, by a growing interest in Cabbala: mystical Judaism. With the roots of this approach firmly implanted, the refugees from Spain took the study of Cabbala forward with a bravado that led them along strange theosophical and messianic paths before the exuberance faded.

The mystical excitement that flowed from its early expression in fourteenth-century Spain to a peak of messianism in seventeenth-century Turkey was not, as some used to think, an aberration in Jewish thought. But the eastern Sephardim injected it with an infectious enthusiasm that pervaded Jewish society in a populist sense, and so strongly that something of the same excitement flowed far afield, infecting even the respectable Jewish burghers of Amsterdam and London who were trying so desperately in other respects to behave with the restraint of the conventional financiers with whom they did business.

The upheavals of the Expulsion found other forms of expression, too, before the emergence of major forces among the Ashkenazim in the North began to supply Jewish life with a new fulcrum. But in the first phase, the Sephardi world came together in the East with a religious self-confidence strong enough to survive the political decline that was to follow shortly.

Messianic stirrings

There are many elements in this brief resurgence of eastern life after the catastrophe of expulsion from Spain. A strong factor, already noted, was the role of the adjacent countries of North Africa in offering a base for reinvigoration that would let many leaders move on ultimately to an intensification of Jewish life in the Holy Land. We have already seen how powerfully this escape valve had been used in the past, particularly in making it possible for distinguished scholars to rally Jewish life there after the 'pogroms' of 1391 in Spain. This was evident especially in the land we now call Algeria, where two refugee scholars – Rabbi Isaac ben Sheshet Perfet and Rabbi Simon ben Zemah Duran – had generated learning and dignity over the whole of the 'Maghreb' (the term, as we have seen, applied to the whole of North Africa west of Egypt).

In the Expulsion a century later, the regenerative influence came this time from Morocco, reversing a long period of poverty and neglect there. A leader in this process was a young refugee rabbi from Spain, Jacob Berab, who carried the torch of mysticism, it might be said, from the extreme west of the Maghreb to the centre of the new Cabbalist revival in the Holy Land itself, in Safed. In this he was reflecting the Jewish mood of the time, as expressed by his teacher Rabbi Isaac Aboab, a member of one of the greatest Sephardi families then and in subsequent centuries.

With the refugees from Spain who were active in Morocco, the Expulsion, as André Chouraqui says in his book on the Jews of North Africa, had come like a searing flame. The suffering of the Jews was not as the punishment of sin, but in the perspective of an apocalypse. The hour seemed to have struck for the initiates of the Cabbala to come out of their basic reserve and to offer, to all, the consolation of the mystery of God.[73]

This is the positive side of the enthusiasm generated at the time by a rabbi like Berab, and carried by him to Egypt and Palestine. Inevitably there was another side expressed in quarrels and factionalism, but still reflecting the high excitement that was to give the eastern Sephardi world the explosive character expressed in the drama of the pseudo-messiah Shabbetai Zevi. Long before Shabbetai's emergence in the 1660s, Berab had shown his own messianism by a campaign he launched to revive the venerable procedures of rabbinical ordination (*semichah*). This, in his view, would enable the throng of rabbis now converging on Palestine to form the great *Beth Din* (court) that was to precede, according to an old teaching of Maimonides, the arrival of the Messiah.

Within major talmudic quarrels that surrounded the *semichah* proposals, one has to note that Berab was also trying to get his own status raised, through *semichah*, by the leading rabbi of Jerusalem. He failed in this; but the issues he raised intensified the dynamics of Sephardi faith. It also had momentous practical results; for among the four rabbis ordained at this time in Safed by Berab himself was Joseph Caro, whom we mentioned earlier as the author of the *Shulhan Arukh*, and as such the scholar who had the most lasting influence on Jewish religious practice from that day to this.

In differing ways Jerusalem, Safed and Tiberias had become focal points for an intensified religious enthusiasm all over the eastern world since the Ottomans had conquered Palestine and Syria in 1516. Business and intellectual leaders from different cities stretching from Italy to the Balkans reflected their local backgrounds in the character of their contributions to this movement; but the overriding factor was the recovery for a short period of the resurgence of Jewish life in Palestine itself.

Sephardi notables

Before this, while the eastern countries were ruled from Egypt by the ex-slave dynasty of Mamluks, there had been a long decline in the position of the Jews in Palestine. The Ottoman conquest of Palestine in 1516 had, to begin with, generated a new spirit, something like 'a golden age' in the view of the historian Hayyim Ze'ev Hirschberg. This reflected to some extent the prosperity that had now burgeoned in the Ottoman Empire, but it was also a reflection of the religious leadership that had developed in the East. One can instance the fact that as soon as the Sephardi communities of the North began to get organized in the seventeenth century, they had to turn to what might be called 'the source' to find men of eminence who could lead them. This emerged, we saw earlier, in the recruitment of Rabbi Jacob Sasportas from the East to lead important communities in the North or West.

At this stage, the Sephardim of the East had a major role in the societies in which they lived, while those in the West were still peripheral. Nothing in the West, for example, could match the financial power and luxurious life-style in Constantinople of the great lady Dona Gracia Nasi; and indeed life in Renaissance Italy or sixteenth-century Constantinople gave room equally for other forms of aristocratic existence more in tune with the elegance of Spain than with the cold primness of Amsterdam. To get a rounded view, one has to see how new life in the East had developed at many levels of society, offering satisfactions both mundane and aristocratic to those Jews closely integrated with their background.

One point of interest, not unrelated to Dona Gracia, is the role of educated Sephardi women in that world. When Dona Gracia took refuge for a time in Ferrara the outstanding personality of the Jewish community was, as it happened, another woman, Dona Benvenida, a member of the wealthy and learned family of Abrabanel which had first settled in Naples after the Expulsion and then, still enormously wealthy, had had to move on to Ferrara. On the death of her husband in 1547, Dona Benvenida had not only continued to run the family business on a grand scale, but had also sustained her husband's role in the world of scholarship, devoting her wealth to this cause as well as to the more conventional help she gave to orphans and the rescue of captives.

The historian Cecil Roth was very eloquent on these themes. Ferrara was the home, he tells us, of two ladies of the great Modena family, Pomona and Bathsheba, who were also directly involved in Jewish studies, Bathsheba in particular being an expert on the Talmud and Cabbala. Appropriately, she emigrated late in life to Safed, which had, of course, become the centre of Cabbala study.[74]

Intriguing in a very different way is the story of the influence exercised at the Turkish court by a number of Jewish women entrusted with running the financial and personal affairs of the ladies of the sultan's harem, and inevitably moving on from this to handling major diplomatic affairs for the sultan himself. A woman in this role had to be intelligent and literate, as well as skilful in languages. She had the title or rank of 'Kyra'; and one in particular, Esther Kyra, who carried out these duties for a very long period, after her husband died, for the sultan and his family, amassed a large fortune (in operating the customs) for herself and her sons, and was laden with honours by the sultan before falling foul of rivals and being executed.

At a different social level but equally expressive of a woman's skill and intelligence in these court circles is the story of a Jewish woman called Esperanza Malchi who was the tirewoman of the chief wife of the sultan, and in this role – or off her own bat – wrote a long letter to Queen Elizabeth of England, sending her via the Turkish ambassador a whole assortment of jewelled necklaces and silken robes, and suggesting subtly, at the end of the letter, that return gifts of perfumed oils, for which England was famous, would be more than welcome. There is no record, as far as we know, of the queen's reply; but one likes to think of Esperanza at least having a good try.[75]

Satisfying lives

Coming down to earth, after these and countless other exoticisms that Cecil Roth scattered so lovingly through his books on Mediterranean Jewries, one looks for more practical illustrations of the satisfactions of life in, say, Salonika or Jerusalem. There are fascinating instances of this in Braudel's book *The Mediterranean*, and even more in the work of the famed Jewish historian of Turkey and the Balkans, Solomon Abraham Rosanes (1862–1938). It was a lively satisfying world, and to evaluate it one must rid one's mind, as Roth points out, of what was 'a mistaken nineteenth-century antithesis between the civilized West and the backward East . . . the humane environment of Christendom and Muslim semi-barbarism'. At the height of her power, sixteenth-century Turkey was superior to the West not only in military power, architecture and the amenities of life, but 'hardly second' in humanity. Wartime massacres by the Turks were not more bloodthirsty than numerous Christian atrocities such as the sack of Rome by the

Emperor Charles V (1535), or the St Bartholomew massacre of
Protestants in France (1572). Though exhausted later by military
campaigns to sustain her now vast empire, Turkey established in her
prime many marks of generosity to subject peoples, especially the
Jews; and the good relationship was mutual.[76] When Suleiman the
Magnificent (sultan from 1520 to 1566) conquered Buda in 1562, the
chief rabbi there treated him as a liberator, which led to a considerable
migration of Hungarian Jews to the Sephardi communities of Turkey.
In another area, it was Suleiman who built the great wall around the
Old City of Jerusalem, which not only gave the Jews living there a
sense of security but also preserved for posterity the only surviving
remnant – the *Kotel* (Western Wall) – of Second Temple times.

Not that all the Jews were content with the Turkish conqueror. The
mysterious would-be messiah David Reubeni, who was active at this
time, thought that the upheavals called for something like a holy war
'to take the Holy Land from his hands'. More generally, however, the
improved economic situation of Palestine, especially in food and
wine-growing, encouraged Jewish immigration. It is thought that
there were about 1,000 Jewish families (say 5,000 persons) in
Palestine at the time of the Ottoman conquest and that the population
doubled within a few decades. In Jerusalem itself the Jews had four
more or less distinct origins: Sephardim coming directly from Spain,
Maghrebis from North Africa, 'Musta'rabs' (Arabic-speaking Jews of
older origins) and Ashkenazim, known to have lived there since at
least the time of Maimonides (twelfth century). Despite this mixed
background, with its heavy Arabic-speaking element, the influence of
the Spanish immigrants became dominant. Elie Eliachar, descendant
of a very old Sephardi family, reports in his memoirs that Ladino
(Jewish–Spanish) became the common language of the entire
community. 'In Jerusalem, right up to the end of the nineteenth
century, it was spoken by all Jews, with Ashkenazim and non-
Sephardi Oriental Jews employing the language in their contacts with
the Sephardim.'[77]

Industrially, the availability of olive oil and chemicals had a
manufacturing spin-off in dyeing and the manufacture of soap; but it
was in Safed, the hill-top town in Galilee, that the most substantial
economic expansion took place, in line with the proliferation of
talmudists, poets and cabbalists. The stimulus was the flow of
immigrants, after 1492, from Spain, often via Salonika. Within a few
years the Jews of Safed were reported as trading in spices, cheese, oil,

vegetables and fruit; but the most solid mark of their industrial prosperity was the development of textiles, in which they competed with the fine looms of Venice itself.

We hear of eight synagogues catering for Jews of different origins living there contentedly. Later, as the prosperity of Turkish lands declined, Safed became less famous for its industry than for the cabbalism that had flowered – or over-flowered – there. By the beginning of the seventeenth century funds were being collected all over the Jewish world to support the now impoverished rabbis and their pupils. There are said to have been 300 rabbinical scholars, eighteen schools, twenty-one synagogues and a large *yeshivah* of a hundred pupils. But the chief activities of the cabbalist 'industry' had now been transported to the large communities in Turkey itself, due in time to produce the messianism personified by the pseudo-messiah Shabbetai Zevi.[78]

Luria and Shabbetai Zevi

At the centre of the mystical faith that was to spread with such power from Safed during the seventeenth century was the remarkable teacher already mentioned, Isaac Luria, who became known as the A-R-I ('the lion'), a name said to be formed from the Hebrew initials of *Elohi-Rabbi-Isaac* – 'the saintly Rabbi Isaac'.

The name indicates the veneration in which he was held. He had been born of an Ashkenazi father and Sephardi mother in Egypt, where he lived in youth as a hermit and poet. The teachings he elaborated, after settling in Safed, centred on the metaphysical problem of how there can be room for man in a universe which is 'filled' by God's presence. His answer was that in the act of Creation, God, though infinite by definition, 'withdrew' or 'reduced' himself (the Hebrew word is *tzim-tzum*) to leave a dark void which represents a form of God's own exile into the recesses of His Being. The gap is indicated by the character of the *sefirot* ('spheres') which were intended for the divine Irradiation. The three upper *sefirot* were able to contain this Light; the six lower *sefirot* were shattered into *klippot* ('husks') when the Light reached them. These *klippot* represent impurity and evil; but they still contain sparks of the divine

Light; and Redemption will come when these sparks are released through Israel's march to moral perfection.*

Jewish mysticism had found expression in fifteenth-century Spain in the book called *Zohar* (Illumination); but in the new developments under Luria it was the expulsion from Spain that supplied a new kind of impetus. The doctrines reflected the longing for Redemption, which was to be led by miracles. As a prelude, one must obey the Torah meticulously. Paradoxically, however, one could also envisage a complete *bouleversement* of ordinary life and its pieties to demonstrate a reversal of natural law; and this became a recurrent element in the life-style of the pseudo-messiah Shabbetai Zevi.

Shabbetai, born in Asia Minor in 1626, had responded from early youth to the mixed expressions of magic and messianism that pervaded the Sephardi world. During the previous century, metaphysical speculation had increasingly included a 'practical' element coming close to black magic (miracles, alchemy, visitations from the dead, intervention of Satan and so on), as well as more 'natural' campaigns to bring about the arrival of the Messiah through risings and warfare. The idea of using warfare had been picked up by the adventurer David Reubeni who, as we saw earlier, had appeared in the 1520s, proposing a war to be fought jointly by Christian countries and the army of his own fantasized Jewish kingdom to win back the Holy Land from the Turks. In a very different spirit, a legend was current among eastern Jews for centuries about a man called Joseph della Reina, who burnt incense before Satan to secure his support for the arrival of the Messiah, and suffered a dire fate for his idolatry. Famous cabbalists of Safed took the legend seriously but gave it different elaborations, leading in the fullest form to a sexual tempting, in which Joseph became the lover of Lilith, the female temptress of the night. The legend grew even more widespread in the eighteenth century, where it was regarded by Jews both as a gripping story and as a parallel to Shabbetai's defeat by Satan when he converted to the Muslim faith.

Shabbetai, though knowing the *Zohar* and Luria's work, was never clear-cut in what he took from cabbalist teachings. His influence flowed, rather, from the charisma of his presence and the magical splendour that grew around him, offsetting the depression and perplexities to which he was constantly subject. He was also promoted

* The most authoritative exposition of the Cabbala is the huge essay (in effect a book) by Gershom Scholem in the *Encyclopaedia Judaica*, vol. 10, cols 489–653, *s.v.* 'Kabbalah'. There is a full exposition, also, in his great biography of Shabbetai Zevi.

through the dialectical skills of his apostle Nathan of Gaza, who spread faith in him as the Messiah to the furthest ends of the Jewish world. In life, he had turned the Law upside-down when the spirit so moved him – for example, by eating on fast days and pronouncing the ultra-sacred name of God – as a free expression of the metaphysical power of the Messiah. Even after his conversion to the Muslim faith to save his life many followers, and especially Nathan, saw this as a positive echo of his former daring. Though the Jewish world as a whole was shattered by this bitter end to the messianic dream, some adherents, who became known as 'Doenmeh', followed him into conversion to the Muslim faith, while still maintaining, as they believed he had done, their beliefs in Judaism.

The Turkish setting

The factual background of the Shabbetai story reflects very well the high and low points of Sephardi existence at this time. In some respects the Jews of the eastern communities had found a stable life, adorned at the top by their notables, from whom they enjoyed reflected pride. In Turkey itself the fame of Joseph Nasi, Duke of Naxos and diplomatic adviser to the sultan, had been carried forward, after his death in 1579, by Solomon Abeneas (or ibn Ya'ish), another great financier born into a *converso* family in Portugal who reverted to Judaism and settled in Turkey in 1585 after a vastly successful business life, which included making a fortune in diamonds, in India. He, too, was created a duke – of the Aegean island of Mytilene; and he has a footnote in English as well as Turkish history as the diplomat who negotiated, for the sultan, the first Anglo–Turkish alliance to resist jointly the expansionist ideas of the king of Spain. In the Jewish sphere he was equally notable, both for his influence at court and in following in the footsteps of Joseph Nasi in trying to rebuild Tiberias as a centre for Jewish settlement.

The Jews of Turkey doubtless derived equal satisfaction from the special place at the Turkish court of the Hamon family, who were physicians to successive sultans for at least three generations, and were very prominent in Jewish life. The first of these Turkish Hamons, Joseph, had been born in Granada. His son Moses (*c.* 1490–1554) was physician to Selim 1 and then to Suleiman the Magnificent, accompanying him on his campaign against Persia in 1554, and bringing back some distinguished Jewish scholars whom he installed in a *yeshivah* named after him. In the third generation of Hamons we hear of a personal relationship with the great ex-Marrano doctor Amatus Lusitanus, who worked in Italy and the Balkans. In the same circle another court doctor, Solomon Ashkenazi, who had been born in Italy, was highly influential in diplomatic negotiations with Venice, and was installed, in effect, as Turkish ambassador to the great city-state.

It is in this ambience that one has to evaluate the complex relationship that Shabbetai Zevi must have had with the Turkish court, being treated at one level as a high representative of Jewry, and at another as a troublemaker whose pretensions to be a kind of king-messiah had to be silenced. H. H. Ben-Sasson catches the mixed atmosphere well in describing in *A History of the Jewish People* the extraordinary background to Shabbetai's rise and fall.[79]

His rise, we are told, was an expression of Ashkenazi as well as Sephardi hope, coming as it did after the massacres of 1648–9 in Poland had plunged the Jewish world into despair. Intense sessions of prayer and strict asceticism spread widely, in line with the fierce writings of Nathan of Gaza denouncing sin and calling for repentance. Against this picture of desolation, the concept of a Messiah spread glory. Even during Shabbetai's imprisonment in Gallipoli in 1665–6 before his conversion, 'there was ample external pomp'. When seized by the prophetic vision, 'he would promise vengeance against the gentiles, and stress that in particular he would avenge himself on the murderers of Poland and Lithuania. When the spirit rested upon him, he would distribute lands, principalities and kingdoms among his followers. In his "court", there was an emotionally charged atmosphere that was almost erotic.'

The faith in Shabbetai as Messiah had come at a time 'when Ashkenazim and Sephardim alike were experiencing the kind of suffering that was termed "the birth-pangs" of the Messiah's coming.' Even in far-off London, the great diarist Samuel Pepys recorded that bets of a hundred pounds were being laid in the City that 'a certain person now at Smyrna would within two years be owned by all the Princes of the East as the King of the World'. In Constantinople itself, belief that this would happen was universal. As Ben-Sasson puts it, 'the Jews who saw Shabbetai entering the sultan's palace thought that he was about to remove the crown from the ruler's head'. When they learnt that he had in fact submitted to conversion there, the blow was unbearable: 'their own crown had fallen from their heads'.

There was a wider significance for Jewish history in the disillusion of this moment. It reflected the onset of a time in which the splendours that had surfaced in different ways for centuries among the communities of the East would increasingly fade. The general factors relating to the decline are not difficult to identify. Externally the Turkish governing power extending through a very large part of this world had begun to fail markedly in political and economic affairs. Among the Jews themselves the historic change in which the Ashkenazim would soon dwarf the Sephardim in numbers and importance was already under way. Yet this general factor left room for great differences within the inner life of the different Sephardi communities themselves, an issue of great significance to their revival later.

There was always a strong contrast, from the sixteenth century on, between Jewish life in the 'central' lands clustered around Turkey and Palestine, and those on either side – North Africa to the west, Iraq–Iran and Central Asia to the east – where for a long time the pattern of Jewish life was one of increasing poverty and degradation. But though these lands had now become weak in contrast to their former strong position in Jewish life, they still emerged in modern times with strongly individual characteristics, whose elements were undoubtedly nurtured in these centuries of 'decline'.

Onset of decline

There was no set pattern even within each country. Morocco, for example, which had far the largest population of Jews in the Islamic diaspora, might have been thought to be uniform in character, especially since it continued to be ruled throughout this period by local Arab dynasties and was never under the distant control of the Ottoman Turks. It may have been partly for this reason, indeed, that Jewish life in Morocco had developed some particularly close contacts with the Arab world in which it lived, evidenced in traditions and folklore. But this did not yield a uniform life. Norman Stillman points out in his book *The Jews in Arab Lands* that 'there were tremendous polarities of tolerance and intolerance, assimilation and isolation, security and insecurity'.[80] Against examples of Moroccan Jews in high places at court and also performing important roles in trade and diplomacy, it was in Morocco's Fez that a special Jewish quarter – the *mellah* – was first set up in 1438. It was declared to be for the Jews' own protection; but this in turn indicates the provocations and even persecutions to which they were subject. In this connection Stillman notes an important contrast between Jewish life in the interior and that in the towns. In the interior 'the Sephardic plutocracy' was in a very strong position, while in the towns the laws against non-Muslims, virtually all Jews, were harsher than elsewhere.

To generalize for a moment, one would say that the crudeness of life in the Moroccan towns encouraged among the Jews a fierce kind of religiosity which survived the centuries. There were strong currents of cabbalistic mysticism within which the Jews found a form of escapism; and they were famous also for their addiction to *mahya*, the local brandy. The only other Muslim country in which Jews were known as hard drinkers was Yemen, where again the *dhimmi* laws were very harsh and the Jews the only *dhimmis* to be found. Yet having drawn this parallel, one sees immediately how misleading parallels can be; for descendants of these two communities in Israel today are attested as vastly dissimilar in social character, the Moroccans tending to be turbulent, while the Yemenites have brought with them a very effective form of social responsibility. In using parallels one has to draw on the whole background, in all its variety.

One sees this demonstrated in the story of another of the eastern countries, Iraq, which also seemed at this point to have gone into decline. The fall of 'Babylon' from its earlier pre-eminence in Jewish life had already been a catastrophic blow to its pride; yet there were periods in which the Jews of Baghdad seemed to recapture their former ease and dignity of life, in ways significant for the future. When the pagan Mongols conquered the Middle East in the thirteenth century and turned for administrative and professional help to all who were available – Muslims, Christians and Jews alike – the result for Jews was a period of unusual freedom and opportunity. Later, under Persian rule, life was harsher for the Jews; but when the Turks, in a war with Persia, took Iraq away from Persian rule in 1534, the old tradition of independence in 'Babylon' seems to have been given some leeway, which must surely have sowed the seeds for the special quality of Jewish life there in later centuries. From this time trade flourished with neighbouring countries, including Palestine; religious teaching and scholarship were strongly maintained; and even though the form of administration under virtually independent Turkish pashas could lead at times to barbarities and flight, it usually left room for the Jews to re-establish their own form of self-government, long a characteristic of Iraq.

Decline is obviously too flat a word to cover the changing life in these varied eastern communities. The true flavour is more likely to emerge by trying to look at individual rather than national stories. The chapter which follows will do this, by listening to the voices of some of the descendants of the eastern communities.

PART FIVE
The Interim Centuries

13 *Varieties of Eastern Experience*

This chapter, though central to the theme of the book, will be a diversion in style, in the sense that it will try to project a general mood by drawing on disparate sources and without strict chronology.

The eastern Sephardim are difficult to present in an orderly progression. The areas in which they appeared overlap with each other, as do the time sequences, mixing up what is medieval with what is part of our time.

Yet one feels the need to pick some illustrative moments or instances from this unorganized pattern; and one way is to listen to the voices of descendants. If one brings in memories from a number of the eastern countries, the flavour of this world as a whole may emerge, while still revealing the variety of Sephardi experience before all these sources began to flow into Israel and be absorbed there.

One knows in advance that one cannot expect to get *pictorial* echoes of Jews in the immediate post-Expulsion era, because naturalistic painting was alien to the Islamic world. The Jews seem to have been poorly represented even in the mixed Sephardi–Ashkenazi world of Italy, where art was practised freely. In this respect the Ashkenazim of the north did better, as is revealed in *Jewish Life in the Middle Ages*, a superb book produced by Thérèse and Mendel Metzger which shows how illustrators, mostly of prayer-books, incorporated a vast range of daily experience, sacred and profane, among the Jews of northern France and Germany.

However, if paintings are not generally available for the eastern countries, the tapestry that one seeks of daily existence emerges in many other forms, including travellers' tales and song. If one sees what can be said in this framework it will not be comprehensive or consistent; but it may still be true to the background.

The voices we shall listen to are from Rhodes, the Maghreb, Iraq, Turkey and Bulgaria, with some talk also of the music which pervaded all the eastern communities. For good measure, I will add at the end an echo from Spain itself which I, though an Ashkenazi, am called upon to record in this instance as a participant.

A descendant of Rhodes

It may be surprising to take Rhodes, a small island off the coast of Asia Minor, as the first example. One is led on because a book by one of its descendants opens up this world in a highly original way.

The Sephardi experience of Rhodes paralleled that of major communities like Salonika in many ways but with elements that gave it a flavour all its own. The geographical position of Rhodes had made it the locus, over the centuries, of a number of crucial wars between Muslims and Christians, with Jews drawn in on different sides, but always independent, and surviving until in our own time the community was destroyed by the Nazis. As a postscript to the story, it was in Rhodes that the armistice talks between Jews and Arabs in 1948 ended open war against the new State of Israel.

For the most distinctive part of the Rhodes story one has to start with the capture of Jerusalem by the Crusaders in 1099, their defeat by Saladin a century later (1187), the many struggles betwen Muslim and Christian forces in succeeding centuries until the knights of Jerusalem ('the Knights Hospitaller') made Rhodes their headquarters in 1309, and turned it into a fortress which they were able to sustain, despite many Muslim attacks, until driven out by the Turks in 1523. At one stage the Jews of Rhodes were ardent fighters for the knights, though they were ultimately glad to welcome the conquest by the Turks. They had become a flourishing community, though not on the scale later attained by the Sephardim. Under Christian rule there had been no influx of refugees from Spain, for obvious reasons; but now, in the ambience of the Ottoman Empire, the Sephardim began to immigrate freely. There were, of course, the usual tensions between 'natives' (Greek-speaking Romaniot Jews) and the increasingly dominant Sephardi arrivals, but the outcome was satisfying. Rhodes became known as 'little Jerusalem', thronged with scholars and financiers, and famous particularly for silk manufactures.

Much of this is typical of the pattern of Sephardi life in the eastern communities; but there are elements that generated a special flavour for its descendants. Here are two or three at random. Going back to the eighth century, there is a piquant anecdote of the Arabs' first conquest of the island, when a Syrian Jew, moving with the Arab armies, bought as scrap the remains of the famed 'Colossus of Rhodes', using 900 camels to carry away the huge quantities of bronze. In a different vein, one hears of the famed beauty of the Jewesses of Rhodes, and of a fulsome tribute to the island by two German rabbis travelling there in the fifteenth century and writing home:

> If the Jews who live in Germany knew a tenth of the blessings which God has bestowed in His people of Israel in this land, neither snow nor rain, neither day or night would be of consequence until they had journeyed here.

More tangible for the descendants of Rhodes is the heritage of Sephardi folklore and song which seems to have been preserved there with particular distinctiveness, perhaps because it was an island community. Here we can draw on the direct testimony of our descendant, Marc Angel, who is currently the rabbi of the famous old Sephardi synagogue of New York. As always, the chain of tradition is fascinating. Rabbi Angel's grandfather left Rhodes at the beginning of this century, like others of his time, to settle and found synagogues in a few cities of the USA, in his case in Seattle, Washington. When the grandson, now a rabbi, set out for the Aegean in the 1970s in search of his roots, everything that he had heard, as carried by oral tradition, came alive with intense force. In the book – *The Jews of Rhodes* – which he wrote on his researches, we hear with special intimacy of the Spanish songs which the Sephardim preserved, and of the background of folk sayings out of which they sprang, a subject which has come under detailed study only in this century.[81]

Any of the Sephardi lands would yield something of the same treasure; but it is good to see this heritage in an individual setting. The folk sayings and the texts of the songs are, of course, in Ladino, a form of fifteenth-century Spanish which the refugees preserved and adapted with accretions from Hebrew and other languages. Ladino had swiftly become the Jewish colloquial speech of all these lands, giving the Jews involved a warm sense of continuity to supplant the strangeness of their uprooting. It was, above all, a 'popular' speech, as distinct from the pure Castilian which some sophisticated Sephardim might speak in Italy, Holland or London. For ordinary Sephardim, Ladino spelt the home they had established in exile. The language was full of poetry and song; and one particular expression of it was the Bible translation and commentary called *Me'am Lo'ez*, which began to be written in Ladino early in the eighteenth century. It was aimed particularly at women, on the assumption that they were not as likely as men were to imbibe this kind of knowledge in their Hebrew studies. In the event it had a much wider social function, passing on the strength and beauty of Ladino from mothers to children, and, as such, was vital to the culture of the Sephardi world until this century.

Forms of the heritage

Yiddish had, of course, some of the same functions for the Jews of eastern Europe; but to judge from the book by Rabbi Angel, the ethos was different in Sephardi lands. The folk sayings have, perhaps, the same wry tone. A number of them, he says, deal with the Jews' self-image: they see themselves as clever and helpful to each other, while recognizing that their 'overwhelming individuality and pride' could often lead to dissension. *Gudio bovo no hay* ('There is no stupid Jew'), is one saying; but this is not a formula for happiness. *El gudio bive riko, muere prove. El grego bive prove, muere riko* ('The Jew lives rich and dies poor. The Greek lives poor and dies rich'). More elaborately, there is another folk saying which seems to have a deeper meaning, if one knew what it was: *El turko demanda sedaka en kantando, el grego yorando, el gudio en malkiziendo* ('The Turk begs for charity while singing, the Greek while crying, the Jew while cursing').

But if some of this seems familiar to an Ashkenazi ear, the text of folksongs can be different: more daring, one might say, more Latin. It became of great interest to Spanish scholars when *romances* sung for generations within Sephardi families were brought into the open in this century, for it was clear that they went back to authentic traditions in Spanish–Jewish life before the expulsions.

The major pursuit of these old *romances* has centred on the large communities, notably Salonika; but the tradition was 'particularly vibrant among the Jews of Rhodes', Angel says (p. 137), quoting scholars who noted 'the astonishing fidelity of the Rhodeslies to the Spanish poetical and musical heritage', and the exceptional number of songs known by the older women. The subjects, we learn, were varied, some dealing with the lives of kings and queens, some with simple folk, happy or sad. Surprisingly, many of the themes were not specifically religious:

Pious Jews and Jewesses did not blush while singing songs of passionate love, even songs which reflected immoral behaviour. One of the songs, *El Rey Por Muncha Madruga*, tells of a king who came into the queen's room while she was combing her hair early one morning. She had been expecting her lover, and thinking that it was he who had come in, sings of two sons she had by the king and two by the lover, with the latter being treated much better than the former.

Turning round and seeing the king, she says that she has been having a strange dream; but the king is not taken in and orders her to be beheaded by day-break. There are other love stories like this, sometimes intimate confessions between a mother and her daughter, sometimes of the despair of a young man whose love is unrequited.

Behind the expanding academic literature that now studies the *romancero*, it is good to recall, in Angel's words, the evolution of Sephardi life that was establishing a new heritage, even in a period of apparent decline:

The Sephardim of Rhodes and elsewhere had a broad outlook on life. They saw no sharp conflicts between the teachings of religion and the singing of the *romances* . . .
Their songs did not bewail their poverty or make them feel sorry for themselves. Rather, the music tended to reach outward. . . . Poetry and imagery were nourished and bore fruit. The tradition of singing helped the Sephardim remain optimistic and happy in spite of the poor settings in which they lived.

A descendant of the Maghreb

Across the Mediterranean in North Africa, the folk-heritage was being moulded with a very different flavour during these post-Expulsion centuries. Here, too, we can examine the testimony of a descendant in André Chouraqui's book *Between East and West*, discovering, in this case, how strongly the Arab–Muslim background had dominated Jewish life, and how essential it is to evaluate this past for an understanding of the present.

Chouraqui, born in Algeria in 1917, has a special claim to our attention in this kind of evaluation since in everything he writes he is clearly drawing on a sustaining empathy with the constituent elements of Jewish experience, no matter how remote they might seem from modern life. If one applies this to the mixed historical experience of the Jews of North Africa, it opens up an issue that is of central importance in Israel today.

It is significant that Chouraqui, who was educated in France in a wide range of Jewish and Muslim studies and received a number of high decorations for his work with the French Resistance, opted nevertheless, after the war, to settle in Israel rather than in France, being one of the few Jewish intellectuals of North Africa to follow this course.

With so many ready to emphasize the truly wretched conditions of the Jews, at various times, in North Africa, one sees in his book a more balanced approach. We are asked, in effect, to take a long-term view, confronting the horrors, which were unspeakable, with another side of Jewish life in North Africa, a long existence which cannot be just shrugged off but demands even today a sense of participation. It is hard, but therefore all the more important, to consider how this 'Moorish' element in the broad Sephardi heritage continued to shape itself during the centuries of 'decline.'

There are times, it is true, when this son of the Maghreb seems to endow Jewish history in North Africa with a strong romantic element merely because it went on for so long. One forgives him all the more readily since many Jews, looking back on the endless story of our people, do not see as he does that survival itself is not the only element in the attachment. In this case, Chouraqui's determination to give descendants of the Maghreb a strong feeling of pride extracts feelings which would otherwise go unnoticed. 'Among all the races of the Maghreb today,' he writes, 'only the Jews, while retaining their own identity, have known the long series of empires that governed this territory from the Phoenicians to the French.' After 2,000 years, the end of the story, with a major element of the population now in Israel, leads him into an almost mystical judgement. The sudden dissolution of the communities 'was the more astonishing because Jewish life had been the one unchangeable constant in all the changing history of the Maghreb. Indeed, one might say that the best way to understand the past and present of the Maghreb is to regard it through the prism of the history of its Jews.'[82]

In this approach, life in the Maghreb as a whole often had a wretched character, for Chouraqui makes no attempt to play down the evils that emerged from this background for the Jews:

The worst miseries of the European ghetto are not comparable to the moral and material degradation that existed in the mellahs of the foothills of the Atlas or of the remote Sahara until they were emptied with the migrations to Israel.[83]

Yet we are left with two themes which we still have to bear in mind. First, the extreme length of this diaspora – 'one which has no parallel in the history of the Jews' – means that it can never be reduced to a consistent story governing everything, but is rather a kaleidoscopic picture, 'countless histories of disparate communities', full of contradictions and paradoxes, and leaving room for endless cultural and special highpoints that give meaning to the story.

A folk Judaism

The other theme governs the texture of life at mass rather than high level. It is not enough to talk of poverty. The Jews of North Africa had developed an attitude to their faith and a rich folk pattern that are dominant in any kind of evaluation.

Here, as in the political background, there was no overall pattern. To some extent the Jews in remote isolated communities maintained an almost biblical life; in ports and towns by contrast they were subject to external influences from Spain, Italy and further afield. Despite these varied influences one can say of all Maghreb Jews that they were deeply rooted in their loyalty to the Jewish faith; but Chouraqui risks some other generalizations that have relevance to descendants in Israel today.

Basically, he says, the Jews of the Maghreb were strictly 'traditional' but not in the aggressive way which characterizes some Ashkenazi circles. In the Maghreb, observance had almost a folk character. Prayers were recited (in the Sephardi style), and there was great respect for Bible and Talmud teachers; but this never had a sectarian tone. They would never have set out to define how the familiar daily acts reflected particular religious principles. 'Everyone knew in general what religious practices were required of him', and one left it at that.

One might quote in illustration a similarly relaxed attitude by a leading Sephardi rabbi in Israel today, who, unlike the Ashkenazi rabbis, was quoted in a newspaper report as seeing nothing sinful in organized public football on a sabbath afternoon.[84] Chouraqui's explanation of the Maghreb attitude is worth quoting:

> The Judaism of the most conservative of the Maghrebi's Jews was marked by a flexibility, a hospitality, a tolerance, that was far removed from the unbending and aggressive orthodoxy that sprang up among European Jewry in opposition to, and defense against, the movement towards reform that resulted from the emancipation of the Jews of Europe at the end of the 18th century. Not only were the historical circumstances different, but so were the nature of life and outlook. The Jews of North Africa, with their ignorance of sectarian disputes and their innate distaste of regimentation, had a touching generosity of spirit and a profound respect for meditation.[85]

If this picture is true, it fits in with another distinctive quality of Jewish Maghrebi life mentioned earlier: that there was a great sense of communication and strong affinities, in folk life, with their neighbours. A vast literature, both personal and academic, has grown up on all these subjects, especially since the heavy immigration to Israel from eastern communities has stimulated the search for roots. For convenience we can look briefly at a few illustrations given by Chouraqui on the Moroccan background, recognizing that this was echoed elsewhere in the Maghreb.

In the Maghreb generally there were long-established channels of communication in language with neighbours, though with a distinctiveness that was always showing through. For a long time, and even in this century, the Jews in some sections of Morocco spoke Berber, echoing the Jewish–Berber links which have indicated to some that the Berbers were originally Jews, and to others vice versa. Apart from this, the Jews of the Maghreb spoke a Jewish–Arabic vernacular among themselves and 'ordinary' Arabic to others though with a somewhat archaic vocabulary derived, it is thought, from preserving older forms of the language within the *mellah*. The same kind of archaism in the use of Spanish became significant, as we shall see, among the Sephardim who had settled in Turkey and the Balkans.

As late as the 1930s, a survey showed that almost half of the surnames of Jews in the Maghreb were of Arabic or Berber origin. The very wide use of Arabic rather than Hebrew first names is a reflection of the same strong identification with the background.

The dress of Maghrebi Jews in these 'interim' centuries is copiously illustrated by what has survived in southern Morocco and southern

Tunisia until modern times. The men wore a long *jellaba*, a one-piece gown with many variants like the *zoha* (a gown worn by rabbis, 'without lapels or collars'), the *behdia* (a long gown 'richly embroidered with forty buttons'), or the *sarawal* ('breeches of satin or wool, narrow or wide according to fashion, and gathered at the waist or ankle').

The clothes of women were even more colourful, and have survived today in families and museums to universal delight. The hugely elaborate wedding-dresses are the most familiar; but the free use of striped silks, lace, gold-braided velours and coloured woollens lent themselves to graceful fashions for girls and young women, with a silk scarf embroidered with gold to encase the face and cover the hair, since 'uncovered hair was considered akin to nudity'.[86]

Links with the Arabs

Though one knows that the Jews were separated from their neighbours through anti-*dhimmi* regulations derived from the Covenant of Omar as well as through separate religious rituals, it is relevant also (Chouraqui reminds us) that 'close proximity permitted a complete interchange of folk-ways, customs and manners'. Like the Muslims, 'the Jews were given to the practices of witchcraft and superstition that belonged neither to the law of Moses nor of Mohammed'. All believed in talismans or other forms of magic to ward off the evil eye. Elaborate rituals of magic were performed by Jews when a male child was born. In another situation, a woman stricken by an inexplicable disease would take part in some highly stylized dance ceremonies, the object of which was to drive out the evil eye.

A particular link of Maghrebi Jews with their neighbours lay in their veneration of saints and holy places:

There were few villages and sites in the Maghreb that did not have the characteristic *kubba* of some local saintling to which the piety of the crowds was directed. The Jews adopted this Moslem custom. Moslem influence on their devotion was so strong that frequently there were no sharp lines between the saints venerated by the Moslems and those venerated by the Jews.

The veneration ceremonies, usually on the anniversary of the death of a local saint or some other outstanding holy man, were gatherings of great excitement known as *hilula* among the Jews. The most fervent occasions of this kind recalled the death in the Holy Land, in the far-off second century, of the legendary founder of Cabbala, Rabbi Simon ben Yohai. His death is recorded as having taken place on a minor feast-day, *Lag B'Omer*, some four weeks after the end of Passover; and on this day there would be massive gatherings all over the Maghreb at local shrines for prayers, feasting and the hope of miracles:

With the approach of the great day, the crowds would get thicker and thicker, entire families arriving from afar on foot, on mule-back. . . . Rich and poor mingled in their thousands in the same fervour; each had come to fulfil an earlier vow by participating in the sanctity of the occasion.

By the light of tapers and oil-lamps in honour of the saint, groups of people stood or squatted reciting psalms or loudly chanting hymns. As the night wore on, there was a tangible feeling among the crowds that the saint had come to life and was in their midst.

There is an undoubted echo of this spirit in the emergence in Israel today of a mass celebration by North Africans of a feast called *Mimuna* (or *Maimuna*) on the day after Passover. In origin, the Jews of some communities of Morocco used to eat fish and other foods while exchanging blessings on this day, perhaps as a substitute for a pilgrimage to the tomb in the Holy Land of Rabbi Maimon, father of Maimonides. In its new vastly expanded form, the *Mimuna* has become a great feast of self-expression for all North Africans in Israel, joyous but also with strong political overtones.

A descendant of Iraq

For contrast, we can turn now to echoes of life in the eastern communities as carried by a descendant – a rather special one – of Iraq. The echo in this case comes from a member of the great Sassoon family, who left behind him a slim volume published in England by his son in 1949 under the title *The Jews of Baghdad*. Where North African Jewish life emerges in the hands of Chouraqui as a colourful tapestry of political and social life, with particular attention paid to the involvement with the Muslim background, the Sassoon book is, on the surface, merely a collection of sketches of the lives of religious leaders going back many centuries, with details often extracted from hitherto unpublished manuscripts or old printed books. But in this approach we get an echo of the disciplined Jewish life that was loyally sustained in Iraq, and that descendants in many other Iraqi families have carried forward into the very different conditions of life in Israel today.

The Sassoon family were clearly a prime example of this spirit in the period we are discussing in this chapter – the sixteenth to eighteenth centuries – even though they were largely taken over into other fields closer to our time. The earliest Sassoon we know by name is Sheikh Sassoon ben Salah (b. 1750); but he was so rich and powerful by then that the family must have been leaders of the community long before this, in centuries with poorer records. Sheikh Sassoon himself was head of the Jewish community for forty years, and chief treasurer of the Ottoman pashas of Baghdad, a familiar combination of roles. He had already built up a great complex of textile mills and factories in India; and when his son David had to flee from Baghdad in 1828 because of the dangerous hostility of a pasha, Sheikh Sassoon followed him, the first stage in the Sassoon diaspora that led them into a vast industrial and trading expansion in India and the Far East within a few decades. As Britain was dominant in this whole area at the time, it was not long before members of the dynasty were finding their way to England to play a mixed – and sometimes exotic – role in the activities of high society. Some were under the special patronage of Queen Victoria's son Edward (later King Edward VII), who found it useful to have rich Jews in his entourage. As time went on, the family moved into politics and other fields. One of them, Sir Philip, made a point of winning the Derby several times. Another, Siegfried, was a poet who expressed a rather un-Baghdadi kind of life in a novel, *Memoirs of a Fox-Hunting Man*.

It might have been thought that the Sassoons had passed out of Jewish life, with Babylon forgotten. But the Jewish strain has a way of surviving. Among the eight grandsons of Sheikh Sassoon was one, Solomon, who held the huge business together in the Far East but was also an ardent Jewish scholar. His wife Flora (herself a Sassoon in origin) took this even further. She managed the business in Bombay after his death, but then moved to England, studied and lectured on the Talmud, and passed on these passions to her son David, author of the book mentioned above. He himself brought together one of the greatest collections of manuscripts of old Hebrew books in the world, and published learned editions of some of them. His son Solomon, who published his father's book posthumously, became a rabbi and settled finally in Jerusalem, where many of the most precious items of the Sassoon collection now form part of the University and National Library.

In sketching the lives of Iraq's Jewish leaders, Sassoon reaches back, inevitably, to Babylonian and Persian times, noting with particular pride the direct descent of Babylon's *resh galutha* from the royal house of King David, and adducing scholarly sources to indicate that there may have been a million Jews in Babylon in the seventh century. The aim is to illustrate the strength from earliest times of community life, with the leading Jew (the *Nasi*) always playing a powerful, if perilous, role with the government authorities.

Contemporary sources

To a Sassoon writing in this style, with ancient centuries as valid as the present, it is intriguing to read of the tribulations of a predecessor like the thirteenth-century Sa'd al-Dawla, who was court physician and vizier to the Mongol ruler, immensely powerful while he lived, but then attacked and executed through the envy of rivals. The special Sassoon touch is that details in the story – say of the descent of a Jewish *Nasi* from King David – are attested through ancient manuscripts adorning the Sassoon collection, which must be a particularly pleasant way of recovering history.

The echo of these centuries comes through more graphically, it must be said, when the manuscripts yield travellers' tales of actual conditions in Iraq. He tells us, for example, of a traveller called Zechariah el-Dahri who visited Baghdad in the second part of the sixteenth century and included the following in his report:

I travelled from Hormuz [Persia] to Babylon, which is situated on the Tigris. I carried 500 musical instruments for sale in order to make joyful the weary and the exiled. After forty days' journey on the sea I landed in Basra, where I boarded a boat for 20 shekels on the Tigris. Passing on the river I saw the grave of Ezra the scribe and that of the prophet Ezekiel. After another forty days' journey I arrived in Baghdad, where all my troubles and sorrow ceased. I hired temporary lodgings with board. This happened on a Friday. I went to the bath to refresh myself. Then I went to the Great Synagogue, where I offered my prayers and read out of the Book of the Lord. I vowed 20 gerah for oil for the perpetual lamp; then I went with the community to fulfil the duty of visiting the sick.[87]

It was always a local custom, Sassoon tells us, to visit the sick after divine service on the sabbath. It is a detail that illustrates the community spirit very graphically.

Voices from Turkey and Bulgaria

One seems very remote in the Iraqi scene and further east from any effect of the expulsions from Spain and Portugal. If one moves on to the centre of the Ottoman Empire in Turkey and the Balkans, where the direct Sephardi influence was momentous, the voices of descendants reflect this overwhelmingly; but though the general Sephardi influence has some uniformity, one hears varied echoes in what descendants tell us, as we saw in considering the unique history of the community of Rhodes.

For Turkey itself one can consider the voice of the historian Abraham Galante, who did more than anyone else to bring to life, through his researches, the astonishing sixteenth-century period in which the refugees from the Iberian peninsula were welcomed and then took over Jewish life in these many lands, creating what can be called a Sephardi world in a literal sense. Galante, as it happened, had a very distinctive life of his own, having been born in Turkey in 1873 at a time when this creaking empire was facing a modernizing revolution. He took an active part in this, but it was as an embodiment of the Sephardi tradition that he made his special mark.

Galante's family had fled from Spain in 1492 to Italy, where they acquired the name Galantuomo. Branches of the family lived all over the Near East, including cabbalist Safed in Galilee, until one branch settled as rabbis in Turkey. By Abraham's time a young man of that mobile interconnected Sephardi world was liable to be proficient, as *he* was, in a host of Near Eastern and western languages. With this, and a strong rabbinical background, he was able to find his way skilfully through mountainous archives of the old empire when he worked as a civil servant, professor and librarian. Out of all this came a huge flow of books and learned articles (mostly in Turkish or French) on the history of the Jews in Turkey, and in particular on the great sixteenth-century Mendes family led by Gracia and her nephew Joseph Nasi, whose power and achievements he could chronicle fully for the first time.

Galante's unearthing of ancient Ottoman archives was enormously valuable in solidifying the material that all historians have subsequently drawn on to get a picture of this vibrant Sephardi world. Yet from one point of view his personal involvement in the practical politics of Turkey in the late nineteenth century may have been a limiting factor, in diverting him from conveying the warmth and colour of the earlier Sephardi age as projected by other descendants. Being split between absorption in Jewish affairs and the local environment has always been a diaspora problem, which was due to be tackled in varying ways in the Sephardi world as Jews began to move towards emancipation.

One finds a particularly interesting illustration of this if one turns from Turkey to adjacent Bulgaria. The picture given of the past by a descendant, Vicki Tamir, in her book *Bulgaria and her Jews*, helps us to understand how it was that the Jews of this country opted so powerfully for migration to Israel in 1948.

Bulgaria was, admittedly, a special case, perhaps because of its unusual position, poised between the Slav and Near Eastern world. Jewish settlements in Bulgaria had begun in early times with the usual overflow from the Byzantine world. Subsequently there had been many Ashkenazi immigrants, with trade connections established from Germany to the East. It was perhaps surprising that the 1492 expulsions from Spain and Portugal took the Sephardi influence so powerfully to what might have seemed a remote country; yet this certainly happened, with Sephardi immigrants flowing in increasingly from Italy, Yugoslavia and Turkey, and becoming dominant rapidly over Ashkenazim and Romaniot. Ladino was soon spoken by all Bulgarian Jews. Many synagogues following the Sephardi rites were built, in some cases, it seems, on Spanish models. Folklore, including the famed *romancero*, expressed the Spanish traditions over a very wide front.

One has a picture from Tamir's book of a very prosperous community in economic terms. Together with those of other Balkan countries, Jewish textile industries in Bulgaria had a virtual monopoly in producing clothing for the janissaries of Turkey. The dyeing business was in Jewish hands. Arguments on commerce (loans, contracts, markets, etc.) came before a Jewish court. Court records and *responsa* document the scene profusely.

Connections on trade and scholarship were intense in the Sephardi world, though with special factors always at work. One archaic survival in Bulgaria is particularly interesting. We learn from eighteenth-century *responsa* that questions were put to rabbis there on the rights of the children of former slaves, a problem arising from the shortage of Jewish women (males usually predominate among refugees), which led young men to purchase female slaves and lead them to conversion. Slavery was still common in the East. Under Jewish medieval law, if a girl slave was taught Jewish law and belief and accepted conversion, expressed ritually in *tevilah* ('ablution'), she was given a certificate of release and then had full Jewish rights. It seems as if some questions on children could arise, as evidenced by the *responsa*; but this footnote to Bulgarian Sephardi life is interesting in its own right and perhaps also helps to explain why so many Jewish descendants of those lands have a blond or red-head colouring. It is obviously not enough to continue to assume rape of Jewish women by fair-haired Cossacks!

Tamir gives us many echoes of the Spanish links in her picture of the busy economic and social life of Bulgaria in this period, but she also opens up a line of thought on this which is worth considering. Most historians writing on the remarkable flow of Ladino folksongs, customs and sayings in the Sephardi world of Turkey and the Balkans concentrate on recovering and analysing the words and the music, a fascinating study which has become very intense and scientific in our time. But how was it, Tamir asks, that this ethnic concentration surfaced in the Ottoman world at that time? In Spain itself, she says, the cultural drive of the Jews had been expressed in two separate forms. On the sacred side, the Hebrew language had been the medium for scholarship and literature, especially poetry; on the secular side, the Jews had identified fully with the language and culture of the host nation. In the Ottoman Empire, by contrast, Hispanic culture, with Hebrew modifications, had itself become a dominant tradition, a matter she finds very puzzling:

What happened on Ottoman soil? Why did a sudden surge of popular energy and folk wisdom combine to create a unique Balkan–Sephardi body of secular humour, sayings, proverbs, songs, writings and customs?[88]

The question has never been explored, she believes, and she offers some ideas of her own. Was it the amalgamation of Romaniot,

Ashkenazim and Iberians that supplied the impulse, or did the peculiar tone and texture of the Ottoman environment provide a fertile ground for non-élitist creativity? Perhaps one should see what happened as a release of 'the Spanish popular spirit, finally loose after years of constraint under the boot of the Inquisition'. These are just conjectures, she agrees; yet something remarkable did happen. The fact is that 'after imposing their language and customs on the indigenous Jews', the immigrants, hand in hand with those new to Spanish culture, 'proceeded to forge what we know as the Balkan Sephardi, a Jew *sui generis*, quite distinct from the Sephardi of Amsterdam or the assimilated "grandee" of the New World'.

The musical traditions

The uniqueness of the Balkan Sephardi in Jewish life must, of course, be seen in proportion. Many customs, sayings and attitudes from that area were found in very similar form in North Africa and other parts of the Arabic–Sephardi world. A striking example is the similarity in the form of wedding practices, the heritage of which was as carefully preserved in Morocco and Yemen as in Salonika. The common feature here is that festive gatherings, accompanied by singing and dancing, would begin days before the final ceremony, and that the happy pair, having been escorted to the bridal bed with the same kind of singing and dancing, would stay indoors for a week before leaving the new home. In all these cases the bride, surrounded by family and neighbour women, would be subjected to many old customs, such as having a henna liquid, prepared by the women, applied to her fingers and toes. The bridal dress was ceremonial in its splendour, an heirloom from generation to generation. There were parallel folk rituals, and the use of herbal and other remedies when no child was signalled in a reasonable time; and the festivities of food, singing and dancing when a son was circumcised had the same wildly ecstatic style. Many of the songs for these occasions have been adapted into forms of Sephardi popular music, sung with light orchestras by matinée idols; but side by side with this researchers have devoted great energy in the Balkan Sephardi lands to recording authentic versions by skilled singers with only the correct accompaniment of drums and perhaps the 'ud', an ancient instrument similar to the lute on which Sephardi Jews – from Greece to Iraq and Iran – became the most expert players.

A descendant who has specialized in this field is the ethno-musicologist Amnon Shiloah, whose family came from Syria, and who, with colleagues in various lands, has deepened the study of old Arabic and Near Eastern music immeasurably. In one of his record-ings, for example, we hear very ancient *bakkashot* (prayer-songs of supplication) which Moroccan and Syrian Jews developed greatly, side by side with songs for the women's pre-wedding rituals as sung in Yemen, and among them *romancero* lovesongs of the most exquisite feeling as sung, say, in Salonika or Sarajevo.[89]

In all these cases we learn now where the music came from. The *bakkashot*, built around medieval Hebrew poetry and lasting well over three hours of a long winter's night when sung, offer impromptu variations of a complex system of vocal and instrumental music in a style which originated in Spain during Muslim rule. The circumcision song we are given is from Tunis, but derives its musical style from the Middle East. The music of the Bar Mitzvah song, sung after his first haircut – 'Do not laugh at me / This is my first song / And if my brother was not dear to me / You would not hear my voice . . .' – is stylistically from Andalusia. The henna song, in honour of the bride who has been led veiled through the village by women holding candles, is Yemeni local music, to the percussion of *tof* (drum) and *sahn* (copper-tray). A Ladino lovesong here, in which a woman laments her lover's desertion, is a traditional Turkish melody. Another, *On a Moonlit Night*, 'is in the Phrygian mode common to many Spanish songs'.

It is clear enough even in these brief references that though the folk background of the Sephardi world did not function in watertight compartments, the influence of the local background was always paramount. In music, for example, one cannot even reach back to the longest continuous settlement of Jews in the Middle East – which was in Iraq – to find a dominant strain that affected all the other areas. Amnon Shiloah has, in fact, examined this very problem with great intensity, but has concluded, in his book on the musical tradition of Iraqi Jews, that old travellers' tales which speak of an unbroken musical tradition in Babylon going back to Temple times cannot be accepted. The recital of prayers and religious poetry, and the cantillation of Bible readings, does seem very old; but this is as far as one can go, in spite of arguments for a link by Saadyah *Gaon* in the eighth century and the acute observations of the traveller Benjamin of Tudela in the twelfth:

The simple fact is that neither they nor we can determine with any certainty what fate overtook the ancient music of Israel, or the age of the melodies that were being heard when they wrote, or are heard today.[90]

The form of the songs

In the end it is the relationship to Spain which raises the most interesting issues. The anthropologist Raphael Patai says, in an essay on Sephardi folklore, that the words of the Ladino ballads, with their strongly erotic character, are derived from old Spanish epics of the eleventh and twelfth centuries which were later cut up into shorter songs in the fifteenth century and adapted by the Balkan Sephardim in this form. It was mostly because they were sung by the Sephardim at weddings that their erotic character was appropriate.[91]

The contrast with Yiddish folksongs is very great, replacing soft sentiment by passion. Here is one, quoted by Patai, that opens innocently enough:

Una ija tiene el reyes,	(The king had a daughter,
Una ija regalada.	A delicate daughter.
Mitiola en altas tores,	He placed her in a high tower,
Por tenerla bien guardala.	To keep her well guarded.)

But the tone soon changes. The princess sends out a slave to entice a 'reaper' passing by to come and help with the wheat and the rye:

> 'Where shall I sow the wheat?
> Where shall I reap the rye?'
> 'In her body sow the wheat,
> And in her lap the rye.'

This is, of course, only one subject, though repeated with many variations. The Spanish style — an 'innocent' opening followed by a very long and leisurely development — is evident equally in songs whose content draws heavily on Jewish Midrashic tales. A choice example is a circumcision song whose subject is the birth of the patriarch Abraham, saved miraculously, by divine intervention, from being put to death at birth by the mythical enemy of the Jews, Nimrod the hunter:

Quando el rey Nimrod, el campo salia,	(When Nimrod the king went out to the field
Miraba en el cello y en la istiaria.	He looked to the sky and the stars.
Vido luz santa en la judiria,	He saw a sacred light among the Jews,
Que avia de nacir Abraham avinu.	For our father Abraham was about to be born.)

When Spanish scholars came across these Sephardi songs in relatively recent times, they began to investigate them with patriotic as well as academic fervour, for they saw in them, and in Sephardi life generally, important keys to their own past. The surprise was that the refugees, driven from their homes at the end of the fifteenth century, had not simply kept alive a nostalgic attachment to Spain, but had, as it were, 'frozen' the form of the attachment at the moment of departure, so that what became their spoken language throughout the Sephardi world had preserved in aspic the Spanish language – and the referential background – of that century. In Spain itself the language had inevitably changed in vocabulary and style during the ensuing five centuries, just as, in England, English moved on from the days of Shakespeare. This by itself made the Sephardim immensely interesting to the Spaniards; but there were ramifications taking it still further.

The Sephardim of the Balkans and elsewhere used, in effect, two 'Spanish-type' languages: Ladino, the universal vernacular, and Castilian, the pure Spanish, which educated Sephardim still retained. Ladino, as noted earlier, was a flexible language that adapted words from Hebrew and local sources, though it remained far more Spanish in character than Yiddish (which had a similar vernacular function) remained German. The mystery of how Ladino spread as a vernacular in the Middle East so powerfully is probably explained by the fact that the Jews in Spain itself had already developed within their own communities a Ladino vernacular. This was based on the Castilian they had originally heard, but which was now somewhat archaic. These archaic elements became a natural part of Ladino and, when identified by Spanish scholars, are naturally of great interest to them. There were thus two forms of old Castilian preserved and used by the Sephardim. One form could be identified in Ladino; the other was preserved when Castilian was used by the Sephardi learned classes, and in this case 'frozen' in the style of 1492.

The more the Sephardi world and its songs were studied by the scholars, the more interesting they became; but the issues were in no sense merely academic. They had, in fact, a most dramatic historical outcome in the 1930s; and I, though only a Litvak witness to the scene, must report it now to round up this discursive story of the Sephardi diaspora.

The return to Spain

The expulsion of Jews from Spain in 1492 had been an act for which the monarch had been directly responsible. The monarchy and its dynastic struggles remained central to Spanish history; but a republic was finally set up in 1931, with a mission to purge Spain from reactionary deeds of the past. The new policy was to give recognition to all elements of Spanish society, past as well as present; and this included re-gathering into Spain those Jews who had been expelled in the past but had maintained their loyalty in language and sentiment. All genuine Sephardim, it was stated, could now return; and as an expression of this new attitude, the government announced that it would stage a great *fiesta* in Cordoba, in April 1935, in celebration of the 800th anniversary of the birth there in 1135 of 'the great Spanish and Jewish philosopher Maimonides'. Lectures would be delivered by Jews and Spaniards alike on all aspects of the Sephardi tradition. The government would offer banquets in honour of the visitors. As a supreme tribute to Maimonides himself, a special bullfight would be staged in his name.

There may have been ironies, but it was nevertheless a supreme moment in Jewish history. The Expulsion of 1492 was being reversed. Even with Hitler now beginning to put into effect his evil plans for the Jews of Germany, the Spanish action generated a tiny ray of hope. Portia's words seemed to say it well:

> How far that little candle throws his beams!
> So shines a good deed in a naughty world.

As the opening day of the *fiesta* drew near, the hotels of Cordoba were awash with Sephardim from Greece, Turkey, Yugoslavia, Palestine and indeed the whole of the Middle East. The Arabic-speaking Sephardim of North Africa had crossed the Straits of

Gibraltar *en masse*. Ashkenazim were equally seized by the drama and had come from far afield. I was present myself as a representative of the University of Oxford.

The first ceremonial reception opened with an elaborate address of welcome in Spanish from the governor of the province; and then the first Jewish speaker rose to reply. He was the chief rabbi of Sarajevo, a bearded man of immense dignity. As he began to speak a shudder went through the Spanish audience. Most of them were scholars and knew that what the rabbi said would be in some sort of Spanish. What they didn't know was what it would sound like. Their faces showed their wonder, and soon they explained. The rabbi spoke a Castilian they had read but never heard, rich and ripe with the archaisms of the fifteenth century. It was as if a dignitary of the Court of Queen Elizabeth had risen to speak in his own language while receiving an honorary degree today at the University of Oxford. Hearing Castilian as spoken by the rabbi was to relive Spanish history in all its glory.

The session came to an end. In magniloquent language the presiding Spanish dignitary invited all present to move into the adjoining hall for a great banquet that awaited us. The most lavish hospitality was to be accorded to the visiting Jews in a huge banquet of lobsters and other choice shellfish. The rabbis recoiled in horror. In five hundred years the hosts had forgotten that shellfish is anathema to orthodox Jews. But it was still only a small hiccup to a great occasion.

There would always be problems in understanding the extraordinary relationship of the Jews to Spain and Portugal. For the most part one had to be content with the magic that had emerged in a golden age of scholarship and poetry, and that had somehow prolonged itself in new forms during what was at first a bitter exile. All the shellfish and bullfights in the world would not disturb the vibrant Jewish echoes of this legacy.

14 *The Colonial Era*

At the beginning of the nineteenth century the two streams of Jewish existence – Ashkenazim in the north, and varieties of Sephardim to the south and east – seemed to have established a set pattern for the future. They had mingled and overlapped in the past, and had always had one common feature: that the vast majority in both cases were impoverished and often persecuted masses. Yet there was a crucial difference. The Ashkenazim – mostly at this time some two million Jews in Russia and Austria-Hungary – were pointed towards huge expansion and modernization, whereas the Jews of eastern lands had shrunk from their earlier domination in numbers and position, and seemed destined for further isolation and degradation.

By the time the century was over the Ashkenazi stream had more than achieved what seemed its certain future. The component in Russia and Austria-Hungary had grown fantastically to more than seven million, out of a total in Ashkenazi lands of more than nine million Jews. Their history had not been trouble free, but they had certainly given decisive evidence of assured economic and social progress. The eastern Jews, in contrast, seemed to have moved still further down the ladder: few in number and bleak in outlook.

Yet a revolution had taken place in the eastern lands during this century; and with hindsight one can see how it established a base on which the descendants of this world would build in the even more troubled times of the century to follow. It is in this framework that we will evaluate briefly in this chapter elements in the eastern scene during the nineteenth century that were positive for the future.

One approach is to build on Bernard Lewis's suggestion that the history of the Middle East in the Islamic period can be seen under the category of three decisive invasions. The first was that of the Arab Muslims in the seventh to eighth centuries, which brought a new religion, a new language and a new political and social order to the

Middle East. The second major transformation is seen fully developed in the conquests of the Mongols and Turks in the thirteenth century, which set up elaborately administered kingdoms and empires, and produced 'a new kind of Islam, more structured, more hierarchic, more concerned with order and with orthodoxy'.[92]

The third invasion was from Europe. It can be seen as beginning quite early in military terms, when the Muslim advance began to be held back in decisive battles, and was followed by successful Christian attacks – and the seizure of Muslim territory – in Spain and Portugal, in the Balkans, and around the Black Sea (by the Russians). This still left the Ottoman Empire as a sprawling giant; but there was a new type of attack – an invasion of influence – which became forceful in the nineteenth century and was destined to bring about a transformation equal in scope to the earlier two.

The European invasion

This European 'invasion' had long been operative as an overflow of the huge international trade that had developed around Ottoman Turkey. In its earliest stage it formalized the guarantees that different rulers began to give each other to ensure that their traders and agents could move in and out of each other's territories free of taxes and dangers to their person. Suleiman the Magnificent (1520–66) had made the first of these agreements with Venice in 1521, and subsequently with other countries. Non-Muslim merchants – Christian or Jewish – arriving from abroad would not be regarded as of *dhimmi* status and would enjoy foreign protection. In time this extremely valuable right spread into 'Capitulation' agreements: the granting of foreign nationality to certain residents, who would thus secure foreign protection. It was not as formal as this when first set up; but by the end of the eighteenth century there were many rights of protection to those engaged in foreign trade, and a readiness of the foreign countries to expand the forms of protection they were willing to extend to non-Muslims in Ottoman lands, as a way of asserting their political influence.

Inevitably there was great rivalry among the Christian countries in winning this influence. It was, in effect, the onset of the colonial era in the Near and Middle East. From the end of the seventeenth century the French had been successful in securing these rights for merchants or agents in Aleppo, where they were known as 'Francos'. By the beginning of the nineteenth century the consuls of the Christian countries – those of France and Austria-Hungary most active at first – were extending their protection freely, a process due to expand greatly in that century, with Russia, Britain and Italy joining in with enthusiasm to play a part in what was to become the dismemberment of the weakening giant. But this form of increasing influence was only one expression of what has been called 'a veritable metamorphosis of the Middle East' in the nineteenth century.[93]

One element in the changing picture was a great increase in the numbers of visitors from Christian countries, partly as a by-product of the expansion of international trade, but also linked to the increased popularity of travel, particularly to classical and eastern lands. The reports that many – mostly Christians – wrote of the conditions they found give a vivid picture, on a much bigger scale than ever before, of Jewish life in these lands. These fascinating writings of scholars, aristocrats, clerics, diplomats and others have been widely published, and are very relevant to understanding the change that was to happen in the nineteenth century; for though the earlier reports are mostly cheerful and admiring of the Jews, the later ones paint a depressing picture, giving one a clear idea of the decline and the need to find ways of making something like a fresh start.

To illustrate, Bernard Lewis prints a letter from a French monk in 1681 describing how 'skilful and hardworking' the Jews of Turkey are:

There is no considerable family among the Turks and the foreign merchants which does not have a Jew in its service, whether to value merchandise and assess its quality, to serve as interpreter, or to give advice on everything that happens.[94]

The emphasis in all these early reports is on the liveliness of the Jews, their devotion to study, and their superiority to the other non-Muslim traders. In time, however, a very different note is being struck. A nineteenth-century writer called Ubicini – typical of many – talks of the Jews as apathetic, indifferent to study, and outclassed by their rivals in lucrative trade. It is admitted that the Jews, unlike these rival Greeks and Armenians, live lives that are free of moral scandal; but they are poverty-stricken and dirty.

Jewish decline

Though other non-Muslims were subject to the humiliation of the *dhimmi* position, the Jew seemed to suffer most. A British traveller in Istanbul in 1828 says this, and contrasts their 'pusillanimity' with the attitude of the Jews in England who would strike back (as expert pugilists) at any insult, whereas in Turkey the smallest children are free and indeed encouraged to throw stones at Jews without reply. If a child spits on a Jew, he must be silent. 'It would be more than his life was worth to strike a Mohammedan.'[95]

What had happened to bring this about after the sense of liberation that had been generated among the Sephardim at their first reception? To some extent it reflected the weakening of the Ottoman Empire, and indeed of the Islamic world as a whole. This was not cushioned for Jews, at this stage, by support from co-religionists from abroad, unlike the Christians who had this help. But the real weakness was among the Jews themselves; and Lewis offers the view that it represented a drying up of the creativity that had found expression in the circumstances of the great immigration of the Sephardim following the expulsions from Spain and Portugal. For a brief period the learning, skills and contacts that they brought with them had stimulated the whole of that world, and had attracted also a flow of Jewish immigration from other parts of Europe. Now all immigration had dried up, and with it the basis of stimulating contacts outside their own community. Their nostalgic preservation of Ladino, which they wrote only in Hebrew characters, had a cutting-off effect, however interesting and charming it might be in folklore terms. The Jews of this world felt no need to speak the local languages or to get involved in local affairs. Their share of international trade had dwindled, partly because of their lack of the support that their rivals received from Christian countries in Europe.

One factor in their decline had been the fiasco of the Shabbetai Zevi drama, which had left most Jews in despair. Another new element was the beginning of direct anti-Jewish accusations, imported from Europe by Christians. This is not to say that there was universal poverty and discrimination, but that there had been a true decline, due to leave a disquieting legacy later.

There was another factor which would, in due course, make the problem more difficult still for the Jews. The European 'invasion' in the form of increased influence from Christian countries began, in the nineteenth century, to open up this world to an awareness of secular education and political freedom in the form of incipient nationalism, all of which presented barriers to Jewish participation. In time, it was the growth of nationalism that was to disturb the position of the Jews most decisively in all the eastern countries.

Everything mentioned here so far had a negative effect on the position of the Jews in the first half of the nineteenth century. Yet a transformation did occur, in different forms and at a varying pace, leading this eastern world, and the Jews within it, towards an emergence from the virtual medievalism that had characterized it.

The fight for rights

It is ironic to recognize that the Jews were due to benefit because many of the 'negative' factors also had a positive side. The increased influence of the Christians in the Ottoman world is an example of this. The *dhimmi* status itself, despite its harsh aspect, had brought some benefits, in that 'protected' non-Muslims could make contacts more easily than others in international trade, and thus were increasingly able, as noted above, to receive the protection of foreign governments at home or when they travelled. Even more directly, the Jews were to benefit when Christian influence from abroad persuaded the Turkish authorities to begin the process of granting civil rights to all their subjects. The landmark was the promulgation by the sultan, in 1839, of an edict giving complete security to 'the lives, honour and fortunes' of all inhabitants, 'irrespective of whatever religion or sect they may belong to'. In 1856 this was taken further in an edict banning from official usage all abusive and derogatory references to non-Muslims. Side by side with this, the introduction of the *millet* (independent religious authority) system gave each individual non-Muslim community official representation through a designated leader. For the Jews, this leader was the *haham-bashi* (chief rabbi).

A further landmark was the reform which abolished the *jizya*, the special tax paid by *dhimmis*, which had always been a symbol of humiliation both as a financial burden and in the way it had to be paid. It was at first replaced by a tax levied ostensibly to relieve *dhimmis* of their new liability for military service; and it was not until 1909 that monetary payment of this kind was finally abolished.

This march towards reform was a clear echo of the emancipation process that had gradually spread in Europe since the French Revolution. In so far as it reached the Jews in Turkey, they were beneficiaries on the backs, as it were, of Christian influence; but it was a slow process. Under the Ottoman system, governors of provinces throughout the empire were virtually independent, and many had no sympathy with the reforms of Constantinople. The issues involved can be seen clearly in the story of the Damascus Affair of 1840, when the benefits and limitations of influence from abroad were fully displayed.

At the basis of the affair lay the importation of European anti-Semitism, which for centuries had included the extraordinary idea that Jews commit murder of gentiles at Passover time in order to use the blood of the victim for ritual purposes. This monstrous libel had not appeared seriously in the Muslim world until in 1840 an Italian Capuchin friar, living in Damascus, and his Muslim servant disappeared. The local Christians, supported by the French consul, accused the Jews of having murdered him to obtain his blood for the Passover rituals. A Jewish barber was arrested, and under torture 'confessed' and implicated a number of leading members of the community. All were arrested and tortured. Two died, one embraced Islam, and the others 'confessed'. Sixty-three Jewish children were taken hostage under the orders of the pasha to force their parents to reveal the whereabouts of the blood.

The story, feeding on latent anti-Jewish feeling among Muslims, spread through the eastern world, leading to riots against the Jews in many places. The news reached the West at a time when leading Jews in a number of countries had already won an assured position and could try both privately and publicly to get the accusations dismissed. James de Rothschild, who was honorary consul for Austria-Hungary in Paris, acted urgently to this end. In London the protest was led by Sir Moses Montefiore, a friend of Queen Victoria and the acknowledged leader of British Jewry.

Montefiore already had a unique position in Jewish and British public life. A Sephardi by birth and related through his mother to the famed Mocatta family, he had married into the leading Ashkenazi family in England and was, through this, a brother-in-law of the head of the English Rothschilds. His own fortune, though not on the Rothschild scale, had risen swiftly through financial operations linked to Britain's growing domestic and international power in the first half of the nineteenth century. In 1824, at the age of forty, he had retired from daily business work with the resolve, inspired by religious faith, to spend the rest of his life in helping his fellow Jews, particularly those in distressed conditions in Europe and the East. Work for the Holy Land was central to this aim; and in 1827, accompanied by his wife Judith, he had made the first of seven visits to Palestine, travelling always with introductions from the British government. After Queen Victoria's accession to the throne in 1837 she, too, always added her endorsements to the visits he undertook to Palestine and elsewhere, to talk directly to foreign dignitaries, including the Sultan, the Kaiser, and the Czar of Russia. He carried on this work for sixty years after his retirement, dying in 1885 after passing his hundredth birthday.

Though Montefiore was quite exceptional in his Jewish responsibility and his political contacts, his position in England reflected to a considerable degree the prosperity and sustained Jewish devotion that had been achieved by Sephardi communities in various parts of the western world – notably in Holland, France and the USA – in sharp contrast to the decline into which the Sephardi masses of the East had fallen by this time. In this respect the Damascus Affair of 1840, and the activities undertaken from the West to help in the East, represent a turning point in the nineteenth century.

Colonial rivalries

The development of the affair was symbolic also in another form, as a reflection of the rivalry that the Great Powers were engaged in to win increasing influence in the East. This helps to explain how it was that in England Montefiore was able to win overwhelming support over the affair, with a mass meeting at London's Mansion House (the home of the Lord Mayor) and denunciations by Parliament and the Church of what was called the 'barbaric treatment' of the Jews of Damascus. By contrast, little was said or done officially in France. France was, by now, the protecting power of Catholics in Syria, and the libel had, in fact, been stimulated by their consul in Damascus. Montefiore was to find, as he sought redress from the governmental authorities in the eastern countries, that France was unwilling to imperil its favoured position there.

This even inhibited the action of leading French Jews to some extent; but the French–Jewish statesman Adolphe Crémieux joined Montefiore in travelling, with their expert 'oriental secretaries', to Egypt, to confront Mohammad Ali Pasha, the powerful governor of

Egypt whose authority covered also Syria and Palestine. The mission was successful in that those charged in Damascus were released. On their journey home the delegation was received in Constantinople by the Sultan, who was persuaded to issue a *firman* denouncing the blood libel in clear terms. It has to be said that, though released, the prisoners were never declared innocent of the charges. The ultimate sadness was that the blood libel now became a familiar occurrence in many Muslim lands, though not in Morocco or Iran, presumably because of the smaller Christian presence.

The colonial rivalries of the Great Powers, which were to have important consequences for the Jews of the eastern communities, had first emerged in clear form much earlier in Egypt. The French under Napoleon had occupied Egypt in 1798–1801, but had been forced by allied British and Turkish forces to withdraw, with Britain emerging in an increasingly strong position of suzerainty as the century moved on. The opening of the Suez Canal in 1869, and Egypt's huge indebtedness to western finance through the profligacy of her rulers, led Britain to assume direct control of the country in 1883. In the First World War Egypt was made a British Protectorate, later becoming a monarchy, with a close British alliance that lasted in various forms until the rule of Nasser.

Against this background the Jews in Egypt had, at first, a nebulous position, but one that offered them new opportunities as increased prosperity under orderly British rule made some mark. Jewish immigrants were attracted from Turkey, Greece and other countries, forming a rich assortment of communities, and exploiting to the full the chance to secure a passport, or some form of protection, from one of the Great Powers. It was a cosmopolitan life in which Jews, rich and poor, found a good footing until the more drastic events of the middle of the twentieth century forced an emigration that ultimately became almost total.

West of Egypt, the main intervening colonial powers were Italy and France, though Spain had important interests adjoining Morocco. To consider Italy first, her direct intervention in North Africa did not begin until 1911, when she invaded Tripoli and subsequently tried to take full possession of the rest of what is now Libya, to forestall German ambitions in the area. Though many Libyan Jews lived in very poor conditions under Italian rule, educational opportunities increased and life was peaceful enough until Mussolini's Fascism enforced anti-Jewish measures in 1936, followed by infinitely worse conditions during the occupation by Nazi forces later. But though these war conditions and later 'pogroms' in Libya inevitably turned the Jews there towards emigration, the earlier life had had satisfactions which left a warm Sephardi legacy for the Jews of Libya.

Influence of the French

Italy's involvements were, however, small in scale compared with the major interventions of France in all the North African countries. The most startling story was of Algeria, where the future of the Jewish masses was changed by France, during this century, as if by a magic wand.

France's intervention here followed the usual pattern of getting involved in trade and then finding a way through one excuse or another to back this up with military force, after which power was retained either through their own rule or through nominees. With Algeria this programme was developed with startling self-confidence. France simply invaded the country in 1830 and issued a declaration guaranteeing freedom to all inhabitants, all religions and all trade and property. For the Jews this alone clearly changed the inferior position they had occupied for centuries in relation to the Muslims there. But there was much more to come. In 1870, after a series of intermediate steps, France issued a decree giving full French citizenship to all Jews 'indigenous to the departments of Algeria', a truly momentous development.

France's plans received further formal expression when she established a protectorate over Tunisia in 1881, and over Morocco in 1912; but by then it had long been recognized that France had become, *de facto*, the dominant trade and cultural power in the whole of the Maghreb, with further influences extending eastward, particularly in Syria. Most of the leading Jews of the West saw this as a beneficent influence on the position of the eastern Sephardim, or at the very least as a way of opening the door to such help. Even if what had happened was patently an expression of French foreign policy, it had the benefit of encouraging similar cultural effort by rival powers. All this helped to take the eastern Sephardim some way along the road to freedom before they were engulfed in the post-war anti-Jewish outbreaks of the Muslim world.

It is important to put French policy towards the Jews of Algeria into historical perspective if one is to understand the later developments of Muslim–Jewish relations in North Africa, and the legacy of bitterness that was left. Though the original declaration of the French when they invaded Algiers in 1830 was in general terms an espousal for all of 'the rights of man', the subsequent policies had within them a more traditional element in which the Jews were being looked on as a separate community, with much internal self-government and rights related to this. They had always been a separate community within the Ottoman Empire, and the French only reaffirmed this at first with the invasion of 1830. The excuse for invasion, as it happened, had turned on the attempt of the Dey (ruler) of Algiers to help Algiers' chief trading company, run by a Jew, Joseph Bacri, to secure money he was owed by France. In argument, the Dey had angrily struck the French consul with his fly whisk. The invasion followed this insult; and now, ironically, it was the French who supported Bacri, setting him up as 'head of the Jewish nation of Algiers', investing him with powers to police the Jews of the city, carry out the judgements of the courts and collect taxes.

Though the change to French authority was to prove momentous, the separate status was sustained even when the Jewish courts fell increasingly under French rule. The Jews were on their way, however, to something entirely new. The first step was a declaration in 1845 giving Jews the same kind of religious self-rule, under a Consistory, that Jews enjoyed in France itself as full citizens. By now the Jews of Algiers had absorbed French culture deeply and were themselves pressing for full French citizenship, as distinct from the status of the Muslims of Algiers. The leading Jews of France, including the very influential Adolphe Crémieux, supported this; and after a long campaign this right was finally given to Algerian Jews by the French government in 1870.

Education and welfare

The concentrated support of French Jews for disadvantaged Jews in other countries, and especially those in the Near East, had received expression in 1860 by the formation of an organization, the *Alliance Israélite Universelle*, which announced that its first aim was to seek 'emancipation' for Jews everywhere, to parallel the status now firmly achieved in western Europe. To give French citizenship to the Jews of

Algeria was, of course, not a normal form of emancipation; but it would always be difficult to give local parity to Jews living in a Muslim country, where a non-Muslim was held to be permanently inferior by the rules of Islam and the custom of centuries. It is true that as the century moved on something like emancipation seemed on its way in some of the *edot ha-mizrach*, but the pattern was very uneven. The Sephardim in the more 'European' communities like Greece or Bulgaria reached towards this with some assurance, in contrast to a self-contained community like Iraq, whose Jews taxed themselves to pay for their own education and welfare, and had a good internal life, even if externally they were, to quote Norman Stillman, 'in a continual state of insecurity'.[96]

It was good, therefore, that the French leaders put civil rights first, embracing, as this did, the challenge to help Jews everywhere and on all subjects. The *Alliance*, with Adolphe Crémieux as its president from 1863 to 1880, had soon become effective. A similar organization, though much smaller in range, was founded in England in 1871 as the Anglo–Jewish Association, working jointly on overseas matters with the representative body, the Board of Deputies of British Jews, headed by Sir Moses Montefiore. All three organizations joined in diplomatic work for the Jews during the Congress of Berlin in 1878, particularly in securing a promise of civil rights for the Jews (mainly Sephardim) in Balkan countries. In due course work for Jews in all parts of the Ottoman Empire was broadened through the co-operation of other organizations, including the Jewish Colonial Association (ICA) founded by the enormously wealthy Baron de Hirsch in 1891, and the American Jewish Committee, established in 1906 by a number of important public-spirited Jews of German–Jewish origin with the same aim.

The expertise of refugee organizations like HIAS (Hebrew Immigrant Aid Society) continued to help some poor Sephardi immigrants from North Africa even after refugee work as a whole began to be concentrated overwhelmingly on helping Jews from eastern Europe, following the massive pogroms in Russia in the 1880s. This emphasis on rescue work was broadened during the First World War to cope with the disastrous effects on Jews of the German invasions of eastern Europe in 1914. A new rescue organization which was founded in America for this purpose in 1914 under the name American Joint Distribution Committee ('the Joint') became of great importance, with its range widened still further in the 1930s when the need arose to rescue the Jews of Germany from the growing Nazi horrors.

But though the need to help the Jews of the eastern lands had now been overtaken by the crises in Europe, the pioneer work of the *Alliance* had already made a decisive mark in the Sephardi lands, particularly in establishing schools in many of these countries through which generations of poor Jews were able to emerge from ignorance and poverty with qualifications that could lead to a more satisfying life in their homelands or overseas.

It is usually said that the Jews of the Muslim world were more literate than their neighbours because of the attention given to reading and study in the religious schools which Jewish boys had to attend. Be that as it may, the key to the future now lay in secular schooling.

The first special school for Jewish boys under a French director was actually opened in Algiers as early as 1832, with a school for girls soon after, both of them without the expected objection of the rabbis. Algeria was, of course, a special case, with Jewish children soon going to French-style state-operated schools and obtaining a high-quality education. It was more remarkable that schools sponsored by the *Alliance*, and teaching 'ordinary' subjects under close control from headquarters in Paris, spread rapidly all over the Muslim lands. The first was opened in Tetuan (Morocco) in 1862, and became a model for all which followed. The curriculum combined religious and all secular subjects, taught in Hebrew, French and the language of the country. *Alliance* schools had opened rapidly in Tangier, Damascus, Baghdad and Jerusalem, together with an agricultural school near Jaffa in 1870. By 1910 there were 120 *Alliance* schools in the Near and Middle East, under a carefully organized system in which prospective teachers, selected from all over this area, were educated in training-schools in Turkey and the *Alliance* seminary in France, and then sent to teach in the local *Alliance* schools, usually in some country other than their own. Emphasis was put, also, on the participation of the teachers in social work; and the reports of the teachers and inspectors from all over the Sephardi world illustrate how actively this side of their work was pursued.

In a sense the spread of these schools (accompanied later by the establishment of some similar schools under English, and then German, sponsorship) was part of a general educational process in which schools operated by Christian missionaries were also very effective in producing an élite cadre of students to play a role in administration and cultural emancipation throughout all these lands.

If it is true, as is often said, that the Jews benefited from this to an exceptional degree, it also sowed some seeds of discord for the future. Christians and Jews alike, Stillman says, came to have a place in the economic life of the Muslim world that was far out of proportion to their numbers or their social status in the general population, and this particularly affected the Jews:

> Their Western ties and their economic success were deeply resented by the Muslim majority. It was this conspicuous over-achievement on the part of some *dhimmis* that would contribute to their undoing as a group in the 20th century with the rise of nationalism in the Arab world.[97]

Forms of protection

This sombre look forward casts a shadow over the nineteenth-century march of the eastern Sephardim towards emancipation, but it must not be allowed to lessen the achievement in its own terms before wholly adverse factors rose destructively. We have already noted that there was no fixed pattern throughout the eastern world, but parallel developments, both favourable and unfavourable, can be clearly seen.

In broad historical terms, it was a bonus that the colonial era, which had started with Napoleon in Egypt and continued in various forms through the nineteenth and twentieth centuries in the form of protectorates, monarchies and mandates, lasted so long. There can be no doubt, Bernard Lewis writes in *The Jews of Islam*, that the original imposition of imperial rule – in British-ruled Aden, Egypt and Iraq; in French-ruled Algeria, Tunisia and Morocco; in Italian-ruled Libya – 'ushered in a new era of Jewish educational progress and material prosperity'.[98] We have noted earlier some aspects of French influence, and one could also cite some positive effects of British influence in these countries.

A perhaps unfamiliar example is the way the British came to express special concern for the Jews of the Middle East and North Africa. This was a reflection, to some extent, of the liberal and humanitarian principles so respected in Victorian England, but it also involved strategic considerations. France and Russia, Britain's two main imperial rivals, had used religion to achieve a special place in the Ottoman world. The French saw themselves as the natural champions of Roman Catholics in Ottoman lands, while the Russians protected Orthodox Christians, both intervening with the Ottoman authorities

RHODES

Above left The entrance to the synagogue in Rhodes, which after the Expulsion had a thriving Sephardi community. Known as 'little Jerusalem', the island was thronged with scholars and financiers and became particularly famous for silk manufactures.

Above right The memorial to the Jews of Rhodes killed by the Nazis in 1944-5.

GIBRALTAR

A Jewish woman of Gibraltar in a fiesta dress, drawn by J. F. Lewis in 1835.

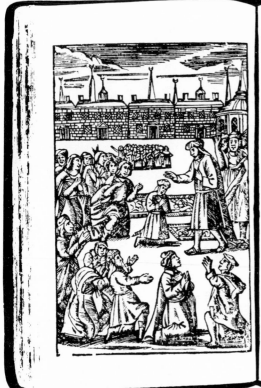

THE
Counterfeit Meffiah,
OR,
Falfe Chrift
OF THE
JEWS
AT
SMYRNA; in the Year 1666.

Written by an Englifh Perfon of Quality
there Refident.

According to the Predictions of feveral Chriftian
Writers, efpecially of fuch who Comment on
the Apocalyps, or Revelations, this Year 1666. was
to prove a year of Wonders, and ftrange Revolutions
in the World, and particularly of Bleffings to the Jews,
either

An illustration from a book about Shabbetai Zevi, 'the false Christ of the Jews', published in Smyrna in 1666.

Above left This Jewish doctor has been identified as Moses Hamon, physician to Suleiman the Magnificent (1520–66). He wears a tall red hat, common among Sephardim in Turkey.

Above right This drawing of a Jewish merchant in Turkey first appeared in a book in 1568. The long clothes were typical of other Turks, but the turban was normally yellow to mark that it was worn by a Jew.

Joseph Nasi (d. 1579), the great Marrano financier who was appointed Duke of Naxos by the sultan of Turkey, sought to establish industry in Tiberias as a way of encouraging Jewish settlement in the Holy Land.

Above Dona Gracia Nasi, Marrano stateswoman, portrayed in a contemporary medallion by Pastorino de Pastorini in 1553. She worked with her nephew (and son-in-law) Joseph Nasi to help the refugees from Spain and Portugal.

Right A Jewish orphanage in Tchorlou, Turkey, 1921, run by the *Alliance Israélite Universelle*.

A lithograph by van Lennep of a Jewish marriage in Turkey, 1862.

An elaborately carved and uptilted tombstone in a Jewish cemetery at Altunizade, Istanbul.

An exhibition of the work of Jewish schoolgirls in Smyrna, 1926.

An Algerian Jewish family, *c. 1900.*

A synagogue in Algiers, from a watercolour *c. 1835–40.*

A sewing class at an *Alliance* school in Constantine, Algeria, 1895.

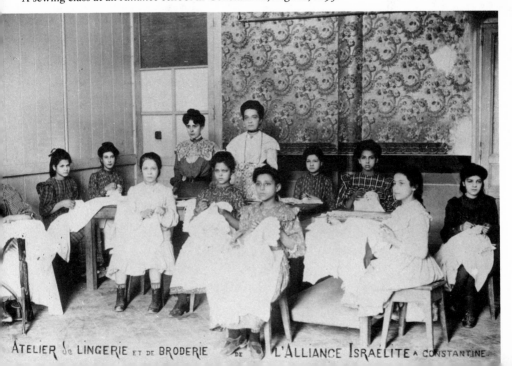

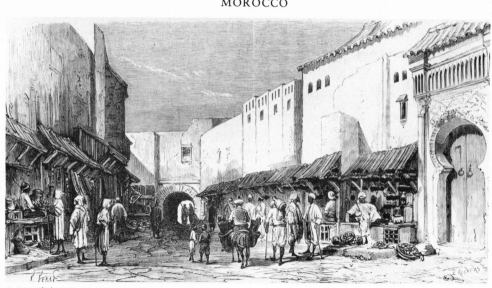

A Jewish bazaar in Tetuan, Morocco, 1868.

A children's school (*cheder*) in Tiznit in the 1930s.

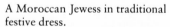

A Moroccan Jewess in traditional festive dress.

The Jewish quarter in Damnat, a village in the Atlas Mountains.

Below A caravan of Jews from the Atlas Mountains going on a pilgrimage to Saint de Ovirgane Anzar.

Left The house of Maimonides in Fez, according to tradition. He had fled from Spain with his parents to escape persecution by the fanatical Almohads and lived in Morocco from 1160 to 1165.

TUNISIA

Above left The Jews of Djerba, a small island off the coast of Tunisia, still survive with ancient traditions intact, notably the *Lag B'Omer* festival celebrated for three days about a month after Passover.

Above Pilgrims to the *Lag B'Omer* festival at the ancient Ghriba Synagogue in Djerba.

Left The interior of the old Ghriba Synagogue, its walls covered with brightly coloured glazed tiles.

The first fragments of documents in the Cairo *geniza* were brought back to England in 1896 and shown to the scholar Solomon Schechter, at Cambridge, who realized their antiquity and arranged for a mass of these fragments, numbering 100,000, to be crated to Cambridge. Schechter is shown here working on the papers in 1898. Scholars everywhere have been enlarging Jewish history through *geniza* study ever since.

An autograph *responsum* by Maimonides (1135-1203) in Hebrew and Arabic, in Hebrew characters, found in the Cairo *geniza*. Maimonides settled in Egypt c. 1170.

A page from the Tenth Book of the Mishnah commentary by Maimonides. This copy from the Yemen was made c. 1295.

A richly decorated Yemenite *ketuba* (marriage certificate), 1794. The Yemenites were fiercely observant Jews.

San'a, capital of Yemen, *c.* 1900. The Jews of Yemen had already begun an *aliyah* to the Holy Land in the 1880s, fired by religious zeal.

A Yemenite family in San'a, *c.* 1930.

The shrine of Ezra the Scribe near Basra.

18th-century brass and glass oil containers from Baghdad. Water was placed in the
glasses and oil was poured in to float on top; a wick absorbed the oil and the flame was lit.

A Boy Scout troup at the Rahel Shahmoon Boys School, Baghdad, 1926.

The opening of a new wing of the Meir Elias Hospital in Baghdad, 1924. Those present include Chief Rabbi Ezra Dangour and his *Beth Din* in traditional dress, and notables of the community in *tarbush* hats.

Operation Ali Baba, 1951: a group of Kurdistan Jews in transit to Israel as part of the massive airlift transporting 120,000 Jews from Iraq by various routes.

Oriental Jews celebrating their first Passover in Israel.

The route for flight to Israel was via Aden, then a British colony. The Aden police are supervising transport here, 1949.

Operation Magic Carpet: Yemenite Jews arriving in Israel at Lydda Airport, 1949.

On arrival, each Yemenite family was given a tent and the minimal requirements for survival, 1949. Health, education, language and training were all obstacles that then had to be surmounted.

A North African family on its way to a new home in a township in Israel.

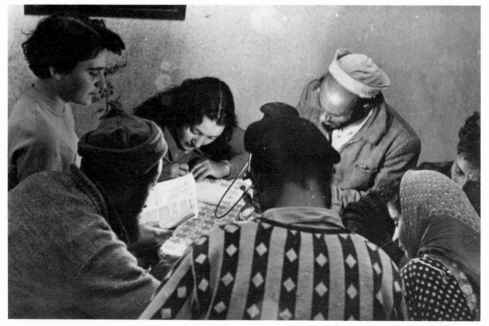

Many oriental Jews, illiterate in some countries of origin, receive intensive schooling after their arrival in Israel.

A synagogue for Bukhara Jews in Jerusalem, as immigrants keep community links in their own synagogues.

The *Maimuna* festival celebrated in Morocco immediately after Passover has become a great folk festival in Israel. Here a young woman is dancing a traditional Moroccan dance at the *Maimuna* celebration in Jerusalem.

whenever they so chose. Britain, as a Protestant country, had no such entrée as religious protector, since Protestants were insignificant in number there. Jews were, however, very numerous; and in 1840 the prime minister Lord Palmerston proposed that Britain should become the protector of Jewish interests, at least in Palestine. This was linked to a remarkable appeal at the time from the highly respected Lord Shaftesbury that the Jews should be helped to make Palestine their national home. Palmerston offered to be the channel, through the newly established British consulate in Jerusalem, for the receipt of any complaints that Jews had of unfair treatment by Turkey or her satellites. The function of British protection, Palmerston wrote, would be to avert 'the violence, injustice, and oppression to which the Jews have hitherto been exposed'. It would also help the Turks, 'because the wealth and habits of order and industry which the Jews would bring with them, would tend greatly to increase the resources of the Turkish Empire, and to promote the progress of civilization therein'.[99]

It was nearly eighty years before Britain could again express something like the same idealism in the Balfour Declaration of 1917; but in the meantime James Finn, the famed British consul in Jerusalem from 1845 to 1862, had carried out the protective policy to the greatest extent possible.

On Britain's record as protector of the Jews, one may note a sharp contrast later between Palestine and Iraq. As holder of the Mandate for Palestine from 1922 on, Britain received many complaints of unfairness from the Jews involved. In sharp contrast, the Jews of Iraq were very content when Britain held the Mandate for Iraq from 1917 to 1932. It proved to be a period of political as well as economic progress for the Jews of that country.

These are merely two examples of the very varied effects of diplomatic protection as exercised by the Great Powers. In more general terms, one sees this aspect of the colonial era as positive in what it gave to the Sephardim of the Near East, supplying a sense of political security to supplement their strong sense of religious security, not yet undermined by assimilation.

All this was to change when the Nazis came on the scene. Whatever had been achieved in the colonial era in improving the welfare and education of the eastern communities was now fiendishly interrupted or reversed.

It is hard to write of the Nazis in the general context of other developments. The effect on the eastern communities will be treated, therefore, in the brief separate chapter which follows.

15 The Nazis and the Uprooting

In considering the Nazi horror, our first thoughts usually go to central and eastern Europe; but it also affected many areas of the Sephardi/ Muslim world, in a variety of forms that were all part of the same demonic force.

Even where the Nazi armies were not actually present, encouragement was given everywhere to stimulating Jew-hatred, often to a pitch of tragedy.

Nazism widespread

One country where this happened to baleful effect was Iraq. Once the British had given up their Mandate there in 1932, the government reverted to some traditional forms of anti-Jewish discrimination; and when the Second World War broke out in September 1939, Hitlerite doctrines were propagated openly throughout the country. A dreadful climax came during a Jewish holiday, the feast of Shavuot, in the early summer of 1941, at a time when a pro-Nazi coup by Rashid Ali al-Jilani had spelt danger for the Allies and had led to the British emerging again to support the 'moderate' government. In this setting, the sudden Shavuot riot led to Jewish property being looted and hundreds of Jews being murdered or tortured, all without government intervention. Firm action by British forces saved the situation; but riots of the same kind, and with the same motivation, broke out subsequently in Syria, Egypt, South Arabia and North Africa, held in check only when the military strength of the Allied forces was in a position to operate in these areas.

The lead in pro-Nazi agitation had been given in the summer of 1940 by the infamous Mufti of Jerusalem, Haj Amin al-Husseini, writing to Hitler to offer full Arab co-operation in fighting the war, so that the Jews of Palestine 'and other Arab countries' could be dealt with by the methods adopted in Germany. He repeated this offer in February 1941, and spent the rest of the war in Germany, doing his utmost to rally support for the Nazi programme of mass murder of the Jews.

Fortunately British forces in Palestine were strong enough to prevent any serious trouble there, and the same was true in Egypt. During the first triumphant drives by Rommel's army across North Africa, Cairo had seemed threatened; but Montgomery's victory at Alamein in October 1942 removed this danger. Many Jewish men and women from Palestine served in the British forces in these areas, which fulfilled their desire to resist the Nazis directly, as well as giving them useful military training.

Jewish experience was of a different order, and mixed with stark tragedy, in other areas of North Africa. Here the benefits which had been conferred in the nineteenth century by the spread of French influence were now reversed, with the takeover of North Africa by the pro-Nazi Vichy authorities.

The one country of North Africa which escaped the full brunt of Nazi influence was Morocco, even though the Jews suffered heavily there for a time. The large size of the Jewish population, estimated at 225,000 in 1939, was partly due to heavy immigration from other eastern Sephardi countries after Morocco had been declared a protectorate of France in 1912. Despite the poverty of the Jewish masses in the cities, life had been prosperous and sophisticated for many Jews, with French influence strong, and the path not too difficult to a French passport. When France fell in 1940 the sultan did what he could to prevent the application of the Vichy anti-Jewish laws to his subjects, but quotas were introduced in the schools, foreign Jews were put into concentration camps, and there were riots, verging on pogroms, particularly after the US landings in November 1942.

The Nazi blight operated with much greater severity in Algeria, where Jews had enjoyed full French citizenship since 1870. Despite or because of this, the rise to power of Hitler in 1933 had stimulated latent Jew-hatred, with a massacre of Jews at Constantine in 1934, and further outbreaks in 1936 when a French Jew, Léon Blum, became Prime Minister of France. For all these reasons the Nazi virus had spread in Algeria; and when France fell the Vichy authorities there were powerful and virulent. Every step was taken to harass the Jewish population of some 117,000. The Crémieux Decree of 1870 conferring French citizenship was immediately abrogated, education in schools and colleges was made impossible, property was confiscated. Detention camps that the authorities set up were maintained even after the Allied landings; and though the citizenship decree was reinstated in October 1943, discrimination in various forms persisted until 1947. To some extent the legacy of this period fuelled the final break of the Jews with Algeria after its independence from France was achieved in 1962.

Transport to the death camps

Sadly, victimization was even fiercer, for a short period, for the Jews in Tunisia. The country had been a French protectorate from 1881, and the Jews had lived there fairly peaceably, moving rapidly towards emancipation, and with ways open to French citizenship from 1910. The first period of the rule of Vichy after the fall of France was mild in its effects compared with the position after November 1942 when Tunis was occupied by the Nazis. Now full German rule ensued, with confiscation of property, fines, the taking of hostages, and the establishment of labour camps close to the battle-fronts. There were heavy casualties, and many Jews were also transported direct to the death camps in Europe.

The ruthlessness of the Nazis reflected the swings on the battle-fronts here and in neighbouring Libya. When the British had taken Benghazi in Libya from the Italian forces, the Jewish community had felt relief. But Rommel fought back; and when the Nazis reoccupied Benghazi in February 1942 a reign of terror followed, with Jewish shops plundered, and Jews deported to labour camps south of Tripoli, where hundreds died of starvation. The pressure was relieved after Allied successes; but once again there was a legacy of anti-Jewish riots and looting which continued even during the period in which British forces occupied the country after the war.

These blows to North African Sephardim, grievous in themselves, were of a different order from the all-out attacks by the Nazis in Salonika, the heartland of the Sephardi world, together with a parallel attack on Jewish existence in Bulgaria and indeed throughout the Balkans.

Greece had been invaded at first by greedy but inefficient Italy. At this stage Jews in the Greek army had been able to play a part in the

Resistance. It was different when the Nazis, impatient with their Axis ally, occupied all Greece in June 1941, dividing the country into three zones under German, Bulgarian and Italian rule respectively. Salonika, in the German zone, was immediately plundered. Huge fines were imposed; the Jews, with yellow badges, were herded into a ghetto; labour camps were established, and transports began to be organized to take the Jews to the death camps. The first transports were in March 1943, with 3,000 Jews transported every two or three days. It added up to 46,000 Salonika Jews deported to Auschwitz and Bergen-Belsen, where the death toll was 95 per cent. Jews in the Italian and Bulgarian zones were also transported. In all 65,000 were sent from Greece, some 85 per cent of the entire Jewish population.

The Bulgarian zone, which covered a large part of Thrace and eastern Macedonia, had been handled with full Nazi enthusiasm. Nearly 5,000 Jews had been transported to the death camps from there, a reflection of the alliance swiftly forged in Bulgaria itself with the Axis powers. Yet a strange aberration has to be recorded. Jews trying to survive in Bulgaria included large numbers from Greece and Yugoslavia. When plans were made to send all, including Bulgarian Jews, to the death camps, protests were heard from some brave Bulgarians. As a result the fiercely pro-Nazi government finally gave way, sending only Jews from 'the new territories'. For Bulgarian Jews themselves, work in labour camps was the substitute. In due course, as it became clear that the Germans were going to be defeated, the Nazi decrees were eased and some Jews began to return to Sofia. In August 1944 all the Nazi decrees were abrogated; Russia marched in as the 'liberator'; and the pro-Nazi government gave way to a 'Fatherland Front'.

The old-established Sephardi community of Bulgaria had, therefore, some survivors; but the experience was not forgotten, and played its part in the decision of the Bulgarian community to opt after the war for emigration to Palestine rather than to try to enjoy the new type of 'freedom' under the Russian-supported government. It is one illustration, but an important one, of the decisions being taken on a much wider front in the Sephardi world which were to result ultimately in an almost total uprooting of the ancient communities, and the settlement of many thousands in the new homeland.

The end of illusion

This would always be more than a simple migration, of the kind undertaken so commonly in Jewish history for trade and family reasons. Under one aspect, it marked a decisive breakaway by Jews from centuries of domination in Muslim lands. Under another aspect, it called for the creation of a new society in the land, Israel, to which most of the uprooted now moved, and in which those of eastern origin became in time the majority.

On the first point, the mass of Jews in Muslim lands had often found a broadly tolerable form of life, with poverty and humiliation softened by the joys of communal existence, and with strong roots of direct affection to lands which had been their home for so many centuries. In this setting they seem to have relied on some good relationships with their neighbours, and to that extent had managed to ignore the underlying low status to which they had been consigned. But now, in the Nazi context, every kind of assumed protection seemed to have been shattered, as was shown by the eager way in which Nazi hatred of the Jews acted on those who had often seemed so friendly.

In every situation in which the Nazis released their horror on the Jews of this world, there were Muslim leaders who stirred up the mobs easily to support what the Nazis were doing, and who continued with riots and worse long after the Nazis had been defeated. It was if the presence of the Nazis, and their supporters the Vichy French, released in the Muslim world a resentment and hatred they had mostly held in check and to which they could now give free expression. It is easy to see this, looking back; and it must have been evident while the release of hatred was actually happening.

This was a period in which the horror was infinitely greater in scope in the Christian countries of Europe; but there is a difference which has to be noted. In itself, the Christian religion makes the love of one's fellow-being central to the faith; and throughout centuries of persecution, culminating in the Nazis, there were always Christians who tried to give expression to this doctrine of Christian love, rescuing thousands, and sheltering them at risk to their own lives. Islam, by contrast, has no such doctrine of love which might lead to tolerance. There could be personal friendships, but outside the faith there was no truth. A *dhimmi* might buy protection, but he had no rights by virtue of common humanity. All this seemed to be underlined as the wartime persecution of Jews was prolonged afterwards in riots and murder. Is it surprising that those exposed to it now felt that never again would Jews allow themselves to live in a subordinate state to rulers espousing this relentless religion?

This decision is palpable when one looks at the scale of the uprooting from Muslim lands. It began immediately after the war, and came into force more strongly, though still fitfully, after the foundation of the State of Israel in 1948. In that year the eastern Sephardim, from Morocco to the Yemen, numbered some 856,000. Within twenty years a pitiful remnant totalling no more than 25,000 was all that was left. About 586,000 had gone to Israel. The rest went to other countries, mostly France, Canada and the United States (see Table 1, p. 271).

One is reminded of the break in Jewish history caused by the expulsion from Spain in 1492; but there was a decisive difference, the second aspect in which to consider the uprooting.

The expulsions from Spain and Portugal took rich, talented and cultured communities into new settings where their talents were welcomed and used by the new host society. This process was developed further when titular Christians of Jewish stock – the Marranos – escaped and rejoined the old faith in European countries and across the Atlantic. Dignified in bearing and with connections everywhere, they brought with them a distinctive self-confidence that was part of their expertise. In sharp contrast, the eastern exiles of our time had left behind a fragmented existence which would be of little use in winning a new and stable place in society.

This is not to say that they were universally poor and unskilled. Education and 'westernization' were, it is true, uneven, but they had made very considerable progress, as described earlier, in all parts of the Sephardi world. Yet the eastern Sephardim were still, in a sense, cut off and unstable. In economic terms, the masses had been poor. In cultural terms, westernization had been erratic in its effects. The growth of nationalism in their homelands had raised new barriers to their feelings of freedom. Hovering over all was the memory of the dark cloud of discrimination, which spelt an inferior status even for those with wealth and power.

In the new homeland the aim would be to resolve all these paradoxes and to cope with the new ones that would arise. Unexpectedly, they were soon on their way to becoming the majority in Israel, yet were still being treated in some respects as if second class in status. Israel would help them to become part of the mainstream of Jewish life all over the world, yet they were still disadvantaged in major ways. In one breath they would now pursue westernization, which Israel symbolized; in another, they would keep alive the ancient traditions that had preserved them in the past, and without which they would be poorer today.

The ultimate paradox, perhaps, was that the Sephardi world itself, of which they were clearly a part, was in no sense a single entity. It had a multitude of different levels of intellect and passion, of pride and prejudice. If their Sephardi origin was comforting and supportive, it would no longer be a solid prop in the old sense. The unified spirit of Israel, expressed in many types of educational, social and personal activity – like 'inter-ethnic' marriage – would reduce exclusive 'props' as well as barriers.

The medieval Sephardi world was to be replaced, not easily, but with a dynamism that would have to find its own new forms.

PART SIX
The Eastern Ingathering

16 Behind the Ingathering

With the proclamation of the State of Israel on 14 May 1948 the basis for a wholly new life was laid for the eastern Sephardim, numbering at least a million at the time, in lands stretching from the Balkans to Yemen, and from Morocco to the Far East.[100] Within a few years a very large proportion of them had settled in Israel, offering a quite remarkable finale to the story we have been following here of wandering and settlement, persecution and achievement all over the Near and Middle East since the days of the Bible more than two thousand years earlier.

We saw in the previous chapter that this startling ingathering had two contrasting aspects. From one angle it was negative, marking a final recognition that Jewish life in these lands, almost entirely a Muslim world, was no longer to be borne. Bitter episodes of persecution there in the Nazi period had merely dramatized the underlying or open discrimination and danger of earlier centuries. A new life had to be sought, and Israel was a refuge available. From another angle, the stimulus was positive, a product of age-old dreams of Zion and of intense work in many of these lands to turn the dreams into reality. Without this positive Zionist stimulus, the brilliant improvisation of the organizers of the ingathering could never have been given reality.

To talk of the ingathering in general terms obscures the immense variety that went into its achievement. In virtually every detail, the past experience of each separate country affected the way in which the ingathering took place and the later course of the settlement in Israel. If, ultimately, ancient differences within the Sephardi and oriental world will be to some extent annealed in Israel, the contrasts will still be potent forces for a long time to come, drawing on many of the diverse and colourful threads of eastern experience that we have grown aware of in this book.

The Zionist preparation

Every one of these countries had a distinctive presence in the Holy Land long before the modern state came into being. This had been built up over the centuries, giving some uniform Sephardi elements. But all was dwarfed with the new arrivals, who came from a wide assortment of backgrounds, and whose interest in Zionism showed up in very different ways.

Even in an apparently uniform area like the Maghreb there was never a set pattern. In the background, certainly, there was a palpable devotion to Zion, overflowing from the Bible and the prayers, and common to Jews everywhere; but in terms of action, the position was now affected by differing responses to French influence and westernization generally. If, on the whole, the Jews there had welcomed the growing penetration by the West into the life of the Maghreb, the effects were not spread evenly. Among some, traditional Jewish life remained strong, with relatively little change outside the big towns; with others, especially in Algeria, education and assimilation weakened the hold of the old faith, and this, Chouraqui believes, was disturbing socially.[101] Adherence to the old rituals had reflected the realities of 'the ghetto-induced attitude of the Jews'. Under various forms of partial emancipation that were now surfacing in North Africa, the traditional institutions could not adapt themselves to the new realities, and this was one cause of the crisis in Judaism that eventually 'led to the virtual extinction of the Jewish communities'.

In this situation Zionism had not made clear-cut organizational progress among the Jews of the Maghreb, even though they kept alive old messianic ideas and sent delegates to the Zionist Congresses. It was a common complaint that Zionist leaders from eastern Europe made little effort to understand the specific traditions and attitudes of the Maghreb Jews, and could not communicate their ideas to them. The Maghreb Jews were, indeed, in an ambiguous position, enjoying much prosperity from the French connection yet not part of French colonial society, cut off even more than before, as specially favoured French protégés, from Muslim society around them, and without strong links at this time to the rest of the Jewish world. This isolated position changed instantly, of course, in 1948, when all the Jews of the Maghreb were seized by a kind of messianic excitement at the founding of the state; but the ambivalence in their position left a legacy after the migration to Israel. The French influence had created an élite who mostly left to settle in France and North America, so that those moving to Israel tended to be poor and ill-educated, as well as uprooted from the warmth of a familiar encompassing society.

Different Zionist stirrings

The contrast is very great if one looks at Zionist ideas, before the state, in Iraq. Key features there were the rootedness of scholarly Jewish life and the forms of responsible self-government in which it had long been expressed. In recent periods, as we saw earlier, there had been painful periods of decline for the Jews of Iraq. Yet even then a galaxy of names is visible, giving a framework to these traditions; and this was reflected in a confident pursuit of Zionist action in the pre-state period.

This tradition of great names spanning learning and wealth went all the way back, despite the periods of decline, to the ancient days of Babylon and Baghdad; and one is not surprised, therefore, to see this élite style at work in the establishment of a powerful Zionist organization in Iraq immediately after the First World War, with leaders bearing names – Somekh, Gabbai, Sassoon and others – that had acquired almost legendary character in the eighteenth and nineteenth centuries, despite the decline of the Jewish position in that period. In many cases the leaders had been in a position to serve as head of the Jewish community with the title of *Nasi* (president) while also helping in the government of Baghdad or in Constantinople itself. In this double – and never conflicting – role, some of the wealthy had been expanding their businesses on a huge scale in India and China, while at the same time founding *yeshivot*, and often enjoying fame themselves as the top *halakhic* experts of their communities. Rabbi Abdullah Somekh (1813–89) was a prime example of this. His nephew Ezekiel Gabbai (1824–96), famed for benefactions on a large scale in Palestine, was merely one of a huge family whose interests had spread over the whole of the East. There are other Iraqi families whose fame is equally widespread. In business (and benefactions) one thinks, with the Sassoons, of the Kedouries in Hong Kong and Shanghai, or of the Yehudas in India and Indonesia. In public affairs, David Saul Marshall became Prime Minister in Singapore.

Drawing on this old and well-established setting, the Zionist organization of the 1920s in Iraq founded branches all over the country, distributing Hebrew books and organizing study groups. When the government began to restrict their activities, especially after the end of the British Mandate in 1932, they went underground and intensified their activities in Hebrew education, arms training and secret emigration, with the help of emissaries from Palestine, including the famed Enza Sereni. In all this one sees courage and devotion that relate to the style of their later mass settlement in Israel.

The contrast is particularly strong between these two countries, Morocco and Iraq, in the ways they found of harmonizing western education and loyalty to the Jewish tradition; but the truth is that every country found a different equilibrium in this field. Iran, for example, might have been expected to be close in style to its neighbour Iraq in the light of the common history of these two countries in the past for long stretches of time, and their remoteness in the nineteenth century from the emancipatory experience of European Jews. In fact, however, the Jews of Persia/Iran were overwhelmingly different.

Iran and further east

In contrast to the strong strains of centralized and responsible self-government which characterized Iraq, the Jews of Persia (it became Iran in 1935) had fallen into an abysmal state under the regime – Shi'ite – of the nineteenth century. Persecution and poverty had prolonged a long-existing eastward emigration towards the neighbouring regions of Afghanistan, Turkestan, Samarkand, Bukhara and India, and in other directions to Kurdistan, the Caucasus and even Egypt. Persia, exotic in itself, was thus the base historically for a continuous diffusion of Jews into 'eastern communities' of even greater variety of work and culture, different in every way, except Jewish loyalty, from the solidly European style of the Jews from the West.

The Jews who moved into these eastern regions at different times became heavily involved in the worlds of their host countries stretching from the Caspian to the Far East, and seem to have lost many of their direct links with the Jewish world of Persia. But they all claimed to be descended from the Lost Ten Tribes (as Persian Jews did), and spoke Persian–Jewish vernaculars, written in Hebrew script. According to Itzhak Ben-Zvi, the second President of Israel and a distinguished ethnographer, in his book *The Exiled and the Re-deemed*, Jews speaking Persian–Jewish vernaculars numbered some 200,000 before the Second World War, including 100,000 in Persia itself, 8,000 in Afghanistan, and 10,000 in Bukhara and Turkestan.[102] These amorphous communities of Jews stretching through Central Asia remind one irresistibly of the Bible's description of the vast audience of '127 Provinces' – 'from Ethiopia to India' – to whom Mordecai wrote, as told in the Book of Esther, to urge them to celebrate their marvellous deliverance from the wicked Haman with the carnival of Purim. But if these Central Asian Jews were only loosely connected to the Iran of our day, they were part of the reservoir of Jews who contributed to the ingathering to Israel. Many from these countries had, in fact, migrated to the land of Israel in earlier times, the most notable instance being the arrival in Jerusalem in 1868 of a group of Jews from Bukhara, and the subsequent establishment of their own famed quarter there in 1892.

But even without this unique overflow into Central Asia, the Jews of Iran were distinctive in themselves by virtue of Persia's fabled heritage from early times of royal splendour, wealth, literature and art. The depths to which the Jewish masses of Persia fell in the nineteenth century was, perhaps for this reason, all the more disturbing to prosperous Jews of England and France – now themselves basking in a new kind of imperial splendour – whose emissaries sent back the dismal news; and this explains why the leaders of western Jewry, already active in trying to help the Jews of the East, made a number of special efforts to ease the condition of the Jews of Persia.[103]

One famous occasion in which they seized an unusual opportunity arose during a tour of Europe in 1873 by an apparently friendly Shah of Persia, Nasr-ed-Din, during which the Jews, led by Sir Moses Montefiore and Adolphe Crémieux, were able to get him to promise to move towards some form of civil rights, if not outright emancipation, for the Jews of his lands. As might have been expected, very little came of this after the Shah's return to his country. Yet if the Jews of Persia *en masse* continued to have a pitiful existence, there were other elements in Persian–Jewish life which it would be wrong to ignore. Many Jews had old-established roots in finance and business that generated prosperity, however narrow its range. Memories of the ancient glories of Persia, and the modern echoes of sophistication and high culture, gave some Jews a very satisfying position that would weaken any decision to leave their country in reaction to the enormous upheavals that were ranging through the eastern Jewish world.

One has to be ready to recognize paradoxes of this kind if one is trying to understand how it was that rather less than half of the Jews of Iran – and almost entirely impoverished Jews – migrated to Israel during the first decade after 1948, compared to the situation in Iraq, where almost the entire community took this step. One soon sees that the two factors isolated earlier – discrimination by Islam and love of Zion – were never the only decisive elements in the decision. Throughout the eastern countries there was also a strong rootedness to be considered. Other things being equal, there was always a tremendously strong desire to stay put in homelands to which one was attached. Many of those who migrated to Israel made the move, and always at great financial cost, only when decisions of government policy left no alternative. These government policies in regard to emigration to Israel often changed and took years to work out, which explains why it was that the ingathering, though it now, in retrospect, has almost an instant air, was, in fact, spread over a fair period of time.

The really positive drive came, of course, from Israel itself, eager for 'instant' immigration, at whatever the cost, to fulfil the Zionist promise; and in every country of the East there were local Zionist workers, sometimes operating freely, sometimes of necessity underground, who had the same total motivation, and often paid for it with imprisonment or even their lives. In every case those involved had to adjust to variations in the local political setting which often changed with startling suddenness. The Jews of Iran, as it happened, were relatively free to migrate or arrange for the transfer of funds in the early period, a facility which could be used, though at heavy cost, for would-be emigrants from neighbouring Iraq. In that country a long-standing straight ban on Zionism, with prison or death penalties equivalent to those applied to communists, was suddenly lifted in March 1950 to those willing to surrender their nationality and ultimately, as it proved, their property. In some countries, as for example in Yemen, the Israeli authorities could arrange for the migration openly, through complicated procedures to be described in the next chapter. In other countries, with Morocco a particular case, its government changed its emigration policy several times, so that the migration from Morocco went in spurts. In the Asian countries proper, including the relatively few Jews affected in Kurdistan or India, there were few legal but of course many personal problems. In Bulgaria the situation was again quite different. Here the Jewish community, which was basically Sephardi, having taken a clear-cut decision to emigrate to Israel, put as much pressure as it could on the Israeli authorities to make the arrangements, in line with what they were already doing to facilitate migration for survivors from the Nazi camps and others in eastern European countries, notably Romania and Poland, where migration was possible to begin with.

The historical dimension

In day-to-day action the ingathering was totally makeshift, using every possible means for exit, travel, health, food, clothing and settlement that could be devised. This inevitably involved immense disturbance and unhappiness, though in retrospect it was a unified, historic achievement whose like had never been seen before. In the light of the overwhelming social, educational and economic problems that surfaced from the beginning and continued to grow, it may seem wrong to look on these problems as of secondary importance compared with the positive revolution in Jewish life in the East that was achieved through the ingathering; yet this must be the verdict.

One man, Itzhak Ben-Zvi, was able to see this and write about it not just in retrospect but in the midst of the turmoil; and there is no better way of getting a sense of the historical dimension of the ingathering than by seeing it with his eyes for a moment, before turning in the next chapter to the practical problems and achievements of the ingathering from the East.

We referred earlier to Ben-Zvi's book, *The Exiled and the Redeemed*, which sees the revolution of the ingathering in the context of his many studies of the eastern communities, so that the change is clear-cut. It is significant, also, that the book was published in 1958, a date which allowed him, looking at the first decade of Israel's existence, to discuss the eastern ingathering in a highly individualistic way. He was himself an Ashkenazi from Poltava in the Ukraine, and a leader among socialist European pioneers who were by nature and experience far distant in spirit from the eastern masses. It is from this position that he asks us to consider the extraordinary role of the *edot ha-mizrach* in the life of the Jewish people, and how the eastern ingathering, expressing this, brings home a theme of Jewish history that cannot be overlooked. If some of the story he tells has been touched on in earlier pages here, in his hands it has special significance in being expressed, at the time itself, by the man who, as President, symbolized what was happening.

'As this book is being written', he says, 'the immigration of the Jews of Iraq and Iran is reaching its peak.'[104] For him these immigrants bring to mind immediately the migration to Palestine of those who returned under Ezra and Nehemiah from the Babylonian Exile 2,500 years ago. He thinks at the same time of the many-sided life of the Jews of Babylon, and of the way they imposed distinction on eastern Jewish life.

Part of their heritage, he recalls, was a system of self-government under their own ethnarchs; and he pays tribute, also, to the sophisticated form of study, ahead of Spanish Jewry, developed by their *geonim*. But this distinction was not all; it was paralleled by their eminence in finance and diplomacy:

Iraq Jews carried the trade of their land to Central Asia, India and beyond; and some of the emissaries of Babylonian and Persian Jews to Bukhara served as viziers in the courts of the emirs and the great moguls of India.

In more modern times Iraqi Jews were contributing ('with munificence') to the *Yishuv* (Jewish settlement in Palestine or Israel) long before the new ingathering, founding villages and *yeshivot*, and helping to foster modern agricultural methods.

Historically, he feels, the Jews of Persia had their own distinction. It was through their emissaries that the Khazars of Asia Minor adopted the Jewish faith in the eighth century. Jewish literature in Judaeo–Persian was of the highest quality, especially in poetry. The Jews of Meshed (in north-east Persia), who were forcibly converted to Islam in the early nineteenth century, 'kept up their underground Judaism no less persistently than did the Marranos of Spain and Portugal'. Persian Jews were among the first oriental Jews to settle in Palestine in the 1880s, 'establishing special quarters (as the Bukharans did) and sending some of their sons to settle to work on the land'.

Ben-Zvi is particularly interesting on the Jews from Kurdistan 'who have been leading their secluded life in the mountainous regions of the country ever since they were deported there by the King of Assyria'. They speak Aramaic (which they call *Targum*), the language of the Babylonian Talmud, and are a hardy race of farmers:

The thousands of Kurdish Jews who came to the land of Israel long before the Zionist movement were among the first agricultural workers in Galilee settlements. They constituted the core of the Jerusalem working class at a time when many of the old *Yishuv* largely depended on the charity of their co-religionists abroad. Even if they did not bring with them financial resources or cultural brilliance, they did bring an exceptional aptitude for physical labour. Their pioneers fought alongside the rest of the soldiers of Israel and are now the backbone of the Jerusalem Corridor settlements.

The ingathering of Jews from North Africa prompts Ben-Zvi to some thoughts of their continued settlement there since the days of the Second Temple, and their unique contribution over many centuries to the integration of Jewish life and culture. Their devotion at a crucial time, he says, helped the Jews expelled from Spain and Portugal to work their way towards the Holy Land, where they made a great mark on Jewish history. In more recent times the Jews of North Africa helped to consolidate the agricultural settlements of Israel in the 1880s, and promoted housing schemes to build up the urban centres of Jerusalem, Jaffa, Haifa and Tiberias. In the same spirit, tribute is paid to the early work in Israel of the Jews from the Yemen, and to the Sephardim from the Balkans and Turkey who transformed religious life in the land of Israel after their arrival in the sixteenth century.

But having extolled the ancient glories and more recent practical work, Ben-Zvi feels obliged to come down to earth. In the current circumstances, he says, the arrivals who have been flooding in cannot be expected to rise instantly to the heights of the past. The immigrants from North Africa had been largely confined so far – he was writing in the mid 1950s – to the less-advantaged Jews of that area. More generally,

oriental Jewry is no longer at the height of that glory on which it stood in its heyday in Andalusia and Babylon: it has diverged from the sources of general Jewish inspiration. Its rich cultural heritage has been somewhat superseded by a rather shallow Levantinism, itself the product of the infiltration of European influence.

This is, he is sure, a temporary phase. Blame lies to a great extent with European Jewish leaders who did not provide the young of oriental countries with the special training that was so successful in eastern Europe. It is a striking admission from one who was himself one of the chief leaders in Europe; and it confirms what was said earlier here about the ignorance of European Zionists of the whole nature of eastern Jewry. Few of them understood the basic facts, and none, it can be said, foresaw the nature and scale of the crisis in this field that would overwhelm Israel's leaders when the state was founded.

Looking ahead in 1958 from the admittedly difficult pioneering period, Ben-Zvi saw the weakness of the oriental Jews being overcome by new and carefully considered policies, which would emphasize 'the uniting rather than the separating elements' of Israeli society. The oriental Jews must be trained

to become free citizens of the State, using one language, and adapting themselves to creative effort. We must train them to leadership. We must bring to the fore their hidden and latent cultural potential, on which we may all draw to enrich the common treasure of our people as a whole.

It will be relevant in the next chapters to see how far this optimistic outlook has been justified in the three decades which followed, and to what extent, also, the emphasis on unity, which seemed natural, has been reconsidered, or should one say enriched, by seeking pride and vigour in diversity.

17 Scale of the Ingathering

It was natural that the new State of Israel should declare an Open Door policy for all Jews as soon as it came to power; but the passion with which this policy was pursued cannot be understood unless one recalls the barriers to Jewish immigration that had been a central feature of Britain's Palestine policy while she held the Mandate, and the desperation that had resulted, especially after the rise of Hitler.

Though the Balfour Declaration of 1917 had spoken generously of Britain using her 'best endeavours' to facilitate the establishment of a national home in Palestine for the Jewish people, this had included a reservation that nothing was to be done which might prejudice the civil and religious rights of the existing non-Jewish communities; and this had been operated from the beginning as an effective bar to substantial Jewish immigration. The authorities specified that it could be pursued only 'under suitable conditions', and where it would not 'prejudice' the rights of other sections of the population. As a result immigration certificates were very limited in number and hedged with strict conditions. The Jews were ready to accept the formula of 'economic absorptive capacity' but saw far greater chances for development than the British would facilitate through the issue of immigration certificates. The proof of the Jewish view came in the 1930s when, for a brief period after Hitler's rise to power in 1933, a more substantial number of Jews were admitted and the economy prospered. But Arab protests mounted; and when this broke into military revolt in 1936, with the full participation of other Arab countries, immigration was again tightened. With war in the air, it seemed to the British government of the day – though not to Winston Churchill – that Arab friendship was a prize that had to be won at whatever cost. The Palestine policy designed to secure this was exposed as a fallacy when war broke out and large elements of the Arab world sided with the Nazis. But in the meantime the very restrictive immigration policy expressed in the White Paper of 1939 was maintained in being. Under this White Paper, total Jewish immigration was to be limited to 75,000 during the ensuing five years, after which no Jews would be admitted to the Jewish homeland without Arab agreement.

In pursuance of this policy during the war, immigration was held to minimal numbers. Refugee ships were turned back under heart-breaking conditions, and this continued even when the opening of the death-camps, after defeat of the Nazis, finally exposed the full horror of the fate that had befallen the Jews of central and eastern Europe. Those who had barely survived the death-camps now clamoured for admission to Palestine. The United Nations and other bodies pleaded for at least 100,000 to be admitted immediately, but all to no avail. In desperation, the Jews gathered any ships they could find, in any condition, to try to get through the blockade maintained by the Royal Navy and land a few survivors. As often as not these boats were turned back, with those intercepted put into camps in Cyprus, and a few, most heartlessly of all, even sent back to Germany. It was against this background that the first act of the new government of Israel was to declare that henceforth any Jew would have a right to a home in Israel.

Unlimited immigration

This policy was announced at a time when the new state was fighting for its existence against invasion by Arab armies. Despite this, it was asserted not as a general principle to be put into practice when the time would be right, but as an absolute priority for immediate action. The atmosphere in which the decision was taken is evoked graphically by the first Prime Minister, David Ben-Gurion, in the book he later wrote: *Israel*. Some members of the provisional government, he says, were unwilling to sanction unlimited immigration because it would intensify the grave problems that already existed; but 'many others' (and we may be sure that he was among them) opposed any kind of limitation.

In the first year fortune seemed to reward the courage of this decision. Jobs were available for the immigrants to replace the men called up for military service. Shelter in the form of some empty housing was also available because many Arabs had fled in response to false rumours spread by Arab propaganda. In the second year of the state, with the flow of immigrants rising to an even greater flood, the situation was still manageable, though employment chances were lessened because men released from the army wanted their jobs back. It was in the three years after this, 1950–52, Ben-Gurion says, that the problems became 'almost unbearable', with grave shortages of housing, food and jobs, and with all the difficulties of the new arrivals coming together cumulatively. Thousands were unemployable because of age or health, disabled with TB or heart disease, or overwhelmed with nervous illnesses linked to their uprooting and the emergency conditions in which they were now forced to live.

If some of the immigrants, especially those from eastern countries, never forgot the troubles of this time, which are described very candidly by Ben-Gurion, he is eager also to present the picture in true historical perspective, emphasizing the triumph of achieving mass immigration and settlement, in which the qualities and initiatives of the immigrants were all-important. In particular, he takes sardonic pleasure in contrasting this achievement with the negativism of life under the Mandate. In thirty years of British rule, the Jewish population of Palestine increased by 394,000; in under four years as an independent state, the Jewish population increased by 690,000.[105] Dramatically, he tells that the crucial decision of the provisional government to allow unlimited immigration aimed at doubling the *Yishuv* in four years. The increase of 690,000 in three years seven months meant that this apparently impossible target was 'more than fulfilled'.

Variety of methods

Ben-Gurion is equally proud that settlement on the land, always central to the pioneering Zionist philosophy, was advanced positively even in this early period. In the last forty years of Ottoman rule which followed the first *aliyah* (immigration) of 1881, thirty-two agricultural settlements had been founded. In thirty years of British rule, with strongly motivated Jews pioneering much land settlement, especially in the form of *kibbutzim* (common ownership), 222 settlements had been founded. This number was exceeded in the first *three* years of Israeli independence (1948–51), with the emphasis in the 273 new settlements shifting from *kibbutz* to *moshav* (private ownership co-operative), and with eastern Jews, as we shall see, due to assume an increasingly important agricultural role.

It seems fair to say that in the very early years of the state, no one foresaw what was to be its major numerical factor: the overwhelming proportion of Jews from eastern countries. In deciding on 'unlimited immigration' the provisional government must certainly have had in the foreground of their minds the desperate position of Hitler's victims in Europe; and this, in fact, is how the ingathering began. The first priority was to rescue the European Jews, 25,000 in number, who had been intercepted by the British authorities and deposited in the Cyprus camps. They were brought across to Israel within a few weeks. It took a little longer to arrange for the movement to Israel of the thousands of Jews scattered over Europe in a whole variety of conditions; but this, too, was given urgent attention. Jews from the death-camps and others now being looked after in displaced persons camps in Germany, Austria and Italy were soon arriving, with the pace quickening as the range of countries widened. In the nine months from May to December 1948, 103,000 were brought in. Almost the same number were brought in during the next *four* months, January to April 1949. The total arrivals of 203,000 in this first year of independence came from forty-two countries. Europe was still prominent, with some 104,000 survivors from Poland (two-thirds of the Jewish population), and 119,000 from Romania (one-third of the Jewish population) arriving. But even when the European immigration was still strong – it was soon to be curtailed – the Sephardi immigration had not only surfaced very quickly, but was effecting a more decisive change in the pattern of the diaspora, by bringing over whole communities. Those arriving from Yemen, some 47,000, left only a few hundred behind. There was a similar mass migration from Iraq, covering 121,000 out of 135,000, much the largest single element in the Sephardi immigration until the mass of Morocco's Jews came in later. From Libya 30,000 Jews arrived, out of a population of 35,000. In Europe itself the major part of Bulgaria's Jews – more than 37,000 out of 45,000 – took a voluntary decision to migrate to Israel.

Immigration from Europe, though complicated in its detail, had been achieved by immense ingenuity, though by what might be called 'normal' methods: the drafting of ships, mostly ancient tubs that could at least make the journey to an Israeli port from an assortment of ports in southern France, Italy, the Balkans and North Africa. There was a makeshift air, also, about the relatively small number who were making their way painfully from India and other countries beyond the

Middle East, in response to what they felt was the arrival of the messianic age. Very different, and more dramatic, was the inflow of the old and substantial Jewish communities of Yemen and Iraq.

The great airlifts

The Jews of Yemen had lived in their distant land for endless centuries, believing, indeed, that their ancestors had arrived after the destruction of Jerusalem by the Romans, or possibly much earlier, as traders from Palestine in the days of King Solomon. They were, however, unlike other distant communities, such as the Falashas of Ethiopia, who nursed similar legendary tales of origin, in that the Yemenites had kept in close touch for many centuries (as we saw earlier) with the established leadership of Israel and Babylon, and preserved in this way a vibrant and rabbinically orthodox Jewish life. As part of their attachment to Jewish traditions, they had responded to Zionist stirrings and begun to make their way to the Holy Land as early as the time of the first *aliyah* in the 1880s; and though those that managed to get there, always under the most primitive conditions, had a somewhat lowly 'class' status during the period of Ottoman and British rule, they had won respect for their character, their folk art and the sincerity of their faith.

In Yemen itself they had continued to live in very poor circumstances, though mostly unmolested until Arab countries far and wide gave active military support in 1948 to the war against the new State of Israel, and expressed this at home in attacking and plundering their Jewish communities. Facing this, and responding also to the messianic emotion embodied in the existence of a Jewish state, the Yemenite Jews set off on foot in thousands towards the port of Aden (a British colony at the time) from which they hoped to travel to Palestine. To help as best they could, Zionist representatives entered into negotiations with the Imam of Yemen, local Arab rulers, and the British authorities in Aden for the promotion of an organized flight. The Yemenite rulers were not averse to the Jews leaving in return for cash payments and the confiscation of Jewish property. In May 1949 an agreement set the rescue in action, which helped the Jews to get to Aden, from where they were flown in round-the-clock flights, by routes avoiding flight over Arab countries, in an operation code-named 'On Eagle's Wings'. By September 1950, when the operation was complete, 47,000 Jews, virtually the entire Jewish population of Yemen, together with some 3,000 Jews from Aden, had arrived in their new homeland.

The immigration from Iraq also involved a massive airlift, though the operation as a whole was vastly different in character, if only because of the size and status of the Iraqi community. As we have seen throughout this book, the Jews of Iraq had achieved a strongly independent Jewish life under prosperous and sophisticated leadership, though with their peaceful existence liable to violent interruption through riots, arrests and even more serious forms of persecution. The Arab war against the new State of Israel in 1948 furnished the occasion for a root-and-branch attack of this kind on the Jews of Iraq, with many Jews imprisoned, others hounded out of business and professional occupations, students barred from universities and, as a final touch, with emigration declared a capital offence. Despite this, there was a trickle of illegal emigration via Iran; but the position suddenly changed when, in March 1950, the Iraqi government announced that Jews who wished to emigrate could do so, provided they registered by 9 March 1950. They would have to surrender their nationality, but could sell their property and receive the proceeds later. Thousands accepted; but when all had registered, the government announced on the following day, 10 March, that all property and bank assets were now surrendered without compensation. An existence of something like 2,500 years was to be ended; and they were to start as an uprooted people, in Israel, without any possessions except their inbred skills and inherent pride.

But how was a community of this size to be transported through blockaded seaways or, by air, over hostile territories? Ultimately, permission was given for a take-off by air from Baghdad, provided there was no direct flight to Israel. The planes were to land in non-Arab Cyprus, after which the refugees would make their way to Israel by air or sea. The flight was code-named 'Operation Ali Baba'. By the time it ended in December 1951, 113,000 Iraqi Jews had been transferred to Israel. Other emigrants had arrived via Iran, bringing the total Iraqi immigration to 121,000, with only a few – perhaps 4,000 – left in Iraq.

Flexible policies

The total immigration to the new state by this time, the end of 1951, amounted to 686,700, a number greater than the entire Jewish population of Israel on Independence Day. To get a concept of what this means in numbers, and to a country still at war, one has to envisage Britain taking in, and then housing, feeding, educating and putting to work forty-eight million people (her population in 1940) during the first three and a half years of the war.

Inevitably there was a distinct slowdown to Israel's immigration after the first massive inflow, partly because immigration from eastern Europe was now cut off, and also because most of the eastern countries now had relatively few Jews left. In Israel itself the difficult economic situation and the mounting problems posed by absorption had forced the government to restrict immigration for a time except in cases of acute physical danger. In the years which followed, however, these factors eased, with immigration rising again to considerable numbers and with a significant new emphasis: that those coming from North Africa now became dominant. The proportion from this source rose from 67 per cent in 1954 to an average of 84 per cent in 1955 and 1956. This new wave brought the total from North Africa in the first decade of Israel's existence to 160,000, outnumbering those who had come in the early years from Iraq and Yemen.

This delayed arrival of Jews from North Africa, especially of the large numbers who finally came from Morocco, enabled the Jewish authorities to put into practice new systems of absorption which they had learnt from hard experience in the first phase, though even these changes still left many problems for later. Difficult as *aliyah* was, it was less lasting than the problem of *kelitah* (absorption), the ramifications of which can be seen in this daunting account by an official of the Jewish Agency, which had overall responsibility:

This second stage involved collecting the immigrants at the port or airfield; providing them with food and lodging; building temporary and permanent housing; finding employment; expanding health services; organizing education. Complete absorption was a task that affected all areas of the country's life and demanded massive financial participation by Diaspora Jewry through the Jewish Agency. In one year, the Agency's staff had to transport 200,000 immigrants from the point of arrival to their new homes. In the first place, most of them were taken to *Sha'ar Ha-Aliyah* (Gateway of Aliyah), a converted British army camp near Haifa, where they were registered, medically examined, inoculated and vaccinated, classified, and sent off to their destinations. An average of 1,000 a day passed through *Sha'ar Ha-*

Aliyah at peak.[106]

To list these processes is, of course, merely a shorthand introduction to the detail of the developments which then ensued. In housing, for example, it was demoralizing in the extreme for the immigrants to be crowded into any kind of squalid shelter that could be found in tents or temporary huts without any access to work or even the minimum facilities for family life; and this led in 1950 to the creation of the *ma'abarah* system, specially built 'camps', adjacent to possible work, in which each family had their own quarters and were responsible for looking after themselves, though with communal facilities including an *ulpan* (a school for learning Hebrew), a children's school, a clinic, social workers and a job centre. Even a large *ma'abarah* could be put up in a few weeks; and crude as the accommodation was, it proved an important transitional stage. By May 1952, 113 *ma'abarot* had been built, with a population of 50,000.

In the earliest stage the employment provided could be 'make-work', such as in road-building or forestry, but valuable none the less in giving the new life a work basis. In the next phase two major changes were carried out. First, the new immigrants were linked to a great expansion of food-growing by the establishment of new settlements, some of them of the *kibbutz* type, but more frequently a *moshav* which worked better for them. The new settlers rapidly found their feet in *moshavim* with the help of skilled agricultural instruction provided by the Jewish Agency. Ben-Gurion, in the book mentioned earlier, found the achievement particularly remarkable with the new immigrants from eastern countries who, unlike those from Europe, had had no training in this field. The value to Israel's economy was very great, turning the country ultimately from costly food-importing to a very profitable food-exporting basis. Though this took time, much of it was set in motion in the early years. Official figures given in the study quoted above show that up to the end of 1953, that is in four and a half years, 347 new 'villages' – including ninety-six *kibbutzim* and 251 *moshavim* – were established, with a population of more than 20,000 families. The importance to Israel was not only in agricultural expansion – covering more than a million dunams of land, growing every kind of product and with rapidly expanding stocks of cattle, sheep and poultry – but also, behind this, the immense achievement of providing a settled home life for masses of uprooted Jews involved in the ingathering.

The other development which soon emerged with this double purpose was to link the immigrants to work and residence in development towns through a system of 'ship-to-village' transfers, without an intervening period of transit-camp life. The concentration here was in industrial expansion, with decent housing and a rewarding social life close at hand. Some of the new towns, especially in the Negev and Galilee, used the *ma'abarot* as nuclei for these developments. In other cases, such as Dimona, Kiryat Gath or Beth Shemesh, the new towns had development town status from the beginning.

Inflow from North Africa

These improved methods of absorption were increasingly available by the time the large influx from North Africa surfaced in the late 1950s. It was clear from the beginning that the background of the North Africans, and especially those from Morocco, would create special problems of adjustment; but there was no clear-cut differentiation for deciding how different categories of immigrant would have to be dealt with. The authorities had always to be ready to absorb new spurts in immigration from eastern Europe or Russia itself, so that the whole process had to be flexible, allotting new housing and jobs to meet the circumstances of immigrants, often to the accompaniment of bitter complaints from those who felt that others were being favoured at their expense. The North African immigrants were soon to be very vocal in this direction, partly as a reaction to the rapid progress that Israel as a whole was beginning to make, with some groups moving ahead, while the North Africans, in their view, were being forced to lag behind.

The Moroccans, in particular, felt a certain stigma in the air for reasons linked to their own history. In the Middle Ages, and indeed up to the seventeenth century, the Jews of North Africa had had a prominent place in Jewish life, as we saw in earlier chapters of this book. They had had a respected place alongside the Jews of the Middle East and Spain as active participants in the renaissance of learning in the Arabic language, and had provided a sustained base for Spanish Jews in various times of trouble, especially after the Expulsion. In the early stages of the opening up of Mediterranean trade to the new opportunities in north-west Europe and across the Atlantic, they had played a lively part; yet as this development gathered force in the eighteenth century, their position seemed to undergo a complete decline. Under fanatic local rulers the Jews were particularly affected, crowded into fetid *mellahs*, and falling into poverty, ignorance and superstition. The French eased conditions in the nineteenth century for North Africa as a whole; but only a small proportion of the Jews of Morocco benefited from this. This cultured élite turned its attention after the war to settlement in France and the Americas, so that when emigration to Israel gathered pace in the late 1950s, the Jews involved tended to be particularly ill-equipped with skills or spiritual strength for the new venture.

We saw earlier that the flow of immigration from Morocco was not consistent, and was finally terminated by the Moroccan authorities in 1960. By 1958, however, some 120,000 had already left for Israel, so that a substantial number of individuals had to be absorbed.

By and large the Maghreb Jews, and especially those of Morocco, were impoverished and illiterate. Though some had skills as leather-workers or silversmiths, most had sustained themselves in marginal occupations as fruit-sellers, porters or pedlars. Their absorption was eased by the fact that by the time they began to arrive in substantial numbers the 'ship-to-village' programme was in full swing, so that they could be guided to *moshavim* or development towns without going back to slum existence. Though some of these settlements were in the far north, the majority were in the Negev; and it was a fortunate development of policy, also, that it had proved to be of value to build the *moshavim* in clusters of three to five villages, with many shared services, such as schools, a clinic, a tractor service, a bank, and so on.

This brief look at the mechanics of the ingathering of the eastern Jews foreshadows some of the problems that were to become manifest later, when the new arrivals ceased to be a current inflow and had to be dealt with in terms of the social background that was now assuming a set pattern. The major factor that dominates all consideration of this is that in the course of the 1960s (perhaps around 1968), the Jews in Israel who were of eastern origin by their own birth or the birth of their parents in eastern lands became a majority of the population. Their high proportion among the post-1948 immigrants, and their tendency, especially in the early years, to have a high birthrate, were the contributing factors. As the children of the new majority reached voting age, this majority was bound to give them, ultimately, a decisive power at election time; and it is clear that when this voting power was exercised heavily in one direction in the 1970s, for reasons which we will consider in the next chapter, it spelt defeat for the Labour Alignment and success for the Likud Coalition led by Mr Begin.

Sephardim and Ashkenazim

This all happened after many years in which the eastern Jews, and especially those from Morocco, had been building up the strong social resentment referred to above. It would never be enough that the party originally in power, the Labour Alignment, had accomplished miracles in absorbing the new immigrants and fitting them into employment, education and social welfare. As against this, the relevant consideration for many immigrants was their lowly place in the class structure, in which patterns of privilege were being sustained and intensified, so that political protest, and even violence, seemed the only way to secure change.

The established pattern that had emerged to promote this was by no means a straight conflict between Sephardi and Ashkenazi Israelis, though this was certainly a strong element. The Sephardi/Ashkenazi distinction had been bolstered through separate – and rival – religious roles under successive governments. This was a major way in which the term 'Sephardi' has come to be used to cover a wide variety of Jews of eastern origin, whose main common feature was that they were not Ashkenazis of European origin. The high place given to religious authority in eastern lands goes back a long way, and it has inevitably led, in the Israeli situation, to the emergence of political parties with rival religious allegiances. This has naturally been increased by the growth in numbers of the Sephardim. They have increasingly felt the need to assert their independence from the Ashkenazi religious parties, who enjoyed a strongly established place in the system, with the patronage of large funds put at their disposal by the government.

Duplication – and rivalry – in this field goes back to the early days of the British Mandate. The British found, when they took over in the 1920s, that under the Ottomans there was one top representative rabbi, *Rishon le-Zion* (First in Zion), who was, naturally for those days, a Sephardi. The British, impelled no doubt by their famed principle of fair play, decided that the Ashkenazi Jews had to be given equal status, and that the selection of the two chiefs should be by voting. The various complicated and troublesome processes through which this was given effect is well described, with appropriate irony, by an English constitutional expert, William Frankel, in his book *Israel Observed*.[107]

The first step of the British was to convene an assembly of rabbis and laymen, which elected a Rabbinical Council of eight – four Sephardi and four Ashkenazi rabbis – who elected from among themselves one Ashkenazi and one Sephardi Chief Rabbi, with equal status. The Council itself was recognized as the sole authority in matters of Jewish law, a role which has continued (with some modifications) under the Israeli constitution, with built-in problems in a country which gives *rabbinical* law in many fields the status of *governmental* law.

For the present position in Israel it is relevant to note that, however fair and democratic the British arrangement looked on paper, it has worked out less neatly in practice. For one thing, as Frankel reminds us, the equal status of the two Chief Rabbis has been known (to put it mildly) to lead to conflict. For another, the Rabbinical Council is not recognized by the extremely orthodox Agudat Israel Party, which accepts only the religious authority of its own Council of Sages. Nor is it recognized by the even more orthodox groups of the old *Yishuv*.

To try to establish something more like parity, the Council has now been enlarged to ten members, elected by a system which involves *local* religious councils, and is 'designed to ensure fair representation of both Ashkenazim and Sephardim'. In the same breath, however, we learn that the four major cities of Israel – Jerusalem, Tel Aviv, Haifa and Beersheba – each have two local Chief Rabbis (one Ashkenazi and one Sephardi); and if they take their tone from the rivalries of the two 'national' chiefs, it may well extend the quarrels that were manifest when, until recently, the two top posts were held by Rabbi Obadiah Yosef (Sephardi) and Rabbi Shlomo Goren (Ashkenazi). The former was born in Baghdad, the latter in Poland: both are recognized scholars and both express, perhaps, their national characters, the former rather quiet in style, the latter somewhat rumbustious.

Variety of attitudes

This leads one to recognize that even if there is an overall Sephardi loyalty among those who fall into this camp, there is a great deal of variety in social behaviour, linked to their pre-state history and the styles of life that had developed in the different settings. It was perhaps to be expected that these national characteristics would be discernible most clearly, and with the greatest contrast, in the two communities, Iraq and Morocco, which have provided the largest influx of immigrants. Jews from the other eastern countries, ranging from Libya to Iran and Afghanistan, seem to have attracted less attention. As Howard Sachar puts it in his authoritative book *A History of Israel,* 'they have adjusted to Israeli life quietly and inconspicuously'.[108] If in this sense they are all similar, everyone particularly likes one of them, the Yemenites, who see 'any life in the Holy Land as a blessing', whose farms are models of diligence and thrift, and whose contribution to Israeli's handicrafts has been outstanding. 'In consequence,' Sachar says, 'the Yemenites have evoked an almost universal, if paternalistic, affection from the nation at large.'

He is somewhat more quizzical about the Iraqis, admiring their sense of pride and purpose, but implying that the high qualities they brought with them could sometimes cause as much trouble to the organizers of the ingathering as did the Moroccans, who had little going for them at the other end of the social spectrum. 'The Iraqis regarded themselves as aristocrats,' Sachar says. 'With all their strength, they resisted the initial effort to hustle them into *moshavim* or development communities. A bare 3 per cent of them became farmers.' As early as July 1951 they organized a large-scale demonstration in Tel Aviv to protest at not being given positions as high-level administrators. 'If once they had held high positions in an Arab land, they insisted, should they not be qualified for similar employment in a Jewish state?'

In the end, 'by protest and persistence', they found appropriate outlets for their qualifications and experience, living mostly in the urban areas, and working largely in finance and the professions. But if they have, in this sense, won through to success by holding on relentlessly to their own traditional standards, it is noteworthy that their leaders have also maintained the same standards of social responsibility for which they were so distinguished in Iraq. In particular, they have given freely of their energy and, where they have it, wealth, to improve the education and welfare of their disadvantaged Sephardi brethren from other eastern lands, in programmes that have concentrated very heavily on helping those from Morocco, whose masses came from such a different background.

The Moroccans were not alone, of course, in being so disadvantaged. A great majority of the Sephardi immigrants were in a parlous situation when they arrived. The family structures of the immigrants were exactly the opposite of the pattern of the early *aliyahs* from eastern Europe which had brought in young, hardy, well-trained idealists, for whom no task would be too great. Here the immigrants, rescued and transplanted *en masse*, included a very large proportion of sick old people and helpless infants. The able-bodied of working age were largely unskilled and ill-educated. Education was, in fact, the nub of the problem. It affected not only the wage-earning power of those who found work – usually in very low-level jobs – but the depressing situation at home, where hordes of infants could learn little of educational value from their harried and illiterate mothers. Crash programmes for the education, on western lines, of Sephardim of all ages as well as children took time to build up to full effectiveness; and in the interim period the earning gap was self-perpetuating, heralding social and political problems that were inevitable.

One has always to remember that throughout this difficult period of transforming half a nation through experience that was foreign to them, the country was fighting war after war to defend its very existence. One is aware also, with hindsight, that those guiding the transformation were themselves having to learn from experience, since nothing had prepared anybody for this unique situation. One of the striking things which emerged, after a time, was that the basic elements of western education, necessary as they were, would not be adequate by themselves to fortify the spirit of the immigrants. The uprooting had left psychological scars which would not be healed by burying old memories and traditions under a blanket of westernization. We shall see this emerging when we look briefly, in the final chapter, at the experience of these first decades.

But having dwelt, as one had to, on the enormity of the task, one stands amazed at the end at how much was achieved in this short time. The steady progress towards higher living standards, and the harmonization of disparate cultures through widespread 'inter-ethnic' marriage and other forms of social mobility, are symbolized dramatically by the emergence of Sephardim of all types – including those from disadvantaged eastern backgrounds – in the high ranks of the Establishment; and this transformation is steadily broadening its base, as we shall see, throughout this section of Israeli society.

18 Experience in Israel

The reminder at the end of the last chapter that the term 'Sephardi' is used in Israel to cover both western-style and eastern non-Ashkenazim has to be kept in mind in the present chapter, where we shall be looking at contrasts between the socio-political experience of different 'classes' in Israel. To spell out the terminology 'Ashkenazi' is clear enough, covering those Jews whose ancestors spread from northern and eastern Europe and across the Atlantic, and who were increasingly emancipated and 'westernized' during the last two centuries. 'Sephardi', in the Israeli scene, includes both those whose ancestors were influenced by a long stay in medieval Spain and Portugal before funnelling out across the Mediterranean, and also those who are linked to long stays in 'eastern' lands stretching from Morocco to the Far East, often overlapping with 'Spanish' Sephardim but essentially carrying a very distinctive history.

A preliminary word has to take note of the social differences between these two kinds of Sephardim. In many cases, 'upper-class' and old-established Sephardim have had the benefits of education and westernized culture in styles that parallel the experience of Ashkenazim. In contrast, most 'eastern' Sephardim have come from much more primitive backgrounds, which has generated special problems of absorption. Yet this gap is by no means static. If one uses the term Sephardim to cover all non-Ashkenazim, it is with an awareness that the trend is towards homogeneity. Indeed it is the essential feature of Israeli life that all the gaps are losing their earlier dominance, both among those covered by the catch-all name 'Sephardim' and in the wider community, where even the old Ashkenazi–Sephardi bifurcation is losing its restrictiveness.

The most obvious signal of this is the fact that 'inter-ethnic' marriage is now a major feature of Israeli life, affecting well over 25 per cent of the population. This is related to the increasing spread of those areas of life – including agriculture, military affairs, science and the law – which are in a basic sense neutral to ethnic considerations. It is essential to stress this at the beginning of this chapter since our main concern, in dealing with social issues, will be to highlight the problems, as distinct from the achievements. The problems have been, and still are, very real, as we shall see; but everything will be out of proportion if we fail to see the wood for the trees. With all the divisions that surfaced during the massive ingathering of the Jews from Arab/Muslim countries, Israel was always a single united country. The enormous varieties of social origins and cultures have been of secondary importance against this basic fact.

Within this overall unity, Israeli society is essentially mobile; and this brings one to another major point in evaluating the experience of 'eastern' Jews since the state came into being in 1948. In the foreground there seemed to be an unbridgeable gap between the Establishment (Ashkenazi plus some old-established Sephardim) and the disadvantaged 'orientals'. But within a few decades, a new pattern developed, in which political, and even some economic, power began to be shaped increasingly by the less-privileged new arrivals. The speed with which this has happened is of paramount significance. A major element in this rapid change has lain in the development of active social policies of the kind that will occupy our attention in this chapter; but quite remarkably it has also been an internal process of self-development in which the new arrivals moved towards whatever outlets they could develop within their means in order to achieve a full realization of their potential in the Israeli scene.

This potential has demanded increasing expression since the 1960s when those of Sephardi origin (using 'Sephardi' in its broadest sense) became the majority of Israel's population. In the dramatic expansion of Israel's Jewish population from 649,000 in 1947 to 3,373,000 in 1982, the Sephardi element was the central feature (see Table 4). This, in turn, represents a complete turn-about in the balance of Israel's Jewish population. In 1947, the Sephardim were 23 per cent of the Jewish population; today they are 55 per cent, a historic change which has restored the position of a hundred years earlier before the heavy inflow of Ashkenazi Jews from eastern Europe began.

The new preponderance of Sephardim has not meant a simple handover of power and influence from one majority to another. The process of change has been many-faceted, with political and social changes criss-crossing from all directions and containing many apparent paradoxes. An over-simplified description would miss this. In the political field, for example, it can be said (quite correctly) that the new state was governed for the first thirty years by heavily Ashkenazi Labour, which had to hand over power, after the general election of 1977, to the Likud Coalition, whose majority owed much to a wave of Sephardi voting for its leader Menachem Begin. But this would be a very superficial description of what happened, and why. Similarly, it is a far from adequate description of the Sephardim to look only at those elements who are ill-educated and disadvantaged, though this has to be brought into the picture. By the same token, it is misleading just to note how the Sephardim have been assimilating to the western culture of the Ashkenazim, but to ignore the maintenance of their own traditions and their increased importance to the general culture emerging in Israel.

In effect, one has to look at the experience of the Sephardim in these first three or four decades in Israel as an interweaving of influences which never point in one direction, and whose weight can be better understood if one accepts from the beginning that nothing can be clear-cut in a society that is as effervescent as Israel's has been.

Sephardi attitudes

It is part of this indeterminate picture that the changing forces due to become explicit later were not fully observable in the first decades and can only be reconstructed, as it were, from what emerged later at general elections (see Table 5). This is particularly true of the Likud's triumph at the general election of 1977, which revealed the long build-up of frustration and anger with the Labour Establishment on the part of the new generation of Sephardim. Another long-simmering process came to the boil in the general election of 1984, which showed a strong movement *within* the Sephardi community towards splinter parties linked to religious loyalties. This was not so much a religious expression as a growing ability, by the leaders of these small parties, to make more of Sephardi distinctiveness, and thus secure a larger share of government funds set aside for religiously-administered patronage of all kinds.

There was a long background, also, to the emergence in 1984 of contrasting attitudes within the Sephardi community to the toughness of policy towards the Arabs on the West Bank. Support for the hawklike policies of Herut came from the poorer sections of the Sephardim, who are said to have felt that Labour's 'pro-Arab' policies for the West Bank would have left the poorest of the Sephardim on the lowest rungs of the employment ladder. By contrast, many Sephardim already well up this ladder found themselves in political sympathy with Ashkenazi Labour supporters of the same socio-economic class, a process which also has taken time to establish itself but is now a feature of the scene.

Most of the Sephardim who are now well up this ladder started life in the dreary and sometimes unbearable physical conditions endured by the mass immigrants from eastern countries, but managed, somehow, to make a success of the meagre educational opportunities offered by this background. In those early years education was, inevitably, only one of the high priorities of the government which, apart from defence preoccupations, had also to provide every immigrant with shelter, medical care and work. In this situation the government's efforts to give education its obviously important place often had very poor results. There was a colossal shortage of educational facilities and qualified teachers in the camps and early development towns. A social contrast, with baleful effects for the future, soon became evident in the superior ability of Ashkenazi children to take advantage of what was available. They had better conditions at home, and their parents could help with guidance and motivation. The contrast was self-perpetuating. Many Sephardi children simply dropped out of school; compared with Ashkenazi children, relatively few went on to high schools, for which fees were required in those days; still fewer went to college. The social effects of this were disastrous. With poor educational backgrounds, Sephardi youth found it hard to get anything but unskilled work or any jobs at all.

Frustration and its results

In time this painful situation began to be eased through special educational programmes for Sephardim who would never, otherwise, break out of this dead end. Starting with programmes at primary schools, this was ultimately extended to special courses for those in the Forces, and, at a higher level, for those who had got as far as college but still could not cope on an equal basis. Later many voluntary groups and agencies would introduce useful programmes to try to bridge the educational and social gaps; but long before these many efforts at harmonization could take effect, there were violent public demonstrations which made the whole country aware of the anger provoked by the sense of discrimination felt by the oriental immigrants. These protests could take various forms, as we saw earlier in mentioning the protest by Iraqis in Tel Aviv, as early as July 1951, at not being given jobs of a calibre equal to their qualifications and experience. Very different, and infinitely more significant, was a riot by young orientals which broke out in Wadi Salib, a run-down suburb of Haifa, on 5 July 1959.

The troubles began in a bar-room brawl to which the police were called, and led to a drunken Moroccan being shot and carried off to hospital. Crowds of Moroccans besieged the police station the next morning, calling for 'revenge'. There were similar riots in other places; and the significance for the future lay in the scale of anti-government organization now revealed. Leaflets and protests were organized swiftly by the Likud Olei Tsfon Africa (Group of North African Imigrants) led by a Moroccan, David Ben-Harouch, who proclaimed in vehement speeches that his own case, of being offered only a shanty in Wadi Salib after his service in the army, was typical of the prejudice against all North Africans, excluding them from a fair place, compared with Ashkenazim, in education, housing and jobs.

The riots were an alert to the government and public opinion, though nothing much came of a committee set up by the government, with Ben-Harouch himself a member, to report on what should be done. In the view of the sociologist S. M. Eisenstadt in his major study *Israeli Society*, Ben-Harouch's wild accusations were counterproductive in giving body to the view held by many that the North Africans were just hooligans, yet the incident unleashed political developments which have profoundly affected the position of the Sephardim. The Ashkenazi Establishment took note, almost for the first time, of the importance of responding to 'ethnic' complaints:

Several specifically ethnic parties emerged at election time, among them the *Likud*, with Ben-Harouch heading its list and claiming that he represented not only the North Africans but all victims of discrimination. The need to include more orientals in major public posts became generally recognized; and in the 1961 election, when some older Sephardi groups supported Mapai, a Sephardi minister was then included in the 1961 cabinet.[109]

Professor Eisenstadt, writing in 1965, could probably not have foreseen how profoundly these early developments would point the way to the transformation of Israeli political life within a few years. Looking back, one can see that Wadi Salib, and the later riots in 1972 of the 'Black Panthers' – young Moroccans again protesting against discrimination, in the style of the riotous blacks in the United States – show up the continuing ethnic gaps during this period, much eased today though still potent.

Growth of the Likud

The most far-reaching consequence of the frustration felt by disadvantaged Sephardim was, obviously, the emergence to power of Menachem Begin's Likud Coalition in 1977, with his central Herut Party heavily supported by Sephardim, particularly the young ones, as a way of showing their total objection to the hitherto monolithic Labour Establishment. This rationale is the only way to explain the social paradox embedded in this particular division.

The Labour Party (Mapai), though always regarded as 'left' in ideology, have now become status quo in aim, and are supported largely by the better-off Ashkenazim. Mr Begin's Herut has always had a strong right-wing tone in economic philosophy (inherited from their almost legendary leader Jabotinsky), yet this is the party that has coralled the support of very vehement disadvantaged voters who might normally have been expected to support a left-wing party. The paradox is certainly explained by their discovering in Mr Begin a great symbol of protest, which he exploited to the full; but some political analysts have gone further by linking the Sephardi support for Herut to the development of a new form of expression in Israel of what being a Jew is to mean in the future.

In this view the early Zionist philosophy, which saw Jews as aiming at 'liberal' progress along 'western' internationalist lines, is replaced by a Herut philosophy which sees the Jews as standing alone, echoing their distinctiveness through the ages, and planning now to hold on to their ancient homeland, without compromise or dilution. The policy of establishing settlements in the West Bank clearly fits into this approach. It removes the relevance of 'right' and 'left' in the usual social sense and puts all the emphasis on a different kind of allegiance, with 'the Land' calling for every kind of loyalty. For some this new kind of surrender to the all-embracing mystique of the Land takes a specific religious form, which is why new Sephardi religious parties like Shas (Sephardi Guardians of the Torah) are naturally at home in the Likud as allies of Herut.

It is not universally accepted, as we shall see, that this new definition of a Jew is a valid projection of issues which are beginning to dominate Israeli politics. Some prefer to give more weight, among Sephardi Jews, to ethnic origins, which create a set of loyalties superseding any generalized concept of what being an Israeli is to mean.

Upsurge of ethnicity

The presence of all these conflicting sentiments is a warning against being too rigid in analysis of the socio-political scene. Dr Sammy Smooha, author of the well-known study *Pluralism and Conflict* (1978), commented usefully on these issues in a recent essay which he called 'The Upsurge of Ethnicity in Israel'.[110]

The early phase of the ingathering, he says, revealed a strong hostility, if not contempt, among Zionist leaders of western origin for the cultural ethos of the Jews of the East – the *edot ha-mizrach*. Of many expressions of this, he quotes two revealing remarks by Ben-Gurion himself. In 1950 he spoke of the new immigrants as 'medley and dust . . . without roots, and without benefiting from the national traditions and vision'. And as late as 1966 he could say, referring to what he believed they expressed: 'We do not want Israelis to become Arabs. We are duty bound to fight against the spirit of the Levant which corrupts individuals and society.'

This polarization, Smooha says, has resulted in many social analysts taking a falsely rigid view of the current nature of Israeli society. Labour, they think, stands for 'innovation and humanism'. The aim is to produce a new type of Jewish life 'which rests on the humanistic values of labour, secularism, tolerance, democratic freedoms, and willingness to compromise in intergroup conflict situations'.

In contrast Likud, especially since their rise to power in 1977, aims 'to fashion a new Jew whose life interests are the nation, tradition, land, power, and messianic in his own absolute right and might'.

Smooha, as we shall see, does not accept this polarization; and he also rejects the views of some analysts that the character of oriental Jews has been immutably conditioned by their countries of origin. The argument here is that they were brought up in authoritarian countries, 'and thus predisposed to parochialism, traditional religion, charismatic leadership, chauvinism, irrationality, messianism and intransigence'. This would argue for a permanent difference from the western Ashkenazim, with an assumption that the Ashkenazim, like the Sephardim, are fixed in outlook, with no change from the old Labour Zionist philosophy which was secular and internationalist in style.

These are, of course, familiar ideas; yet they have become misleading clichés, Smooha believes, insofar as they are applied rigidly to the Israeli situation. The Ashkenazim have long modified their earlier domination by a Labour ideology; and Likud ideas are only partially conditioned by the oriental origin of its adherents. The really significant approach, as was suggested earlier, is to see at the centre the underlying common aims of all sections of society, whose unity beneath the surface is far more important to the future than a concentration on political rivalries would indicate.

It is essential to register the centrality of *Israeli* ideas, both in politics and cultural expression, before one can give full weight, as one must, to all-important differences in social attitudes and traditions. The underlying unity is so 'natural' that it can be overlooked unless spelt out. To sum it up in a sentence, it draws, in *Jewish* terms, on the language and literature that was kept alive for 2,000 years, and in *social* terms on what is recognized in the twentieth century as the so-called 'Protestant Ethic': the biblical values of justice under law and unhampered freedom. The commonality of the Jewish 'core-culture' has been expressed throughout this book; it is a single stream of historic consciousness which overrides any differences of regional origin. It is relevant to mention in this connection that even in religious teaching, which might have been thought to follow differing Ashkenazi/Sephardi traditions, the *halakhah*, as distinct from local custom, is uniform. The leaders of the new religious party Shas (Sephardi Guardians of the Torah) all studied at Ashkenazi *yeshivot*, as did the leaders of the Sephardi Morashah Party.

There is another uniformity worth mentioning. The social difference visible in a pronounced way in the early Israeli years is mostly a matter of timing. Both 'western' and 'eastern' Jews of Israel had their origin in poor societies, one in eastern Europe, the other in oriental lands. Each responded to the science and liberalism of the nineteenth century as soon as they got a chance; but one response was a generation before the other. Today the same one-directional process is continuing, but with the differences in timing very visible – and often violent – on the social scene.

The persistent gap

It is not much comfort to those affected by this difference in timing to recognize that in the long term those Sephardim who are upwardly mobile, socially, are reinforcing a visible trend towards harmonization of the economic classes. Nor is it really correct; for though an increasing section of the disadvantaged orientals have been greatly improving their education and economic status, the Ashkenazi sector has also been going ahead at the same time, and perhaps even at a faster rate.

This has resulted in a frustrating social block that gets increasingly hard to remove. The orientals who emerge leave behind an ethnic working class who generate a continuing image of oriental back-wardness. Official figures reinforce the general impression. The *per capita* income of the average Ashkenazi household was twice that of the Sephardi average in 1981.[111] Educationally, Jews of Asian/African origin had an average nine years of schooling in 1982 compared with eleven for Jews of European/American background. Even when orientals had an extra year or two of schooling, it could not open up a clear road to college or other higher qualifications: among those of Asian/African origin 10.3 per cent had some college education compared with 33.5 per cent for European/Americans.

Figures used by the sociologists in this form of analysis demonstrate radically the dimensions of this gap. Ashkenazim dominate the top occupational categories, whereas the lower-skilled or unskilled are overwhelmingly oriental. In the middle, employment as technicians, schoolteachers, shopkeepers, etc., is about balanced; and it is in this group, comprising about one third of the Jewish population, that social mobility, as reflected above all by inter-ethnic marriage, mostly takes place.

We shall look later at the fields in which the emergence of Sephardi leaders in various forms has clearly narrowed the gap. It still stands four-square in Israeli life, with its most potent reality expressed in politics; but though it is a problem in an obvious sense, it has also an encouraging side in the stimulus it has given to produce a variety of policies to come to terms with it.

Factors that will help

Because the ethnic aspect is so central, observers can be tempted to compare it with manifestations of what seem the same social problems in other countries, such as the presence, say, of disadvantaged black immigrants in Britain; but if some remedies can be similar, there is a crucial difference which makes the Israeli 'ethnic problem' unique.

The Sephardi–oriental Jews are not 'foreigners' to the existing body politic: they have been confronted by something which seems new, but they are in fact fully part of this new world by virtue of their history and kinship. Mutual adjustments are difficult for the time being because of the socio-economic circumstances which have made barriers difficult to lower; but the barriers *can* fall and, paradoxically, this will happen all the more successfully when the cultural differences of the past are given full weight rather than being passed over.

This seems to be the lesson emerging in a far-ranging study called *Studies in Israel's Ethnicity*, edited by Dr Alex Weingrod of Ben-Gurion University.[112] In his introduction to the studies in the book which examine, in sociological terms, the baffling difficulties that the oriental immigrants have experienced, Weingrod tries to explain why it is that though their economic standards have improved so positively, the original assumptions of harmonization as a natural consequence have given way to a new emphasis on ethnicity. There are several reasons behind this, he says, which have little to do with inequality. It emerges, in fact, as people get better off and look for new methods of self-expression:

Ethnicity is not embedded with a social or cultural system but tends to find organisation and expression in certain specified situations. Ethnicity is a resource that can have political, economic and symbolic use and meaning. People join as ethnics when it suits their interests.

From another angle – and most interestingly – the persistent problems of adjustment for the oriental Jews are seen by one of the contributors, Judah Matres, in the context of the particular effects on them of rapid changes between successive generations, a process which is called, in sociologist lingo, 'inter-generational social mobility' (ISM). As a rapidly developing country, the whole of Israel expresses ISM on a 'massive' scale; yet 'this has not yet resulted in a substantial reduction of ethnic socio-economic inequality'. A sociological study conducted in 1974 shows, he says, that whereas some 60–63 per cent of all Israeli Jews aged 25–34 had more education than their fathers, only 20 per cent of oriental Jews whose fathers had 'blue-collar' jobs had got into 'white-collar' jobs. The underlying reason for the far greater success of Ashkenazi non-orientals in rising from a low background is that even where there is a 'break', eroding their ethnic origin, they still have a heritage of 'resources' (knowledge, experience, contacts and skills) which promote continuity. By contrast, 'the mobility of the Asian/Africans tends to be independent of older generation resources, and introduces discontinuity'.

This diverse effect of ISM on Ashkenazim and Sephardim is central, says another contributor, Eliezer Ben-Raphael, to the way the ethnic political parties began to emerge so forcefully in the 1970s, reversing the expectation that the obviously strong economic betterment among the Sephardim would rule this out. Studies show, he says, that 'about a quarter of the oriental population are now in middle- and upper-class occupations and that this proportion is increasing'; but this, strange to say, is precisely why the other orientals left behind have turned to the exploitation of their ethnicity. All are conscious of belonging to a specific group by origin, and 'when some move out, those remaining in oriental *edot* (communities) evolve as Ethno-classes'. And here it becomes relevant for politics to see how the upwardly-mobile of different origins look back on their respective ethnic links.

A study conducted in 1978–9 examined the views of a representative number of upwardly-mobile Yemenites and Moroccans living in good city conditions. It showed that the striking contrast in their attitudes went back to the societies from which they had emerged. Yemenite society, despite widespread poverty, had been 'conservative and cohesive'; Moroccan society had been 'characterized by cultural and communal disorganization after fifty years of French colonialism'. Today both 'identify with the primordial identity of the group' but see themselves as 'different'. The Yemenite thinks of himself as more religious than the group; the Moroccan as less. The Yemenites emphasize the family more than they think their group does; the Moroccans less. Most significantly, both think that ethnicity is more important for the group than for themselves. Whatever their old links, they feel a considerable affinity now for the Ashkenazim. Their Jewish and Israeli identity comes first for 60–80 per cent, followed by their link to their country of origin, and finally their awareness of themselves as oriental.

Relations to politics

Given these attitudes, it is not surprising that these upwardly-mobile orientals kept themselves apart from the emergence of ethnic political parties. The figures in the survey on this are quite decisive: ethnic parties were opposed by 85 per cent of the Yemenites and 91 per cent of the Moroccans. For themselves this indicates a strong self-assurance; they see their future as socially identified with the Ashkenazim, hoping to have left the oriental image behind. But for the remaining orientals, their departure means that the ethnic parties have lost potential leaders which, Ben-Raphael says, 'explains the political weakness of the *edot* compared with their weight in the population'.

Their growth in political power has nevertheless been remarkable, for if the small parties with various allegiances or links with the orientals are still only marginal, they have played a crucial role in transforming government by the single dominant Labour grouping (the Alignment) into what is basically a two-party system, with the Likud (built around Herut) as the alternative. The distribution of support shows that two thirds of Alignment voters in 1981 were Ashkenazim, while two thirds of Likud supporters were Sephardim.[113] Looking to the future, however, it is significant that Sephardi support for Likud was stronger among the second and third generation of immigrants than among the first. In 1981 the Sephardim, though 55 per cent of the population, were still a minority as voters because of a high proportion of children in their numbers. As these grow to voting age, the political balance may be affected, though this depends on how far the upwardly-mobile orientals remain attached to ethnic grouping.

A relevant factor here is the lack of solidarity *within* the orientals, reflecting differences in origin and religious outlook which have stimulated an almost non-stop development of splinter parties. An interesting angle on this is to note that the Iraqis and Yemenites, who were the early political activists among the Sephardim, found that their leadership was never accepted by the Moroccans, and that the Iraqi masses, in turn, refused to accept the Moroccans as equals and felt closer to Ashkenazi Jews.

Overall, perhaps, it has worked better for Sephardim to exercise their influence under one of the two major 'umbrellas'. Labour

(Mapai) was the first to take Sephardim into the government, and they still have powerful supporters, like Yitzhak Navon, from the Sephardi side. We are told indeed that ambitious Moroccans like David Levy sought careers first in Mapai, but found the top positions occupied and so turned to Herut where they could rise as Sephardi leaders.[114] In the immediate wake of the 1984 election, of course, the leaders of both blocs came together in a national government led by Shimon Peres, with posts given also to some 'splinter' leaders. To hold office as prime minister is itself a favouring factor which can override earlier analyses, as Mrs Meir and Mr Begin found, so that the balance within the leadership of the nation may well be subject to further change as time goes by.

Local and national politics

Much more assured, in relation to the political outlook, is the upsurge of Sephardi leadership at the municipal level. Here the creation of development towns with a substantial number of orientals certainly laid a basis for the reversal of the earlier position, in which local government and patronage lay heavily for years within the purview of the Labour Establishment; but as always in local politics, success was more likely to come when a leader with unusual personal qualities could make the most of a potential take-over. This is always a situation with more than local significance. Among many cases in which it had already happened, the recent emergence of a young Moroccan, Elie Dayan, as Mayor of Ashkelon, is a particularly interesting example in that it brings so many issues together in one setting.

Dayan, born in Morocco in 1944, fought his way up the educational ladder against all the obstacles spoken of earlier, in order finally to win a degree in law from the Hebrew University in Jerusalem. Throughout these early years he worked passionately in Ashkelon for nursery schools and other special programmes to help children from illiterate homes to find a way to equal opportunity. The Sephardim of Ashkelon lived in a very ill-provided sector separate from the comfortable Ashkenazi homes of what had been mainly a resort town. Locally, he defied the entrenched Establishment with promises of immediate introduction of his special programmes the day after he was elected. Nationally, he joined the launching of Tami, an openly ethnic party led by Aharon Abuhatzeira, member of a long line of revered rabbis of Morocco, and able because of this to retain the total loyalty of his Moroccan followers. (This happened even when he was arrested and sent to prison for alleged embezzlement of funds provided by the government for educational and social purposes handled by religious bodies!) Tami won three seats in the 1981 election and joined Mr Begin's coalition in order to get a large share of the religious funds, long distributed by the mainly Ashkenazi 'National Religious Party' which had supported the Labour Alignment. With ethnic parties apparently growing, it was fully expected that Tami would at least hold this number of Knesset seats at the election of 1984. Elie Dayan was number three on the Tami list which indicated a seat in the Knesset and an open road to the future. In the event, Tami won only one seat in 1984. The Sephardi sentiment had moved, as noted earlier, to specifically religious parties, and notably to Shas led by a new figure: Rabbi Yitzhak Peretz, born in Casablanca in 1946 and brought to Israel under Youth Aliyah in 1950.

This criss-crossing of developments reflects the volatility of the Sephardi–oriental background, with Elie Dayan as a good illustration. Though high on the Tami list, he is only one of a growing cadre of well-educated young men and women of oriental origin who, as a newspaper account puts it, are still 'seething with frustration and bitterness at the discrimination and inequality that they perceive in Israel society', and have plunged into a huge variety of social campaigns to redress this balance.* Tami itself is said to be financed by very large contributions from wealthy Sephardim resident in Switzerland, England and America; but in addition, numerous social projects in many other areas are financed by individual patrons who believe that it is of supreme importance to give disadvantaged Sephardim a better chance in Israel.

At the local level a visit to Dayan's office with its heady atmosphere of bustling reform reminds one of the style of Mayor La Guardia's office in New York at the height of his fame. He, too, had thrown out

* The extraordinary scale of these projects is described in a detailed review by Charles Hoffman (*Jerusalem Post*, 28 April 1984) entitled 'How Tami Bestows Party Favours'. To summarize, Tami's grants finance Hadar (a religious vocational training network), Moreshet Dorot (an association which organizes social and cultural activities to promote oriental–Jewish culture), Mifras (a scholarship fund for needy students in schools, *yeshivot* and colleges), Leket (a publishing house for literature of importance to oriental Jews), Meorot (to finance Sephardi religious instruction neglected by the Ashkenazi system), Nahlat Avot (a fund to promote new *moshavim* for Tami members), Maoz (welfare services for the aged), and many more.

the established 'bums' (to use his term) in order to exercise patronage in the cause of justice as *he* saw it. One is frequently aware, looking at the problems of the ingathering, of how much is being accomplished by the inspiration and charisma of local leaders in this way, and often without the overhang of national politics, and the corruption that this can generate.

Programmes for bridging the gap

A very good illustration of this, completely different in character from the national involvement of even an attractive mayor like Elie Dayan of Ashkelon, is seen in a programme called 'Bridging the Gap', which is based at the University of Haifa, but owes its success to the quiet but irresistible dynamism of just one woman, Arlette Adler.

The programme was founded in 1974 to reduce the gap, in the development areas around Haifa, between disadvantaged Sephardim and the relatively privileged Ashkenazim. The solution was seen from the beginning, in familiar terms, as the need to raise the abysmally low level of education among most Sephardim; but the method adopted in this case has been highly original, in arranging for those who have already had the privilege of a university education to move out into the development towns and tutor selected pupils who can benefit, if given a chance, from this personal relationship. The system is financed through scholarships provided by donors, which enable graduates of the university to go out as 'consuls' to work in this way in development towns, and also provides finance for study at the university for those who are prepared to help pupils with learning difficulties. This is merely the basic outline of a programme which has broadened out into a multi-dimensional series of interrelated activities that now affect the whole region, and bring in adult education, women's groups, social advice centres, music, drama, dance and the arts generally, with special interest in the varied expression of Sephardi culture from Yemen to Morocco.

There is a political aspect to the programme in that the 'consuls' sometimes work in senior positions in the educational services and local authority departments. Graduates of the courses have been extremely active in local elections, being involved in a variety of parties, with many moving on to local government offices as mayors, chairmen and deputies of local councils. But by all reports this vastly useful programme has kept clear of the potential dangers of political involvement, and has taken shape, one is ready to believe, through the devotion and personal style generated by Arlette Adler.

Original as the Haifa programme is, it is, of course, only one of many which have developed ingenious ways of trying to bridge the gap. One, still in an experimental stage, has concentrated its attention on dealing with the low level of education among many young orientals by involving them in special courses during their period of service in the Forces. If successful, this could rescue the Sephardi young from what is, for most of them, a dead-end position in the Forces, confined as they are to menial jobs because of their lack of adequate schooling, compared with the Ashkenazim. A few figures document this. On average, 58 per cent of the total in the Israel Defence Forces (IDF) have completed twelve years of schooling. The figure for the Sephardi element is 26 per cent. The most depressing aspect of this low position for the Sephardim is that it deprives them of incentives to volunteer for fighting roles and other special tasks through which promotion is secured. The result shows up in the relative position in higher ranks. An IDF source stated, in 1981, that though the percentage of officers from lieutenant-colonel upwards of Sephardi origin had greatly increased, it was still only 3 per cent as against at least 53 per cent of the Sephardi Jews in the total population.

These figures emerge in a very frank study of this project commissioned by the IDF and entrusted to Professor Maurice Roumani, chairman of the Elyachar Centre for Oriental Heritage Studies at Ben-Gurion University of the Negev at Beersheba.[115] The project, which is called 'The David Education Unit' in tribute to David Ben-Gurion, is one of a number established by the IDF 'to advance the social and military status of the weaker sectors of the Israeli population, most of them of Asian/African origin'. Within the IDF itself there had been a division of view on whether the Forces exist just for military purposes or whether the presence of the disadvantaged should be exploited to rehabilitate those who, if special courses succeeded, could be established at higher levels within the Forces, and then get better jobs in the country at large. In adopting experimentally the second alternative, the Unit moved from a 'minimum' model, in which a recruit is put into work closest to his existing qualifications, to a 'maximum' model 'which requires investment in the individual in order to bring him to the highest possible position he can fill on the basis of his potential'. In choosing recruits for the courses devised, the aim has been to tackle the very low social standards found (inadequate homes and schooling, weak oral expression, poor symbolic conception, slow reflective thinking) by courses in 'areas unknown to the soldier' (e.g. history, political ideas, literature) aimed at personal 'enrichment', 'the enhancement of self-image' and 'the improvement of reciprocal ties with society'.

There could hardly be a better way of bringing out – and tackling – some of the problems inherent in the ingathering. One virtue of Professor Roumani's study is its frankness: it reports the total frustration expressed by many of the participants at their low positions in the army and life in general, their feeling of being wasted, and the doubt of many that anything in the course would help them in their future life. Within this, there were some who responded positively and with an increase in motivation. One test was that whereas before the course 80 per cent had opted for unskilled jobs and only 10 per cent for fighting units, the latter figure rose to 32 per cent after the course.

To get a balanced picture of the social world that has emerged from the ingathering, one has to confront the depressing factors that are embedded in all honest reports of this kind, with the encouraging sign that the low image of themselves held by the Sephardi–orientals, as well as by a large sector of the public at large, is being confronted all the time by positive projections. This must certainly be an element in the fact that the Sephardim (using the term in its broadest sense) have moved forward not only in political power, which is partly an expression of their frustration, but in cultural esteem, which works from within.

The oriental heritage

Professor Roumani's work at Ben-Gurion in the field of the oriental heritage is a potent example of this. A great range of courses presented by the history and language departments of the university in numerous aspects of Jewish sociology, history, philosophy and literature, has been enlarged by the Elyachar Centre with courses related specifically to the historical and cultural backgrounds of individual countries – ranging from North Africa to India – whose story is now enriching the stream of Israeli culture, thus removing barriers of origin that existed when the state emerged. The ramifications of this approach go far beyond the campus of Ben-Gurion, however appropriately it is established there; for a similar endeavour, though at a different level of education, now exists in a government programme for all the schoolchildren of Israel, established under a Knesset directive in the 1970s. In putting this programme into action the Knesset realized that it was, in effect, a conscious reversal of the earlier outlook which had assumed that the many diverse strains within the people of the ingathering could be harmonized by a 'melting-pot' approach. Ironically, David Ben-Gurion himself had urged in 1951 that all cultural sources had to be integrated to build up the new nation. It was only by the actual experience of the ingathering that the limitations of this approach emerged for all to see.

For nearly three decades the social upheaval which we have surveyed here in the life of the oriental immigrants made it increasingly evident that behind the economic problems there had been a spiritual débâcle. The immigrants and their children had found Israeli ideals encased in a western Ashkenazi framework. This had been disastrous in confirming a lower status for those from Sephardi backgrounds, which affected the way the Sephardim were treated and instigated a loss of their own pride and self-confidence. The Knesset recognized in 1976 that this had to be countered by a major programme which would produce for all schoolchildren, Sephardi and Ashkenazi alike, a picture of their history which took all sources into account. The main thrust would be to bring out in a new way the history embodied in the Sephardi–oriental cultures, much of which had been obscured during recent centuries of decline; but it would also present Ashkenazi culture without the taint of materialism so commonly assumed, and thus harmonize all aspects of Jewish tradition.

Israel, in this new view, has to establish a unified outlook which at the same time gives full expression to the different heritages which were once so colourful in Jewish life everywhere. The contrast with the old approach can be expressed in a brief sentence. Until the new approach, the traditions of the Sephardi–oriental world were regarded as peripheral to the central theme: 'ethnic' in the sense of being charmingly different; now all sources are ethnic, and all belong with equal importance to the rich tradition that Israel represents.

Operationally, the programme has functioned since 1977 as part of the Ministry of Education and Culture, with government funds. In its first decade it has established a flow of children's books, posters, films and other audio-visual products of a vast range, linked to communal activities that have generated delight as well as instruction, with an unknown world brought to vibrant life. A report on the first decade by the current Director, Dr Nissim Yosha, defines very carefully the balance between integration and diversity:

There is no attempt here to work for the total preservation in the state of Israel of bygone lifestyles of various diaspora communities; such a position has almost no adherents in any stratum of Jewish society in Israel, apart from a few esoteric groups of specifically Eastern European origin. The new consensus does not neglect the original objectives of ingathering and integrating the Exiles ... but will proceed with the concomitant fostering of various particular elements: a selective approach concerning the form of the various heritages will be employed, along with examination of their relevance to modern Israeli society.

Cultural traditions

It is important to note that though this form of the Oriental Heritage Programme is directed heavily towards schools, it inevitably draws on a wide variety of other programmes in the same field where special expertise and enthusiasms are given full rein. The work of Bezalel in the art field is a clear example. Oriental music and dance is another. The books and magazines published on the Cairo *geniza*, and the learned writings of Goitein, Hirschberg and Scholem on the Middle Ages (heavily drawn on in this book), are invaluable source material. In dealing with individual countries, the traditions of Salonika – 'the Jerusalem of the Balkans' – are intensively pursued in alliance with the Federation of Greek Immigrants in Israel. The folklore traditions of North Africa have been increasingly given national significance in Israel by a great expansion of the celebration of the *Maimuna* festival immediately after Passover with considerable financial support provided by the World Sephardi Federation, and with the enthusiastic support of Israel's political leaders, both Sephardi and Ashkenazi.

The importance of all this activity to the future of the ingathering becomes evident when one moves on from 'populist' expression of the oriental heritage to the great range of scholarly research and writing that accompanies it at a different level. To list a few of the institutions engaged in this, there are the *Misgav Yerushalym* (research institute run jointly by the Sephardi communities and the Hebrew University), the 'Centre for the Study of Babylonian Jewry' in Or Yehudah, the

'Jeshurun Institute' (on Yemenite Jewry), the 'Centre for the Study of North African Jewry', the 'Ben Zvi Institute', and so on. The Jews from every country with oriental links and interests issue bulletins dealing not only with Persian, Bukharan, Moroccan, Tunisian and other 'national' festivities, but including anthologies of literature, poetry and memoirs, together with long-established annuals, like *Shevet va'Am*, which achieves the highest research standards.

The cultural range has been widened still further, of course, with the arrival of the Jews from Ethiopia. The Sephardi rabbinate has been in the lead, as one would expect, in recognizing the new immigrants as true Jews, due to make their own mark as they are absorbed into their new home.

Upsurge of Sephardi leadership

Without some awareness of the immense activity in Israel in giving expression at all levels to the cultural strains of the oriental heritage, one would miss an essential ingredient in the remarkable change that has emerged so clearly, since 1977, at the political level. We discussed earlier some of the factors which made so many of the young Sephardim in those days identify with Mr Begin's Herut Party, surprising at first glance but very understandable when their continued resentment is allowed for.

The result in the last few elections, as set out in Table 5, show that there has been no set pattern to this development. Sephardi sentiment has been moving along different channels with no prediction possible on how the political balance will take shape. The high posts now held by many Sephardim are more significant for the future, of course, when one sees a leader of disadvantaged origin – like David Levy – break through, or when a Yemenite like Yisrael Kessar rises to the top in the ultra-responsible work of the Histadrut, in succession to Ashkenazi leaders.

Men, so far, have been more prominent, though women have increasingly made their mark in many fields. Among the men, one notes that Yitzhak Navon, member of an old Sephardi family resident in Israel for ten generations, was President of Israel from 1978 to 1983, and on re-entering parliamentary politics became Minister of Education and Culture, and a Deputy Prime Minister, in the government headed by Shimon Peres. There were, in fact, six Sephardim in Peres's cabinet of 1984, including, besides Navon, David Levy, born in

Morocco, as Minister of Housing and Industry and with the rank, also, of Deputy Prime Minister; Mosheh Nissim of Iraqi origin, Minister of Justice; Rabbi Yitzhak Peretz, born in Casablanca in 1946, Minister for Home Affairs; Mosheh Katzav (of Iran), Minister of Labour; and Mosheh Shahal (of Iraq) Minister of Energy and Infrastructure.

The new Speaker elected by the 1984 Knesset was Shlomo Hillel, born in Iraq in 1923, an immigrant to Israel at the age of seven and a member of the Labour Party. Among his many political activities, he did a great deal to help Jews to emigrate clandestinely from Arab countries; and it is of note that an earlier Speaker of the Knesset, Yisrael Yeshayahu, was also a Sephardi, born in Yemen.

The Chief of Staff of the Forces since 1981, General Mosheh Levi, was born in Tel Aviv in 1936 of an Iraqi family. An earlier holder of the post was General David Elazar, born in Yugoslavia of an old Sephardi family. The commander of the Israeli navy is Avraham Shushan, born in Turkey. These top posts are the apex of a very great number of high-ranking officers of Sephardi extraction.

Abraham Halima, a Justice of the Supreme Court, was born in Iraq. Eliahu Mani, member, like Yitzhak Navon, of one of the oldest Sephardi families in Israel, is a member of the Supreme Court. In terms of power in Israel, as mentioned above, a post of top responsibility is Secretary-General of the Histadrut, the Trade Union Federation. Yisrael Kessar, born in Yemen in 1931, was elected to this post in November 1984.

If one lists a few names of important Sephardim of different origins, it is not intended to be complete but merely illustrative of the process. This applies, for example, to mayors and deputy mayors of development towns, often a stage towards political activity on the national scene. In this category one can mention Mosheh Katzav, Minister of Labour and described, when Mayor of Kiryat Malachi, as 'an authentic representative of the second generation of the immigrant townships'. In parallel, one thinks of Rafi Suissa, appointed to the important post of Prison Commissioner in 1985, who immigrated from Morocco in his teens, became Mayor of the development town Mazkeret Batya and then a member of the Knesset. There is the same pattern in the career of Jacques Amir, who was Mayor of the development town Dimona and then entered the Knesset. Aharon Abuhatzeira, mentioned earlier as leader of the heavily Moroccan party Tami, had been Mayor of Ramleh before being elected to the Knesset and given a ministerial post in Mr Begin's government of

1981. To mention two others in this stream: Eliyahu Navi, Mayor of Beersheba, the 'capital' of the Negev, is by origin from an Iraqi family. Elie Dayan, a Moroccan by origin and Mayor of Ashkelon, was mentioned earlier as one of the rising political activists.

In the professions there are numerous Sephardim eminent in medicine, including the heart surgeon Dr Maurice Levi, born in Bulgaria; Dr Shmuel Shaltiel, born in Salonika and Professor of Immunology at the Weizmann Institute; and another member of the Mani family, Dr Mosheh Mani, Professor of Medicine at Tel Aviv University and appointed president of the university in 1983.

Among numerous Sephardim in high academic posts, we have already spoken of Professor Roumani, born in Libya, at Ben-Gurion University. One might also cite two professors of history at Tel Aviv University: Shlomo Ben-Ami, born in Tangier, and Yehudah Ninni, of Yemenite origin. Among young scholars at the Hebrew University is Dr Michael Abitbul, of North African origin and a specialist in the communities of that area. In music we noted earlier the distinguished work of Professor Amnon Shiloah (he has a Syrian background) in recovering folk music and analysing the place of Jewish music in the Near Eastern world. At Haifa University there is Dr Jacob Mansour of Iraq, who is famed in the field of Arabic linguistics.

Lists of this kind could be extended almost without limit. They would have to include Sephardim prominent in the political field but moving in and out of direct governmental work. An outstanding example would be Mordecai Ben-Porat, born in Iraq in 1923. Ben-Gurion entrusted him with the task, after 1948, of helping to organize the mass immigration from the Arab countries; and later, after resigning from his post as Minister without Portfolio in the Shamir government, he was, among other things, chairman of the World Organization of Jews from Arab Countries.

In a cognate field one would mention the interesting career of Eli Amir, who was brought to Israel from Iraq in the exodus of 1951 and absorbed by Youth Aliyah. He drew on this experience (as we shall see) in writing a very appealing novel; and there is a pleasing appropriateness also in the shape of his 'official' career. Having experienced absorption at first hand, he rose first to become Deputy-Director of the Ministry of Absorption and was then, in 1984, appointed Director of Youth Aliyah, directly responsible for the lives and education of thousands of children, including those who were rescued from Ethiopia.

There are many other assorted realms of public life in which those descended from various Sephardi backgrounds have made a particular mark in Israel. One example is Victor Shemtov, who retired in 1985 from his final post as Secretary-General of the left-wing party Mapam, after being at the heart of affairs in major realms – military service, agriculture, the kibbutz movement and labour politics – since his immigration from Bulgaria in 1939. His family had moved to Bulgaria from Spain after the expulsion of 1492; and behind his passion for Zion and his labour ideology, he was deeply attached to the country which had sheltered his family for centuries, noting always that the Bulgarians, almost alone, refused to deliver its Jewish citizens to the death-camps during the war and granted them the freedom to emigrate to Israel after the foundation of the state. His work for years in holding Mapam, with its Marxist links, in a close, if troubled alignment with Mapai (Labour) illustrates the point made earlier: that Labour continued – and still continues – to draw much strength from Sephardim, despite the move of young orientals, in recent years, towards Herut.

Discursively again, one can pick on many others of this world whose careers have been of special interest. To name a few, one might start with the Sephardi architect Mosheh Safdie, famed for his 'Habitat' concept and designer of important buildings in Jerusalem. In a different field, one can note the work of the Recanati family in establishing and building up the Discount Bank of Israel, whose huge resources have played a major role in Israel's economic development. This family who migrated from Spain to Italy after the Expulsion and thence all over the Near East, belongs to the classical tradition of bankers, doctors, scholars and rabbis which has surfaced on many pages of this book. Different again, there is the diplomatic tradition embodied in the Sasson family of Syria. Eliyahu Sasson, born in Damascus in 1902, immigrated to Palestine at the age of eighteen, and was for many years the leading participant in Zionist and government circles on every aspect of Arab–Jewish diplomatic issues. Appropriately his son Mosheh Sasson was appointed the second Ambassador to Egypt when diplomatic relations were established after the Sadat visit. In a post of major responsibility, Obadiah Sofer, Ambassador to Paris, is Sephardi, as indeed is the Grand Rabbin of France.

Even from these names alone it is clear that the mixed Sephardi background has yielded people of all ages and origins, fully engaged now in a flexible process which will increasingly blur the originally sharp social and class distinctions. Within this process, an extra dose of dynamism will be manifest among the leaders of Sephardim who are, or feel, disadvantaged, or who have particularly strong political views on the future character of Israel. Among women, one thinks of Geulah Cohen, of Yemenite–Moroccan parentage, immensely active in the Tehiyah Party. Shoshanah Arbeli-Almozlino, of Iraqi origin, is now a Deputy Minister of Health. Miriam Taasa-Glazer, also in the Knesset, is of Yemenite origin. Spoken of as perhaps a future leader is Meir Shitrit, Moroccan-born Mayor of Yavneh and member of the Knesset. Of splinter-party leaders who are likely though not certain to support Likud, there is the young rabbi Nissim Ze'ev, born in Iraq in 1952, and organizer of the very successful movement within the Sephardim that seeks to secure political power under a religious label, in contrast to the more secularist slant of the Moroccan Tami Party. Rabbi Ze'ev looks to his teacher, the former Chief Sephardi Rabbi Obadiah Yosef as mentor; and though not in the Knesset, he emerged in 1984 as Deputy Mayor of Jerusalem, at the age of thirty-two.

The inner transformation

To get a different measure of the process, one has to be ready to turn aside from concentration on public affairs and be ready to listen to other Sephardi echoes in the life of Israel. Most of the names emerging in the last few pages have tended to be of those whom one expects to read about in newspapers, where the emphasis, all too often, is on wars and the threat of wars. The ingathering we have spoken of took place in this context, yet at the same time it relates, as we have seen, to a huge slice of time going back thousands of years, in which the everyday dramas surrender to the deeper thoughts which come to us as Jews.

It is not easy to give this feeling some reality when we are overwhelmed with the latest headlines; yet a book on Jewish history is always an attempt to lift oneself into that timeless world. How doubly true this is when the subject of the book reaches back, as this book does, to the earliest period in which the concept of being a Jew began to take shape.

Beyond the newspapers one expects to find these feelings expressed in art forms. The continuous appeal to us of the Bible shows how we can dissolve our immediate concerns into timeless concepts that have been at the core of Jewish history. This feeling comes to us also in music and poetry. One might expect to find it also in fiction, the magic literary form through which the society we live in is given a greater reality through the imagination that the novelist invests in it.

In some ways, music and the dance have been more expressive than the other arts in conveying a specific influence of the Sephardi background. This may be because their appeal can be direct and expressed without too much straining for effect. In music, the name that comes to mind is of the Yemenite Bracha Zefira, whose work is not only attractive in itself but has had a seminal influence in leading 'serious' music towards oriental motifs which have helped to create an Israeli musical style. The Spanish–Ladino tradition in music has also been greatly developed through the pioneering work of Yitzhak Levi of Jerusalem in recording *hazzanut* (liturgical singing) and folk-song from this tradition on a very large scale. This was taken further (as was noted earlier) by the recordings made by Amnon Shiloah in the Balkans of some old people who are virtually the last survivors. All this Sephardi and oriental music, recovered and developed, has been sung by a whole host of very popular singers, with Yehoram Gaon outstanding, and women singers ranging from Shoshanah Damari to Offra Haza.

In dance, the Yemenite tradition is particularly well known, going back to the work of Gurit Cadman, and put on an established basis by Sarah Levi-Tannai, founder of the Inbal Dance Theatre. The wide appeal of dance is illustrated by the fact that it is strongly supported by the Cultural Centre of the Histadrut, which brought together eighty-two dance troupes of ethnic communities during 1983.

The reflection of the Sephardi–oriental background in poetry and fiction has come out less directly. One could almost say that in these forms of expression the overriding unity of current Israeli experience has so far dwarfed in power the separate strands of memory which different groups have brought with them to Israel.

There are, however, aspects of current writing in which the Sephardi background has to be singled out. In the forefront, of course, is the form of the language which is now assured and 'natural' as a common medium, offering all who have grown up with it the same double source: the ancient language which is still in the air in traditional forms, and the language of the street which is something entirely new. This last point is particularly fruitful for its effect in poetry. The poet T. Carmi makes the point in the introduction to his splendid *The*

Penguin Book of Hebrew Verse that the giants of the past who 'resurrected' Hebrew poetry in the nineteenth century had no experience of Hebrew as a truly natural spoken language. The Ashkenazi pronunciation of Hebrew made it impossible for them to understand the tonalities and rhythms of medieval Hebrew poetry. Even Bialik, who led the way in helping Hebrew to recover 'from its stroke of amnesia', was only partially successful in recovering 'the patterns of stress that had marked biblical verse and parts of the early *piyyut* in Palestine and Italy'. The 'traumatic' change for Hebrew poetry came when Hebrew 'moved' to Palestine in the 1920s and adopted fully the Sephardi pronunciation. It was invigorating for Hebrew when the Ashkenazi style was replaced by 'the harsher beat' of the Sephardi style. Though the older poets (including Bialik) found it hard to make the transition, the medium which emerged released the poets from the tight bonds of the past and allowed them to become part of the modern movement in exploring the 'ordinary' aspects of their experience in wholly uninhibited words.[116]

The same naturalness with the 'new' language is, of course, a powerful weapon in fiction; but in both cases the broad Jewish or Israeli themes seem to have superseded any concentration on the Sephardi/Ashkenazi hiatus which has been a strong issue in the later sections of this book. This is not to say that the oriental background has not been a stimulant for some writers. Nissim Yosha, in his ten-year report (mentioned earlier) on the work of the Cultural Programme mentions books by oriental writers themselves (such as Yehudah Burla and Yitzhak Shemi) and by Europeans interested in the background (like Haim Hazaz). He concedes that this was not a strong movement until the 1970s and 1980s, but, in his view, it is now gathering pace. The Centre has, with other units,

encouraged and enabled scores of writers and artists to give expression to particular works anchored in the heritage of Oriental Jewry. Of the many writers and poets who have published in recent years, several have actually risen to prominence in this field: Amnon Shamush, Shlomo Avio, Erez Biton, Ya'akov Ya'akov, and others.

One would expect that the first stage in the development of fiction from this background would make a feature of reportage; and this indeed is the approach of the novel by Eli Amir mentioned earlier (*Tarnagol Kaparot*), which describes in almost autobiographical terms the experience of being uprooted from Iraq and settled, with great family tensions, in Israel. The same background surfaces, though in a very different way, in a major novel by the Baghdad-born Sammy Michael called *Refuge* (1977); and there are other novels of reportage. But in creative Israeli fiction today the underlying issues conditioning the approach of the novelists seem to reach, as in poetry, towards a background of deeper significance. At one level this is always (as in all serious fiction) an exploration of the individual psyche, but this is often shot through in Israel with the problems of national conscious-ness. As one critic, Leon Yudkin, puts it, the individual's physical setting generates a state of perplexity, in which he is 'unable to take his roots for granted as other nationals might do, and constantly having to define his connection with the country and the outside world, and then refine any original definition'.[117]

Bestriding this, the Arab–Jewish relationship is, one might say, the abiding question which forces its way to the surface in much Israeli fiction, sometimes treated naturalistically but expressed more often in symbolism, so that it becomes the vehicle in which the individual sets out his own deepest feelings of love and fear. In telling the story, the novelist is quite likely to draw on remembered (or historical) backgrounds which used to be predominantly East European and may now yield to oriental backgrounds used in this same imaginative or mythical way; but though this can give fiction great appeal, the writer strikes home more powerfully with the common themes that dominate this small 'perplexed' country, where every novel of personal drama is liable to flow into a symbolic expression of some sense of guilt or fear at being a victim (or even a hero) in the midst of conflict. In the novel *Refuge* mentioned above, the issues of 'perplexity' are widened because the immigrants from Iraq are torn between loyalty to the country (Israel) which has given them shelter, and the appeal of revolution, in which they are at one with 'the enemy'. In the way of novels, this inevitably becomes a perplexity of sexual attachments.

One is obliged to look beneath the surface in this way in trying to live with the dramatic return of eastern Jews to the land in which the original creativity of the Hebrew people first found expression and which now looks forward to a fresh start. At one level it is fair to tell this story with an eye cocked to the historical drama; at another, it is the perplexity of personal living which has to be explored, most notably through the immediacy of poetry but also in fiction that lets all the interior doubts emerge, either naturalistically or symbolically.

Ironically, perhaps, one ends this book on history with a wish to find it overtaken by some grand exploration in fiction of the great theme that lies embedded in the return of Sephardi and oriental Jews to their original homeland. One cannot predict what form this might take; but it is not too much to expect a great book to emerge in a form that will let us absorb this mystery into our being.

The riddle which would find expression in this way is how an emerging society like Israel will allow its citizens to become fully integrated while keeping their identity as individuals. The tug-of-war between unity and variety has been, in effect, the central theme of this book. In one approach, the socio-economic factors are paramount, with the educated and affluent of different ethnic origins having more in common with each other than with their ethnic kin. But strong as this is, one has the feeling that varied cultural traditions in Israel will always continue to find new and rich forms of expression. This will not happen in rigidly separate areas but through the kind of cultural fusion that is already becoming manifest. Israel is too lively a society to surrender the colour and vibrancy that have always found new forms through the long history of the Jews.

Statistical Tables

1. *Jews in Arab countries*

	1948	1976
Morocco	265,000	17,000
Algeria	140,000	500
Tunisia	105,000	2,000
Libya	38,000	20
Egypt	75,000	100
Iraq	135,000	400
Syria	30,000	4,350
Lebanon	5,000	500
Yemen	55,000	1,000
Aden	8,000	0
Totals	856,000	25,870

Source: Maurice Roumani, *The Case of the Jews from Arab Countries* (1983 edn), p. 2.

Note: Figures given in other sources vary in detail, though the general sense is the same. In *The Double Exodus* by Terence Prittie and Bernard Dineen, for example, which compares 1948 with 1973, Syria is given as 45,000, falling to 4,500; Morocco falls from 300,000 to 30,000; Tunisia from 23,000 to 9,000. An article in *Enc. Jud.*, vol. 15, col. 1448, states that there were 71,000 Jews of Tunisian nationality in 1946, and that this number had fallen to 7–8,000 by 1968. To extend 'Eastern Jews' beyond 'Arab countries', one must include Iran, among others. The Jews in Iran are said to have fallen from 95,000 in 1948 to some 40–60,000 by 1973. Kurdistan Jews fell from 12,000 to 2–4,000.

2. *Immigrants to Israel, by period of immigration and last continent of residence* (in thousands)

1948–52	Total	Asia	Africa	Europe	America and Oceania
	1721.4	350.4	409.0	793.3	143.0
of which					
1948–51	686.7	237.3	93.9	326.8	5.1
1955–7	164.9	8.8	103.8	48.6	3.6
1961–4	228.0	19.2	18.0	23.4	2.0
1969–71	116.5	19.7	12.0	50.6	33.9
1972–4	142.8	26.8	102.8	6.8	6.3
1975–9	124.8	11.8	6.0	77.2	29.3
1980–2	46.8	5.4	3.7	23.9	13.6

Source: Statistical Abstract of Israel 1983 (Figures include tourists who changed their status to immigrant or potential immigrant).

3. *Fertility rates in Israel, 1948–75*

(*Definition:* 'Number of children that would be born to 1,000 women if they experienced no mortality up to the end of the reproductive period and were subject at each age to the age-fertility rates of the surveyed calendar year.')

Average for years	Israel	Jews born in Asian/ African countries	Europe/ America	Jews	Muslims	Christians
1948–9	3.57	4.47	3.20	3.25		
1950–3	3.52	6.09	3.10	3.91		
1954–7	2.83	5.61	2.64	3.63	7.6	4.7
1965–7	2.78	4.41	2.52	3.35	9.4	4.4
1972–5	3.01	3.75	2.75	3.17	8.2	3.7

Source: Roberto Bachi, The Population of Israel, Institute of Contemporary Jewry, Hebrew University of Jerusalem, Demographic Centre. Prime Minister's Office, 1974.

4. *Proportions of Israel's population*

	1950	1960	1970	1980	1982
Total population (thousands)	1,370	2,950	3,022	3,922	4,063
of which: Jews	1,203	1,911	2,582	3,283	3,373
Percentage born in					
Israel	26	37	46	56	58
Asia/Africa	22	27	26	19	18
Europe/America	52	35	28	25	23

Source: Statistical Abstract of Israel, 1983

5. *Israel's general elections*
(Knesset: 120 seats)

	1969 (7th Kn.)	1977 (9th Kn.)	1981 (10th Kn.)	1984 (11th Kn.)
Labour Alignment	56	32	47	44
Likud: Herut and Liberal	26	43	48	41
Independent Liberal	5	1	—	—
Dem. Movement for Change (Shinui)	—	15	2	3
National Religious Party	12	12	6	4
Agudat Israel Party	4	4	4	2
Poalei Agudat Israel	2	1	—	—
Communist	4	5	4*	4*
Arab Lists	4	1	1	—
Citizen's Rights	—	1	1	3
Tami			3	1
Shas			0	4
Tehiya			3	5
Morasha			0	2
Progressive			0	2
Yahad			0	3
Kach (Kahane)			0	1
Ometz			0	1
Various	7	5	8	—

Source: Compiled from David B. Capitanchik, *Israel's General Election 1984* (Institute of Jewish Affairs Research Report, London), No. 8 (July 1984); No. 9 (September 1984).
* Called *Hadash*.

6. *Projections of Israel's population for 1993 (on 1973 base) in millions*

Assumptions*	Jews 1973	Jewish Population 1993 A	B	C	Non-Jews 1973	1993
	2.8	3.6	4.1	4.6	0.5	1.06
All Israel	3.7	3.7	4.6	5.2		
Percentages of population	1973		1993			
Jews	85	77	79	81		
Muslims	11	18	16	15		
Jews by origin 1st and 2nd generation	1973		1993			
Asia/Africa	57.7	61	54	46		
Europe/America	48.3	39	46	54		

Source: Bachi, *op. cit.*
* Assuming immigration p.a.: A = 0; B = 25,000; C = 50,000. B most likely.

Bibliography

(Section A lists a few general books on Jewish history for the background. Section B mentions books on specific aspects of the theme of this book.)

A. General

Baron, Salo W., *A Social and Religious History of the Jews* (New York) 2nd edn, 16 vols to date; see especially vol. VIII and vols. XII–XV
Ben-Sasson, H. H., and Ettinger, S. (eds), *Jewish Society through the Ages* (London, 1971)
Ben-Sasson, H. H. (ed.), *A History of the Jewish People* (Cambridge, Mass., 1976)
Finkelstein, Louis (ed.), *The Jews: Their History, Culture and Religion* (New York, 1960), 3 vols
Goldstein, David, *Jewish Folklore and Legend* (London, 1980)
Morag, Shelomo, Ben-Ami, Issachar, and Stillman, Norman A. (eds), *Studies in Judaism and Islam* (Jerusalem, 1981)
Seltzer, Robert M., *Jewish People, Jewish Thought* (New York, 1980)
Silver, Daniel Jeremy, and Martin, Bernard, *A History of Judaism* (New York, 1974), 2 vols

Illustrated, lavishly
Kedourie, Elie (ed.), *The Jewish World: History and Culture of the Jewish People* (New York, 1979)
Lange, Nicholas de, *Atlas of the Jewish World* (Oxford, 1984)
Metzger, Thérèse and Mendel, *Jewish Life in the Middle Ages* (Fribourg, 1982)
Rubens, Alfred, *A History of Jewish Costume* (London, 1973)
Wigoder, Geoffrey (ed.), *Jewish Art and Civilization* (Fribourg, 1972), 2 vols

B. Individual subjects

Albaz, André E., *Folktales of the Canadian Sephardim* (Toronto, 1983)

Angel, Marc D., *The Jews of Rhodes* (New York, 1980)

Angel, Marc D., *La America: The Sephardic Experience in the United States* (Philadelphia, 1982)

Ashtor, Eliyahu, *The Jews of Moslem Spain* (Philadelphia, 1973–9), 2 vols

Baer, Yitzhak, *A History of the Jews in Christian Spain* (Philadelphia, 1961–6), 2 vols

Barnett, Richard (ed.), *The Sephardi Heritage* (London, 1971)

Baron, Salo W., *The Jewish Community* (Philadelphia, 1948), 3 vols

Baron, Salo W., *History and Jewish Historians* (New York, 1964)

Barzilay, Isaac, *Between Reason and Faith: Anti-Rationalism in Italian Jewish Thought 1250–1650* (The Hague, 1967)

Bat Ye'Or, *The Dhimmi: Jews and Christians under Islam* (Brunswick, N.J., 1985)

Beinart, Haim, 'The Converso Community in 15th Century Spain' and 'The Converso Community in 16th and 17th Century Spain' in Barnett (ed.), *The Sephardi Heritage* (London, 1971)

Ben-Ami, Issachar (ed.), *The Sephardi and Oriental Jewish Heritage* (Jerusalem, 1982)

Benardete, Mair José, *Hispanic Culture and Character of the Sephardic Jews* (New York, 1982)

Ben-Zvi, Itzhak, *The Exiled and the Redeemed: The Strange Jewish Tribes of the Orient* (London, 1958)

Blumenthal, David R., *The Commentary of R. Hoter Ben Shelomo to the Thirteen Principles of Maimonides* (Leiden, 1974)

Braudel, Fernand, *The Mediterranean and the Mediterranean World in the Age of Philip II* (London, 1972–3), 2 vols

Bright, John, *A History of Israel* (London, 1972 edn.)

Capitanchik, David B., *The Israeli General Election 1984* (Institute of Jewish Affairs, London, 1984), 2 parts

Carmi, T. (ed. and translator), *The Penguin Book of Hebrew Verse* (London, 1981)

Castro, Américo, *The Structure of Spanish History* (Oxford, 1953)

Castro, Américo, *The Spaniards* (California, 1981)

Chouraqui, André N., *Between East and West: A History of the Jews of North Africa* (New York, 1973)

Cohen, H. J., *The Jews of the Middle East, 1860–1922* (Jerusalem, 1973)

Cohen, Mark R., *Jewish Self-Government in Medieval Egypt* (Princeton, 1980)

Deshen, Shlomo and Zenner, Walter P. (eds), *Jewish Societies in the Middle East* (Washington DC, 1982)

Eisenstadt, Samuel N., *Israeli Society* (London, 1967)

Eliachar, Elie, *Living with Jews* (London, 1983)

Epstein, Isidore, *The Responsa of Rabbi Solomon ben Adret of Barcelona (1235–1310) as a Source of the History of Spain* (London, 1925)

Epstein, Isidore, *The Responsa of Rabbi Simon ben Zemah Duran as a Source of the History of the Jews in North Africa* (London, 1930)

Fischel, Walter J., *Jews in the Economic and Political Life of Medieval Islam* (London, 1937)

Frankel, William, *Israel Observed* (London, 1980)

Frankel, William, *Survey of Jewish Affairs 1983* (London, 1985)

Franklin, Myrtle and Bor, Michael, *Sir Moses Montefiore 1784–1885* (London, 1984)

Freidenreich, Harriet Pass, *The Jews of Yugoslavia* (Philadelphia, 1979)

Gilbert, Martin, *The Jews of Arab Lands: their history in maps* (Board of Deputies of British Jews, London, 1976)

Goitein, S. D., *Jews and Arabs* (New York, 1964)

Goitein, S. D., *A Mediterranean Society* (Berkeley, 1967–78), 3 vols

Goitein, S. D., *Letters of Medieval Jewish Traders* (Princeton, 1973)

Goldstein, David, *The Jewish Poets of Spain, 900–1250* (London, 1965)

Haddad, Heskel M., *Jews of Arab and Islamic Countries* (New York, 1984)

Hirschberg, H. Z., *A History of the Jews in North Africa* (Leiden, 1974), 2 vols

Hitti, Philip, *The Arabs* (London, 1948)

Hyamson, A. M., *The British Consulate in Jerusalem 1838–1914* (London, 1938–47)

Hyamson, A. M., *The Sephardim of England, 1492–1951* (London, 1951)

Ibn-Gabirol, Solomon, *Selected Religious Poems* (tr. I. Zangwill) (Philadelphia, 1923)

Jackson, Gabriel, *The Making of Medieval Spain* (London, 1972)

Kalderon, Albert, *Abraham Galante* (New York, 1983)

Kamen, Henry, *The Spanish Inquisition* (London, 1965)

Kochan, Lionel, *The Jew and his History* (London, 1977)

Lewis, Bernard, *The Jews of Islam* (London, 1984)

Liebman, Seymour B., *New World Jewry 1493–1825: Requiem for the Forgotten* (New York, 1982)

Lipman, Sonia and V. D. (eds), *The Century of Moses Montefiore* (Oxford, 1985)

Littman, David, 'Jews under Muslim Rule: the Case of Persia', *Wiener Library Bulletin* (1979), vol. xxxix, N.S. 49–50

Maccoby, Hyam, *Judaism on Trial: Jewish–Christian Disputations in the Middle Ages* (Brunswick, N.J., 1982)

Maimonides (Moses ben Maimon), *Guide of the Perplexed* (Chicago, 1963)

Mann, Jacob, *The Jews in Egypt and Palestine under the Fatimid Caliphs* (Oxford, 1920) 2 vols

Michman, Joseph, *Dutch Jewish History* (Jerusalem, 1984)

Narkiss, Bezalel, *Hebrew Illuminated Manuscripts* (Jerusalem, 1969)

Netanyahu, B., *The Marranos of Spain* (New York, 1967)

Neuman, A. A., *The Jews in Spain during the Middle Ages* (Philadelphia, 1921)

Newman, J., *The Agricultural Life of the Jews in Babylonia* (Oxford, 1932)

Noy, Dov, *Folktales of Israel* (Chicago, 1963)

Patai, Raphael, *Sephardi Folklore* (Herzl Institute, New York, 1960)

Patai, Raphael, *The Vanished Worlds of Jewry* (New York, 1980)

Prinz, Joachim, *The Secret Jews* (New York, 1973)

Rabinowitz, Louis, *Jewish Merchant Adventurers* (London, 1948)

Read, Jan, *The Moors in Spain and Portugal* (London, 1974)

Roth, Cecil, *A History of the Marranos* (Philadelphia, 1932)

Roth, Cecil, *The Jews of Venice* (Philadelphia, 1946)

Roth, Cecil, *The House of Nasi: 1. Dona Gracia* (1947); *2. The Duke of Naxos* (1948) (Philadelphia, 1947–8)

Roth, Cecil, *The Jews in the Renaissance* (Philadelphia, 1950)

Roumani, Maurice, *From Immigrant to Citizen: The Contribution of the Army to National Integration: The Case of Oriental Jews* (The Hague, 1979)

Roumani, Maurice, *The Case of the Jews from Arab Countries* (Jerusalem, 1983)

Ruderman, David B., *The World of a Renaissance Jew . . . Mordecai Farrisol* (Cincinatti, 1981)

Sachar, Howard, *A History of Israel* (Oxford, 1976)

Sassoon, David Solomon, *A History of the Jews in Baghdad* (Letchworth, 1949)

Scholem, Gershom, *Major Trends in Jewish Mysticism* (New York, 1954)

Scholem, Gershom, *Sabbatai Sevi* (Princeton, 1973)

Scholem, Gershom, *Kabbalah* (New York, 1974)

Sharf, Andrew, *Byzantine Jewry* (London, 1971)

Shiloah, Amnon, *The Musical Tradition of Iraqi Jews* (Jerusalem, 1983)

Shohet, Nir, *The Story of an Exile: A Short History of the Jews of Iraq* (Tel Aviv, 1982)

Smooha, Sammy, *Israel: Pluralism and Conflict* (Berkeley, 1978)

Stillman, Norman A., *The Jews of Arab Lands* (Philadelphia, 1979)

Strizower, Shifra, *The Children of Israel: The Benei Israel of Bombay* (Oxford, 1971)

Sutton, Joseph A. D., *Magic Carpet: Aleppo-in-Flatbush* (New York, 1979)

Tamir, Vicki, *Bulgaria and her Jews* (New York, 1979)

Twersky, Isadore, *A Maimonides Reader* (New York, 1972)

Udovitch, Abraham, and Valensi, Lucette, *The Last Arab Jews: The Communities of Jerba, Tunisia* (London, 1984)

Weinberger, Leon J. (ed. and translator), *Jewish Prince in Moslem Spain:*

Selected Poems of Samuel ibn Nagrela (Alabama, 1973)

Weingrod, Alex, *Studies in Israel's Ethnicity* (London, 1985)

Werblowsky, R. J. Zwi, *Yoseph Karo: Lawyer and Mystic* (Philadelphia, 1977)

Yerushalmi, Yosef Hayim, *From Spanish Court to Italian Ghetto* (New York, 1971)

Yerushalmi, Yosef Hayim, *Zakhor: Jewish History and Jewish Memory* (Seattle, 1982)

Yogev, Gedalia, *Diamonds and Coral: Anglo–Dutch Jews and 18th Century Trade* (Leicester, 1978)

Yudkin, Leon, *1948 and After: Aspects of Israeli Fiction* (Manchester, 1984)

Zimmels, H. J., *Ashkenazim and Sephardim . . . as reflected in the Rabbinic Responsa* (Oxford, 1958)

Reference Notes

(Abbreviations: *Encyclopaedia Judaica*: *Enc. Jud.*; *Babylonian Talmud*: *Bab. Tal.*)

1 See Table 4. The Tami (Moroccan) Party was reduced from 3 seats to 1; on the other hand, Sephardi religious parties increased represent-ation: Torah Guardians from 0 to 4; Morasha from 0 to 2.

2 André E. Albaz, *Folk Tales of the Canadian Sephardim* (Toronto, 1983).

3 There is an intriguing account of this by E. A. Speiser in his introduction to the Anchor Bible *Genesis* (New York, 1964).

4 For a fuller account, see 'Assyrian Exile' by Abraham Malamat in *Enc. Jud.*, vol. 6, col. 1036, and references there.

5 John Bright, *A History of Israel* (London, 1972 edn), p. 345.

6 For editing in Babylon, see *ibid.*, p. 350; for editing after the Return, see Martin Noth, *The History of Israel* (London, 1960), pp. 295–7.

7 Elias Bickerman, 'The Historical Foundations of Postbiblical Judaism', in Louis Finkelstein (ed.), *The Jews* (New York, 1970), vol. 1, p. 77.

8 Bab. Tal. *Kiddushin*, 71a. The phrase in the saying is: 'All are dough . . .', a technical term from the Mishnah indicating a mixture of pure and impure material, and therefore second-rate by definition.

9 Bickerman, *op. cit.*, vol. 1, p. 75.

10 Superb examples in T. Carmi (ed. and translator), *The Penguin Book of Hebrew Verse* (London, 1981), pp. 195–232.

11 References are given in a classical article on pre-Islamic Persia by W. J. Fischel in *Enc. Jud.*, vol. 13, cols 306–8.

12 J. Newman, *The Agricultural Life of the Jews in Babylonia, 200–500 CE* (Oxford, 1932).

13 S. D. Goitein, *Jews and Arabs* (New York, 1964), p. 51.

14 Max Weinreich, *History of the Yiddish Language* (Chicago, 1980), pp. 48–52.

15 Isidore Epstein: *The Responsa of Rabbi Solomon ben Adret of Barcelona (1225–1310) as a Source of the History of Spain* (London, 1925); and *The Responsa of Rabbi Simon ben Zemah Duran as a Source of the History of the Jews in North Africa* (London, 1930).

16 Philip K. Hitti, *The Arabs* (London, 1948), p. 53.

17 The burdens and humiliations are described in detail in a new study: Bat Ye'Or, *The Dhimmi: Jews and Christians under Islam* (New York, 1985).

18 Goitein, *op. cit.*, p. 105.

19 *Ibid.*

20 Bernard Lewis, *The Jews of Islam* (London, 1984), p. 56.

21 Excerpts from both books (and further references) are given conveniently in E. N. Adler, *Jewish Travellers* (London, 1930).

22 Américo Castro, *The Spaniards* (California, 1981), p. 9.

23 The two source-books of Yitzhak Baer's archive material appeared in Berlin in 1929–36. The English edition of his classical study, *A History of the Jews in Christian Spain*, appeared in 1961–6 (Philadelphia), 2 vols.

24 *Ibid.*, vol. I, p. 47.

25 Leon J. Weinberger (ed. and translator), *Jewish Prince in Moslem Spain: Selected Poems of Samuel ibn Nagrela* (Alabama, 1973).

26 *Ibid.*, p. 55.

27 It used to be thought that he was born in Toledo; for Tudela, see *Enc. Jud.*, vol. 10, col. 355, quoting Jefim Schirmann, with references.

28 T. Carmi, *op. cit.*, pp. 333–52. This is the source also for the translations from Moses ibn Ezra.

29 S. D. Goitein, *A Mediterranean Society* (California, 1967–78), vol. II, pp. 302 ff., which gives copious sources drawing on the *geniza*.

30 Lewis, *op. cit.*, p. 99.

31 Goitein, *A Mediterranean Society*, vol. I, pp. 281–95.

32 S. D. Goitein, *Letters of Medieval Jewish Traders* (Princeton, 1973), p. 26.

33 *Ibid.*, p. 220.

34 H. Z. Hirschberg, *A History of the Jews in North Africa* (Leiden, 1974), vol. I, p. 9.

35 Quoted by Hirschberg, *ibid.*, vol. I, p. 165.

36 Baer, *op. cit.*, vol. I, p. 79.

37 *Ibid.*, p. 82.

38 *Ibid.*, p. 91.

39 *Ibid.*, p. 95

40 *Ibid.*, pp. 102–5.

41 *Ibid.*, p. 123.

42 *Ibid.*, vol. II, pp. 139–43.

43 *Ibid.*, pp. 138–50 and 170–232.

44 Epstein, *The Responsa of Rabbi Solomon ben Adret*, pp. 95–6.

45 Baer, *op. cit.*, vol. I, p. 2.

46 *Ibid.*, pp. 178–9.

47 Haim Beinart, 'The Converso Community in 15th Century Spain', in Richard D. Barnett (ed.), *The Sephardi Heritage* (London, 1971), vol. I, p. 425.

48 Baer, *op. cit.*, vol. II, p. 96.

49 *Ibid.*, p. 126.

50 See Beinart, 'The Converso Community in 15th Century Spain' and 'The Converso Community in 16th Century and 17th Century Spain', in Barnett (ed.), *op. cit.*, pp. 425–56 and 457–78 respectively.

51 *Enc. Jud.*, vol. 8, cols 1380–1407. For the other figures quoted, see *Enc. Jud.*, vol. 15, col. 240.

52 See I. S. Révah, 'Les Marranes Portugais et L'Inquisition au XVIme Siècle', in Barnett (ed.), *op. cit.*, pp. 479–526.

53 *Las Excelencias y Calumnias de los Hebreos.* Isaac's life and work are portrayed in a warm-hearted study by Yosef Hayim Yerushalmi, *From Spanish Court to Italian Ghetto* (New York, 1971).

54 Discussed by Salo W. Baron, *History and Jewish Historians* (New York, 1964), pp. 111–14.

55 Yosef Hayim Yerushalmi, *Zakhor: Jewish History and Jewish Memory* (New York, 1982), pp. 57–8.

56 *Ibid.*, p. 60, contradicting the earlier view in standard works that he fled to Italy, where he came under the direct influence of the Renaissance. Ibn Verga's philosophy came, Yerushalmi says, 'from the Iberian cultural milieu closest to him'.

57 Lionel Kochan, *The Jew and his History* (London, 1977), pp. 38–9.

58 Bezalel Narkiss, *Hebrew Illuminated Manuscripts* (Jerusalem, 1969).

59 Cecil Roth, *The House of Nasi* (Philadelphia, 2 vols, 1947–8), vol. I: *Dona Gracia*.

60 Fernand Braudel, *The Mediterranean* (London, 1972–3); see especially pp. 436–7, 638–41, 800–26.

61 See Révah, *op. cit.*

62 See Epstein, *The Responsa of Rabbi Simon ben Zemah Duran* . . .

63 The Jamaican Jew Isaac de Lousada (d. 1857) was descended from the seventeenth-century Spanish New Christian Duke de Lousada, chamberlain to Charles III. He succeeded in getting this title revived in 1848. According to Cecil Roth (*Enc. Jud.*, vol. 15, col. 1166): 'this is the highest title of nobility ever granted to a Jew in the West'.

64 André N. Chouraqui, *Between East and West: A History of the Jews of North Africa* (New York, 1973), pp. 92–5.

65 S. D. Goitein, 'The Jews under Muslim Rule before 1492', in Elie Kedourie (ed.), *The Jewish World* (London, 1981), p. 185.

66 See an exceptionally interesting book by R. J. Werblowsky, *Joseph Karo: Lawyer and Mystic* (Princeton, 1977).

67 This is described in detail by Cecil Roth in his affectionate study, *The*

Jews of Venice (Philadelphia, 1946), pp. 9–33.

68 Cecil Roth makes these points in *The Jews in the Renaissance* (Philadelphia, 1950), pp. 13–22.

69 A detailed account of this fascinating trade is given by Gedalia Yogev in *Diamonds and Coral: Anglo–Dutch Jews and 18th Century Trade* (Leicester, 1978).

70 Braudel, *op. cit.*, vol. I, p. 638.

71 *Ibid.*, p. 640.

72 Yogev, *op. cit.*, pp. 15–20.

73 Chouraqui, *op. cit.*, p. 104.

74 Roth, *Dona Gracia*, p. 68.

75 *Ibid.*, p. 107.

76 *Ibid.*, p. 104.

77 Elie Eliachar, *Living with Jews* (London, 1983), p. 12.

78 Michael Avi-Yonah in *Enc. Jud.*, vol. 14, col. 627.

79 H. H. Ben-Sasson, *A History of the Jewish People* (Cambridge, Mass., 1976), p. 705ff.

80 Norman A. Stillman, *The Jews in Arab Lands* (Philadelphia, 1979), p. 78.

81 Marc D. Angel, *The Jews of Rhodes* (New York, 1980).

82 Chouraqui, *op. cit.*, p. XVI.

83 *Ibid.*, p. XVII.

84 In a long interview in the *Jerusalem Post* (5–11 August 1984) with Rabbi Yitzhak Peretz, leader of the Shas Party in the Knesset, an official of the party said: 'The average Shas voter goes to synagogue on Shabbat morning and to the soccer game in the afternoon.' Rabbi Peretz was quoted as saying that he accepted this characterization. He defined the attitude of the Sephardi voter as: 'Even if his observance of the *mitzvot* is minimal, the average Sephardi, deep down, wants Eretz Israel to be built up in accordance with the Torah.' The Shas Party (Sephardi Guardians of the Torah) became prominent in the 1984 general election by rising from no Knesset seats to four, in contrast with the more secular Moroccan party, Tami, which fell from three to one seat.

85 Chouraqui, *op. cit.*, p. 61.

86 *Ibid.*, pp. 65–79.

87 David Solomon Sassoon, *A History of the Jews in Baghdad* (Letchworth, 1949), p. 101.

88 Vicki Tamir, *Bulgaria and her Jews* (New York, 1979), p. 66 ff.

89 *Morasha*, Folkway Records: New York Album No. FE 4203 (New York, 1978).

90 Amnon Shiloah, *The Musical Tradition of Iraqi Jews* (published in Israel by the Institute for Research on Iraqi Jewry, 1983).

91 'Sephardi Folklore' in *The World of the Sephardim* (Herzl Institute, New York, 1960).
92 Lewis, *op. cit.*, p. 108.
93 Stillman, *op. cit.*, p. 95.
94 Lewis, *op. cit.*, p. 140.
95 *Ibid.*
96 Stillman, *op. cit.*, p. 102.
97 *Ibid.*, p. 101.
98 Lewis, *op. cit.*, p. 172.
99 See A. M. Hyamson, *The British Consulate in Jerusalem 1838–1914* (London, 1938–47), on the work of the famed consul James Finn.
100 The numbers depend on the definitions used. Maurice Roumani (*The Case of the Jews from Arab Countries*, 1983, p. 2) speaks of 856,000 'in Arab countries' in 1948. Howard Sachar (*A History of Israel*, 1976, p. 396) speaks of 1.7 million Jews 'in Islamic countries' in 1939.
101 Chouraqui, *op. cit.*, p. 248.
102 Itzhak Ben-Zvi, *The Exiled and the Redeemed: The Strange Jewish Tribes of the Orient* (London, 1958), p. 9.
103 See David Littman, 'Jews under Muslim Rule: The Case of Persia', in *Wiener Library Bulletin* (1979), vol. XXXIX, New Series Nos 49–50.
104 Ben-Zvi, *op. cit.*, p. 14.
105 *Enc. Jud.*, vol. 9, col. 533, gives a larger figure, 483,000, for Jews settling in Palestine 'during the entire period of the Mandate'. Ben-Gurion's smaller figure of 394,000 may be net, after allowing for emigration. Whatever the discrepancy, the general thrust of the comparison remains valid.
106 From a detailed account of *aliyah* and absorption by Rabbi Zvi Zinger (Yaron) of the Jewish Agency in *Enc. Jud.*, vol. 9, cols 508–46.
107 William Frankel, *Israel Observed* (London, 1980), p. 203.
108 Sachar, *op. cit.*, p. 419.
109 Samuel N. Eisenstadt, *Israeli Society* (London, 1967), p. 309.
110 Sammy Smooha, 'The Upsurge of Ethnicity in Israel', in William Frankel (ed.), *Survey of Jewish Affairs, 1983* (London, 1985).
111 In giving these figures in the essay mentioned in note 110, Smooha points out that the Asian/Africans should not be thought of as destitute. The Asian/African *household* income was 81 per cent of the European/American, but contained more workers and wage-earners per room, reflecting their poorer housing.
112 Alex Weingrod (ed.), *Studies in Israel's Ethnicity* (London, 1985); references here from various essays.
113 See David B. Capitanchik, *The Israeli General Election 1984* (published by Institute of Jewish Affairs, London), Part 1, July 1984; Part 2, September 1984.

114 David Levy explained in an interview in the *Jerusalem Post*, 25 March 1983, that he saw the future for Herut after the results of the election for the local council in Beth She'an in 1965 in which he ran under the Herut label for the first time and won the seat.

115 Professor Roumani, born in Libya, is the author of a study of the army's role in Israel entitled: *From Immigrant to Citizen: The Contribution of the Army to National Integration: The Case of Oriental Jews* (The Hague, 1979).

116 Carmi, *op. cit.*, p. 41.

117 Leon Yudkin, *1948 and After: Aspects of Israeli Fiction* (Manchester, 1984), p. 149.

Glossary

aliyah	immigration to Israel
aljama	Jewish community council in Spain
arrabi mor	Chief Rabbi in Portugal
bakkashot	prayer-songs of supplication
cabbala	mystical teachings
dhimmi	'protected' non-Muslim by virtue of having own scripture
edot ha-mizrach	eastern communities
Exilarch	ruler in Exile
galuth	exile
gaon (plural: *geonim*)	rabbinic leader
geniza	a cache of old papers discovered in a synagogue room in Old Cairo
get	bill of divorcement
haham-bashi	Chief Rabbi
hajj	pilgrimage
halakhah	Jewish religious law
hegira	flight (in Islamic history)
jizya	poll-tax paid by *dhimmis*
kelitah	absorption
kharaj	poll-tax of *dhimmis* in Turkey
kibbutz	common ownership village
Knesset	Israel's Parliament
limpieza de sangre	purity of blood
ma'abarah	temporary camp for immigrants
Maghreb	North African countries west of Egypt
megurashim	refugees
mellah	Jewish quarter in North Africa
millet	independent religious authority
moshav	private ownership co-operative
Nasi (plural: *nesi'im*)	president
Nagid (plural: *negidim*)	representative leader

pekidim	assessors
piyyut	poetry for synagogue services
resh galutha	Head of Exile
responsa	answers to *halakhic* queries
semichah	rabbinical ordination
sofer	scribe
takkanah (plural: *takkanoth*)	regulation
toshav	resident
ulpan	school for learning Hebrew
wergild	compensation
yeshivah	Talmud academy
yichuss	pedigree
Yishuv	Jewish settlement in Palestine or Israel

Index

Repetition of a page number, or a figure 2 in brackets after a page number, means that the subject is referred to under two different headings on that page.

Chaim Raphael has taught at Oxford and the University of Sussex and served in Foreign Office and Treasury posts for some years, including many in the U.S.A. A distinguished author, his books include *A Feast of History* (a widely read study of Passover and the Haggadah), and the charming *Memoirs of a Special Case*. His most recent book, *The Springs of Jewish Life*, was the joint winner of the Wingate Prize for 1984. As a diversion, he writes mystery novels under the pseudonym Jocelyn Davey.